A *Refugee*
at
HANOVER TAVERN

Presented by THE HANOVER TAVERN FOUNDATION

A *Refugee* —at— HANOVER TAVERN

THE CIVIL WAR DIARY OF *Margaret Wight*

Edited by SHIRLEY A. HAAS & DALE PAIGE TALLEY

THE History PRESS

Published by The History Press
Charleston, SC 29403
www.historypress.net

First published 2013

ISBN 978-1-5402-2166-7

Library of Congress CIP data applied for.

CONTENTS

FOREWORD

In the decades following the Civil War, authors and publishers embraced
a trend in which the standard short title of a book often preceded an
enormously long subtitle, usually cluttered with multiple clauses separated
by semicolons. Some extended titles exceeded one hundred words. That
practice died an unlamented death with the advent of information-filled
dust jackets. A century ago, *A Refugee at Hanover Tavern: The Civil War Diary
of Margaret Wight* would have been an ideal platform for a prolonged
subtitle of prize-winning dimensions. Her diary follows multiple threads
of interest.

"The Travails of a Confederate Mother" would be one appropriate
subtitle. With a son in the hard-fighting Army of Northern Virginia, Mrs.
Wight monitored military affairs with a patriotic enthusiasm frequently
subordinated to maternal worry. By the time her diary commenced in 1863,
she already had seen two of her children die in service. Her own immediate
circumstances, and those of her extended family scattered across central
Virginia, kept her fortunes tied to the progress of the Confederacy. Every
ebb and flow of the campaigns between 1863 and 1865 had some direct
effect on her life.

Perhaps more than anything else, "Hanover County in Wartime"
accurately defines this journal and its importance. The United States, as
presently configured, contains nearly 3,100 counties. There cannot be more
than a half-dozen of that number that have any legitimate claim to being as
history-laden as Hanover. In a community already proud of its rich heritage

by the 1860s, it might seem surprising that so few residents seized the opportunity to chronicle their Civil War experiences. But Civil War material from county residents is scarce, particularly anything contemporaneous to the events. The final census taken before the Civil War enumerated fewer than 7,500 white residents in Hanover. Subtract the many children from that sum together with the large number of families driven out by the devastating presence of the armies in Hanover in 1862, and the pool of eligible writers by 1863 must have been small indeed.

Mrs. Wight's musings offer a valuable reminder of just how much the Union cavalry raids north of Richmond alarmed everyone in their path. Historians know that the mounted dashes into Hanover County in May, June and July 1863, February and March 1864 and March 1865 ultimately produced no permanent results. For a resident facing those incursions, free from a historian's hindsight, they had a chilling immediacy fraught with unknown and potentially life-changing consequences. Some of the most valuable content in *A Refugee at Hanover Tavern* is the description of "The Blackberry Raid" in June through July 1863, and Mrs. Wight's perilous encounter with General Philip Sheridan's raiders at Beaverdam Station in May 1864—"the most exciting scene I ever witnessed," she asserted.

A disappointing aspect of the journal emerges from one of its great strengths. Many of the places familiar to Mrs. Wight in her daily wartime life survive today. A century and a half later, history-minded Hanoverians relish their own proximity to those same interesting and important sites. They embrace the connection to their predecessors through the local landscape and its history. Mrs. Wight lived in the dignified old Hanover Tavern; she attended church in Taylorsville and in the hamlet of Hanover Courthouse; she rode the rails through Ashland and Hanover Junction. She had the opportunity to more fully describe those places—but she did not do it. A detailed paragraph from her pen documenting the appearance of Hanover Tavern, for example, would be priceless. Like most diarists, Margaret Wight wrote in her journal for herself and for her heirs, not for us, and we must be grateful for the very many good things she left behind.

Robert E.L. Krick
Glen Allen, Virginia
June 2013

PREFACE

The Hanover Tavern Foundation was established in 1990 with the mission to preserve, interpret and utilize Hanover Tavern as a historic, educational, community and cultural resource center for the enjoyment of all. We had no idea what it would take to save the rapidly deteriorating historic building located just fifteen miles north of Richmond on U.S. Route 301 in Hanover County. What we did know was the Tavern was truly of national significance and worthy of restoration.

The original tavern had been the home of Patrick Henry, and had been visited by George Washington, as well as numerous other influential and important figures in American history, and played a supporting role in the Revolutionary and Civil Wars. The historical marker located in the yard reads:

> John Shelton opened the first tavern at the permanent site of Hanover Courthouse about the 1750s. The current tavern's earliest segment dates from about 1791. The tavern prospered with the establishment of the stage coach line until the railroad diverted business in the 1830s. An essential component of the social life of Hanover County, the taverns attracted many important people, including Patrick Henry, Lord Cornwallis and George Washington, among others. Several enslaved African Americans from the tavern complex were accused of participation in both Gabriel's Rebellion of 1800 and the Easter Plot of 1802. In 1953, the Barksdale Theatre was established here.

Fifteen years later, with a fundraising investment of $5 million, Hanover Tavern was stabilized, restored and enhanced. It was ready for two hundred more years of community service. Today within this cultural site, The Hanover Tavern Foundation offers school field trips, educational history programs, exhibits, tours, music, professional theater performances and family-oriented special events to all of central Virginia, as well as the touring public.

The Tavern is a lively place, hosting temporary exhibits and both a monthly speaker and music series. It is a destination for motor coaches and tours, those in search of professional theater and excellent dining, as well as a beautiful venue for weddings, receptions and parties. There are guided and self-guided tours focused on architecture, the development of the building, interesting people and important events. A Hanover County–based Civil War exhibit recognizes the contributions not only of local citizens, but also those who came as combatants. There are numerous children's programs throughout the year.

To cover the costs of programs, building maintenance, utilities and staff, the foundation must continue to fundraise. Money raised through grant writing, donation requests, rentals and large events enables the foundation to continue to give back to the community with engaging, entertaining and valuable educational programs for all ages.

We are most proud of our fourth-grade Standards of Learning–based history field trip program, which hosts thousands of students each spring. During the field trip, students learn about the Colonial Period, Revolutionary War and Civil War history by moving through learning stations located at the historic Courthouse and Tavern, interacting with fascinating living characters from the past.

Hanover Tavern has been the center of life for Hanover County since the eighteenth century. Thanks to the restoration efforts and ongoing educational programming provided by The Hanover Tavern Foundation, the Tavern continues to serve as a cultural resource center for the use and enjoyment of all. We encourage you to see us online at http://www.hanovertavern.org to plan a visit to the Hanover Tavern.

David Deal
Executive Director
The Hanover Tavern Foundation
2013

ACKNOWLEDGEMENTS

The Hanover Tavern Foundation is grateful to the following individuals whose time, energy and expertise helped to bring this project to the printed page.

Researchers on this project were the beneficiaries of the generous commitment of time, energy and knowledge of Robert E.L. Krick, a Richmond-based historian and author of *Staff Officers in Gray*. Mr. Krick's knowledge of the Civil War in the Eastern theater is perhaps unparalleled.

Obtaining images for the book was made possible by the following:

- Jim Burgess, ranger and museum specialist, Manassas Battlefield Park, Virginia, for the photographs of the Charles R. Norris Virginia Military Institute coatee.
- Charles R. Norris's family, who gave generous permission to use two of their photographs of the Charles R. Norris Virginia Military Institute coatee.
- Joseph D. Kyle, PhD, who did early research on the family of Margaret Wight and helped to locate the daguerreotype images of the Wight family children.
- Robert E. Haines, who gave permission for the use of the rare daguerreotype of the Wight children.
- Janice Tallman, administrative assistant for the Ohio Historical Society, whose persistence helped us locate the image of Camp Chase Prison.

- Marianne Martin of the Colonial Williamsburg Foundation provided digital images of the Geddy House and Nicolson House.
- Tad Thompson and Mary Edmunds for images of Tuckahoe Plantation.

Research help was provided by:
- Judy Ledbetter and Sherry Tyler of the Charles City County Center for Local History
- Mary Laura Kludy, archives assistant at the Preston Library, Virginia Military Institute
- Katherine Wilkins and the library staff of the Virginia Historical Society
- Linda Angus Trucchi, who provided early work on the diary transcription
- Shannon Pritchard, owner of Hickory Hill Plantation in Hanover County
- Rosanne Shalf of the Ashland Museum
- Austin Howlett of The Hanover Tavern Foundation, who made the maps and genealogy charts

Finally, the editors wish to thank Barbara Rose, former president of The Hanover Tavern Foundation Board of Directors and tireless supporter of this work.

INTRODUCTION

The publication of Margaret Wight's diary during the sesquicentennial is significant for two reasons. First, this book's production acknowledges the importance of the Civil War 150 years after it ended. Second, Mrs. Wight's writings present a rare analysis and commentary on the adaptations, adjustments, changes, sacrifices and strategies for survival that many Americans—especially women—had to employ during the nation's most horrific war. To call this work a feminist history, however, would be a cliché. Circumstances dictated Mrs. Wight's actions and thoughts.

A skillful writer, Mrs. Wight's images and words were meant as a legacy to her children and grandchildren. The diary is, however, a valuable resource for historians that reaches far beyond her descendants. The commentaries contained in the three volumes provide critical observations about the dilemmas that she, her family and her country faced as each day brought new challenges. Her comments touch on many of the topics historians look to today as they develop deeper understandings of the Civil War beyond the battlefield. Margaret Wight speaks to the constant travails of having to move from place to place and the emotional, psychological and social changes she had to endure as war was brought to her doorstep. She presents a harsh assessment of those who began the war and, in particular, of those who profited from it. With dispassion she discusses matters of commerce, economics, safety and the machinations of war. Her reflections concern children, education, disease, health and the disorienting events that seemed to characterize each day of the war for her and her family.

Margaret Wight's diary is a quintessential primary source written with both unconscious awareness and absolute clarity. The work uncovers the activities and thoughts of a real person surviving the affects and effects the Civil War had on her life and the lives of those she loved. While the diary might carry her name, it is really a history of life on the home front. This volume is important in its precision and powerful in its specificity. In many ways, Margaret Wight writes her own Civil War history.

Alphine W. Jefferson, PhD
Professor of History and Director of Black Studies
Randolph-Macon College
2013

Chapter One

COLONIAL BEGINNINGS

The discovery and first reading of any Civil War diary can prove exciting. The diary of Margaret Copland Brown Wight is no exception. This important primary source adds substance and meaning to the Civil War experience in central Virginia from 1863 through the end of the war in 1865. Over a decade passed before Mrs. Wight completed her final reminiscences. Each volume of Margaret's narrative reveals the circumstances of her life and those of her extended family as they coped with the challenges of a pivotal period in American history. Yet the work fails to provide the reader with genealogical details of her family, both before and after the war. In an effort to put "branches with leaves" on her family tree, space was allocated in this volume for disclosure of familial ties. Some of the genealogy of Margaret Copland Brown and her husband, John Wight, are included in the sections that follow.

The Nicolson, Geddy, Copland, Brown and Wight family lineages reach back both to colonial Virginia and the Massachusetts Bay Colony and carry forward a line of distinguished craftsmen, lawyers, merchants and community leaders. The image of a family that contributed so much to the early history of the United States stands in ironic contrast to a family caught in the dissolution of the Union they helped to establish. As the investigation into these families progressed, it became clear that the ancestors of the diarist and her husband represented an opportunity to explore not just the years contained in her diary, but also more than two hundred years of the American experience. Genealogy at its best is very much a work in progress,

Colonial Settlement Patterns of Margaret Wight's Family. Geddy, Nicolson, Copland and Brown ancestors settled in some of early Tidewater Virginia counties such as Middlesex, Charles City, Surry, James City and York as early as 1654. The map reveals three distinct peninsulas from the mouth of the Chesapeake Bay northward. The main concentrations of early settlers of Colonial Virginia were to be found along the great rivers of Eastern Virginia. *Hanover Tavern Foundation*

and any genealogical research depends heavily on documented fact—such records and artifacts as exist, the memories of our elders and the sometimes risky hypothesis that attempts to make sense of sparse evidence. Most of the information used herein is from the work of other genealogists. Therefore, a conscientious effort was made to present facts as accurately as possible while encountering restraints of time and space. Although the following genealogy is a fraction of what has been discovered, it helps to put the family in context. It also reminds us all that we do not live just in our own era but are the beneficiaries, and sometimes victims, of all that has come before us.

Virginia Ancestors of
Margaret Copland Brown Wight

Many American history books reveal the details of the early discovery of Virginia, which includes settlement of the Jamestown colony. In 1698, after a fourth devastating fire, the colonial capital at Jamestown was moved inland. A more favorable location, known as Middle Plantation, was chosen on a Virginia peninsula between the James and York Rivers. In the following year, the new capital was renamed Williamsburg in honor of England's King William III. Royal Governor Francis Nicholson (of no known relation to Margaret Wight) laid out a plan for the new town. The public buildings, broad streets, a public square and some original residences remain in the restored center of Colonial Williamsburg today. Three generations of Mrs. Wight's family are known to have lived in Williamsburg and surrounding counties before and during the Revolution.

According to the governor's plan, the main thoroughfare through the town would be the ninety-nine-foot-wide Duke of Gloucester Street. Houses were to be built on a half-acre of land and set back a certain distance from the street. At the western end of the wide avenue would be the College of William & Mary; at the eastern terminus, a grand capitol building. The home of Virginia's British governor was erected at the end of Palace Street. The town developed slowly, but by 1710, significant progress was

Colonial Williamsburg of the Geddys and Nicolsons

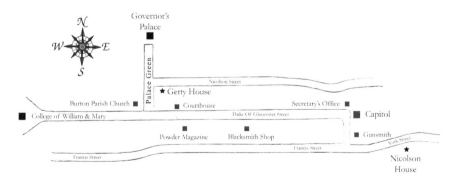

Geddys and Nicolsons in Colonial Williamsburg. The Geddy House is opposite the Palace Green. The Nicolson tailor shop and home are shown on the extension of Francis Street (York Street). Margaret Wight's grandfather, John Brown was employed in the office of the secretary of the colony. The Secretary's Office is next to the capitol. *Hanover Tavern Foundation*

Geddy House in Colonial Williamsburg. Located on the Palace Green across from Bruton Parish Church, the two-story house is one of the original buildings in the Historic Area of Colonial Williamsburg. James Geddy (II) owned the property from 1760 through the Revolutionary War era. He built the house, which was both residence and business for the Geddys, in 1762. The low-pitched roof and absence of dormers are unusual features, as are the door and balcony above the front porch. *Colonial Williamsburg Foundation*

evident. Along Duke of Gloucester Street, merchants opened shops that sold imported goods from England. Government officials and wealthy families who owned plantations in the countryside built fine homes in town. Seven days a week, the town's busy Market Square was crowded with carts filled with eggs, meat, milk, oysters, fish and local produce for sale. Four times a year, Virginia's highest courts held sessions in Williamsburg that resulted in increased population of the town and its taverns.[1]

Meanwhile, more and more immigrants from England, Scotland and other parts of Europe settled in the town. These new arrivals, some of Margaret's relatives, were hardworking and anxious to create good lives for themselves. By order of King George I of England, Williamsburg became a city in 1722, which grew to have slightly more than two hundred houses and a population around two thousand people, half of whom were slaves. By 1760 Williamsburg was well-established. Though the "townfolk" were not all British by birth, they were still British subjects who bought British goods in the shops, observed British laws and lived with the royal governor as their neighbor. Compared to the rigid social structure of English citizens, people in America were less confined to their stations in life. Virginia certainly had a wealthy class, called the gentry, but the "middling sort," as they were called—the merchants and artisans (or craftspeople) of Williamsburg and the small farmers on the outskirts of town—could become wealthier and move up in social status.[2]

From this setting, three known generations of Margaret Copland Brown Wight's family would emerge. Early records clearly establish the presence of Margaret Copland Brown Wight's relatives, especially the Geddy family in colonial Williamsburg. The Colonial Williamsburg Foundation's vast research has authenticated the city residences and businesses of Margaret Copland Brown Wight's ancestors. Archaeological evidence from excavated sites further documents their trade as accomplished gunsmiths, jewelers and silversmiths.

James (I) and Anne Geddy

Evidence suggests that James (I) and Anne Geddy emigrated from Scotland during the 1730s and established a home and business in Williamsburg. Geddy was primarily a gunsmith but also worked in wrought iron and cast brass. Before 1738, James (I) and Anne acquired two lots adjacent to the Palace Green, where he established a business that grew to be quite successful. When he died in 1744, the inventory of his estate revealed that Geddy had created a comfortable lifestyle for a Virginia craftsman of the era. After his death, two of his sons, David and William, carried on the gunsmith business. Two other sons, James (II) and John, both became silversmiths.[3]

James Geddy (II) and Elizabeth Waddill

In 1757, James Geddy (II) married his first wife, Elizabeth Waddill, sister of the noted goldsmith and engraver William Waddill. James (II) and Elizabeth Geddy had seven children. Published records clearly substantiate the business activities of James Geddy (II) in Williamsburg before the Revolution. Other varied accounts further reveal his associations with local officials and residents. "By the 1760s James Geddy was a mature thirty year-old respected member of the Williamsburg community. He was appointed by the Hustings Court to appraise final estates and to settle accounts. In August of 1760, James (I)

Geddy's widow, Anne Geddy, deeded one half of her husband's lots to her son, James (II). In 1762, James built the house that remains today[4] as one of the original buildings in the Historic Area of Colonial Williamsburg. In 1767 he was elected a member of the Common Council. On March 22, 1772, John and Elizabeth's daughter, Nancy (also called "Anne") married John Brown."[5] They would become Margaret Wight's paternal grandparents.

The Colonial Williamsburg Foundation describes James Geddy (II) as being Williamsburg's best-known colonial silversmith. Excavations in Williamsburg have produced what are believed to be samples of the Geddy family's work. Among the discoveries are engraved silver table spoons and brass furniture hooks.[6] Articles published in the *Virginia Gazette* expand the body of knowledge about the Geddys' life in Williamsburg before the Revolution. Personal accounts and business ledgers catalog a varied clientele who crossed the threshold of the shop, which was busiest during sessions of the House of Burgesses and the county courts. Two clients are of particular interest. An account entry on December 7, 1766, shows that Geddy mended two fans for George Washington. Thomas Jefferson noted payment to an apprentice of James Geddy on May 2, 1769. Other receipts show that Geddy provided a full range of services, making small silver items, engraving work (on knee buckles), repairing silver and gold items (spoons, seals and jewelry), repairing watches and selling jewelry.[7]

Information regarding any official involvement of James Geddy (II) in the Revolution was not found from the limited research conducted. However, it is known that by 1776 many colonists and their leaders wanted to declare independence from England. "Not all colonists shared rebellious ideas. Many loyal British subjects moved out of Williamsburg to farms or plantations. Others moved back to England";[8] neither of which seems to have occurred among Margaret's known ancestors.

> Geddy stayed in Williamsburg during the early part of the Revolutionary War. Between June 1774 and November 1776 he provided various services recorded in the account day book of Paul Carrington. It appears that James was ready to leave Williamsburg, a year later when he advertised on 2 May 1777 to sell the houses and lot where he lived. Brother-in-law William Waddill had already moved to New Kent County. The ad stated that if the properties were not sold before 10 June, they would be auctioned. However, they were not sold, nor were they auctioned; Geddy must have revised his plans for a December departure. He

probably left Williamsburg as planned in December 1777, but returned for the winter legislative session to settle outstanding accounts [as revealed in other documents].[9]

The December 1778 deed of the Williamsburg house referenced Geddy as jeweler of Dinwiddie County, confirming that he and his wife, Elizabeth, had settled there on a four-hundred-acre farm on the Nottoway River, thirty miles above Petersburg. The Geddy family would later relocate to Petersburg, which may have been prompted by the deaths of James's wife, Elizabeth, and their two children, sometime between 1783 and 1784. James (II) settled into the Petersburg community, where he married for a second time (another Elizabeth) in 1784. That same year, he was elected to the Petersburg Common Council and still held the position in 1796.[10] When Margaret's paternal great-grandfather died on May 12, 1807, at the age of seventy-six, he had seen five children grow to maturity; both of his sons had followed him in the silversmith's trade. James (II) had also seen all his children marry, including his eldest daughter, Nancy "Anne" Geddy, who would become Margaret Wight's paternal grandmother.

NANCY ANNE GEDDY AND JOHN BROWN (II)

Nancy Anne Geddy (also known as Anne Geddy) married John Brown (II), Margaret Wight's paternal grandfather, on March 22, 1772, in Williamsburg. Efforts to discover details about John Brown (II) have been somewhat disappointing. It does appear that "John Brown, the son of John and Judith Brown, was born on October 4, 1750, in or near Williamsburg. When he married Nancy Anne Geddy John Brown was employed in the office of the secretary of the colony. Three years later he was appointed clerk of the Court of Mecklenburg County and was sworn into office before the court's justices July 10, 1775. While in Mecklenburg, he served as an officer in the Virginia militia."[11] Another source cites that "he learned the skills of a court clerk as an apprentice in the office of Benjamin Waller, the clerk of the colonial General Court of Virginia."[12] It is apparent that his service in "the office of the secretary of the colony" put Brown in Williamsburg, where he and Nancy Anne might have become acquainted. After their marriage, they probably remained in Williamsburg until John began his duties as clerk in Mecklenburg County in July 1775.

Although John Brown held the clerkship of Mecklenburg from July 10, 1775, until February 9, 1795, he relocated to Richmond in 1781 when he was appointed clerk of the General Court of Virginia. He must have maintained both posts during the fourteen-year period between 1781 and 1795, as he did not resign from the Mecklenberg courts until 1795. A nineteenth-century clerk in Mecklenberg commented about John and Nancy Anne Geddy Brown's residence in Richmond. It "faced on Broad Street and ran back on 9th Street to the little Catholic Church facing Grace Street. Mr. Brown was a good gardener and took a great deal of interest in the vegetables he grew in the back of his residence."[13]

Details about all of John and Nancy Anne Geddy Brown's children are scant. Evidence indicates "they had two daughters and three sons." Their eldest son, John H. Brown was born in Mecklenburg County and would become the father of diarist Margaret Copland Brown Wight. Their youngest son, James, was auditor for the state of Virginia for more than forty years.[14]

The personal life of John Brown (II) remains somewhat of a mystery, but his professional career is well-documented. It seems he made Virginia's court system his life's work. He was the clerk of the court of appeals, the highest court in Virginia, from 1785 until his death in 1810. From 1789 to 1793, Brown was the clerk of the District Court of Richmond, as well as clerk of the Court of Chancery in 1787.[15] In December of 1792, Margaret's grandfather was elected a common councilman for the city of Richmond, but he declined to serve. In 1795, Brown was appointed by the General Assembly to a committee that also included such notables as George Wythe, John Marshall, Bushrod Washington and John Wickham. This group of eminent lawyers set about to collect and superintend the printing of the Virginia acts concerning land transactions. Thomas Jefferson gave the men access to his own library of law books and urged the committee to expand its focus to include all the statutes of Virginia from the time records had been kept to 1792. This advice was accepted, and the General Assembly of Virginia arranged several years later to have William Waller Hening edit the *Statutes at Large of Virginia*,[16] a well-known reference for historians.

Mrs. Wight's grandfather associated with John Marshall on other occasions. In 1797 and 1798, President John Adams asked John Marshall to take a delegation to France to soothe tensions between the French and U.S. governments that had been mounting since the end of the Revolution. John Brown accompanied him, along with other members of the delegation, including Charles Cotesworth Pinckney and Elbridge Gerry. When the

Nicolson House. The house and business of Robert Nicolson was built between 1751 and 1753 on the outskirts of town (on what is York Street today). Unlike most of the properties in Colonial Williamsburg, the Nicolson House was privately owned and continuously inhabited until the Colonial Williamsburg Foundation purchased the property in 1964. Only minor work was necessary in and around the house before turning it into a private residence for Foundation employees. *Colonial Williamsburg Foundation*

French government refused to meet the delegation unless it paid enormous bribes, Marshall refused, causing the XYZ Affair.[17]

Original manuscripts of John Brown's reports concerning the assessment of court costs, the technicalities of appeals and other clerical matters relating to the court of appeals from 1791 to 1799 are among the Library of Virginia's collection. Brown's reports were published in the *University of Richmond Law Review* in 1977.[18]

John Brown died in Richmond on November 2, 1810, a year after the birth of his granddaughter, Margaret Copland Brown Wight. His obituary, printed in the *Daily Richmond Enquirer* said he was "a gentleman much respected." His wife, Nancy Anne Geddy Brown, had died fifteen years earlier in 1795, leaving her husband a widower who never remarried.

WILLIAMSBURG MATERNAL ANCESTORS

After establishing the presence of Margaret Copland Brown Wight's paternal ancestors in Williamsburg, both before and after the Revolution, evidence also revealed one line of her maternal ancestors were there as well. Various documents and the research of the Colonial Williamsburg Foundation provide details about the life of Mrs. Wight's maternal great-grandfather, Robert Nicolson.[19]

ROBERT NICOLSON AND MARY WATERS

The family of Margaret Wight's maternal great-grandfather, Robert Nicolson, entered the Virginia colony as early as 1654, probably from Scotland. The families lived in several of the Tidewater counties, including James City, Surry, York and Charles City. The Nicolson surname has at least two different spellings, which makes research a challenge. Variations occur in the historic records, and attention should be given to the absence of an *h* in the name of Mrs. Wight's ancestors. Evidence reveals that Margaret Wight's great-grandfather who married Mary Waters of York County about 1747 was the fourth generation of Robert Nicolsons from Surry County.[20] By 1752, they had moved to Williamsburg, where Robert bought two half-acre lots, built his home and opened his first tailor shop.

> These lots on the outskirts of town, less expensive than those within the city limits, were the setting for a neighborhood of craftsmen and young men just starting their careers. The Nicolson House, owned by the Colonial Williamsburg Foundation since 1965, was built circa 1751–1753 on what was, at that time, the fringes of Williamsburg. The house began as a small three-bay structure. Around 1766, as Nicolson's family and business grew, he added a two-bay extension on the western end of the house. Structurally, the house has essentially remained the same for the last 200 years. Margaret's great-grandparents had seven children, five of whom were born while they were living in the house on Francis Street. Of their children, Robert, Jr. became a noted surgeon during the Revolutionary War: George, became mayor of Richmond, and Thomas became the publisher of the *Virginia Gazette* and General

Advertiser. There were also three other sons, William, John and Andrew. The couple's only daughter, Rebecca…[21]would later marry Mrs. Wight's grandfather, Charles Copland.

To help augment his income from the tailoring shop located across the street, Nicolson took in lodgers. An advertisement in the March 28, 1755 edition of the *Virginia Gazette and General Advertizer* showed that one of his boarders proposed "to teach Gentlemen and Ladies to play on the Organ, Harpsichord, or Spinett; and to instruct those Gentlemen that play on other Instruments, so as to enable them to play in Concert. Upon haveing Encouragement I will fix in any part of the Country." It is likely that Nicolson continued to accommodate tenants in his home. The next reference found regarding Nicolson's boarding practice is seen when he advertised in the *Virginia Gazette* on September 12, 1766, for lodgers:

WILLIAMSBURG, SEPTEMBER 12, 1766
GENTLEMEN who attend the General Courts and Assembly may be accomodated with genteel LODGINGS, have BREAKFAST and good STABLING for their HORSES, by applying to ROBERT NICOLSON

In 1773, Robert Nicolson moved his business into the center of town, buying a shop on Duke of Gloucester Street. Besides tailoring services, Nicolson's shop served as a subsidiary post office and a general store.[22] Nicolson was prominent in civic affairs, serving on one pre-Revolutionary committee with such prominent fellow citizens as George Wythe, Peyton Randolph and Robert Carter Nicholas, Sr. He was appointed in 1775 as an agent for the Fredericksburg Gun Manufactory to receive much-needed old brass to provide arms for Virginia troops. He also performed wartime services as a tailor, employing soldiers in his shop to make uniforms for the state, and served as merchant for the "Publick Store" located in Williamsburg.[23] In December 1774, Margaret's great-grandfather "was named on the Committee of Safety for Williamsburg, said Committee naming Williamsburg as the rendezvous for the troops of the colony. Patrick Henry, the Commander-in-Chief arrived there September 20, 1775, six months after making his famous 'give me liberty or give me death' speech. He selected the field back of William & Mary College as their camping ground."[24] After the Revolution, Robert Nicolson may have sought to again supplement his income. In 1783, he was listed as a tax collector for the city.

It can be assumed that the Nicolson's youngest daughter, Rebecca, remained with her family in Williamsburg during the events of the Revolution. She would, therefore, have had firsthand accounts of activities, especially considering some of the responsibilities of her father. Almost a decade after the start of the Revolution, Rebecca Nicolson married Charles Copland in 1786. This couple would become Margaret Wight's maternal grandparents. Rebecca's mother (and Margaret's maternal great-grandmother), Mary Waters Nicolson, died October 10, 1793. She was buried at Bruton Parish Church, the records of which show that six of Robert and Mary Nicolson's children were baptized there between 1749 and 1766. Robert Nicolson died in 1797 and is buried at St. John's Episcopal Church in Richmond, Virginia.[25]

COPLAND ANCESTORS

Margaret Copland Brown Wight would know only one of her maternal grandparents, Charles Copland. But determining the facts of his lineage proves challenging, as there are major gaps in the information available to document the lines of this family. Therefore, some Copland genealogists have used speculation and rough hypotheses to bridge gaps. To further compound the problem, the matter of variable surname spelling emerges. One genealogist commented that "any researcher of Copeland genealogy quickly encounters and is often confused by the various spellings of the family surname. To name but a few: Copeland, Coupland, Copland, Cooplande, Cowplande and Coplen. Most of these differences seem to have arisen because of the generally imperfect state of literacy among our ancestors and the keepers of their records, at least up through the early years of the nineteenth century. People pronounced the name one way and officials recorded it the way they thought it should have been spelled based on what they heard."[26]

The most plausible theory regarding the lineage of Charles Copland links him to:

> William (III) Copland, who was born in 1687 in Middlesex County, Virginia. It seems that William traveled to Chowan County, North Carolina prior to his father's 1712 move there, where he met Sarah Champen (or Champion). They were married around 1705. He and Sarah had five children. William Copland served as

a constable for Chowan County sometime before 1715. Orange County, North Carolina records show he was called to serve on a jury in December 1752, shortly before his death in 1753. His range of movements between Virginia—as far north as Middlesex County—and North Carolina encompassing Tidewater Chowan County and Piedmont Orange County suggest that William was a man of some means who had a wide scope of business interests.[27]

It is believed one of William's sons was Peter Copland, born in 1728, who later married Elizabeth Gatewood. An ad in the *Virginia Gazette* in 1783 provides a probable link to Margaret Copland Brown Wight's maternal grandfather, Charles Copland. Peter may very well have been Charles Copland's father when examining that article, which read "To be SOLD to the Highest Bidder, For ready money, on Friday the ad day of January next, At the Plantation where Peter Copland, deceased, lately lived in Charles City. All the household and kitchen furniture of the deceased; also the crop of corn and fodder, the flock of cattle and sheep, a riding chair and harness, a light wagon, and six Negroes. The sale to begin precisely at eleven o'clock. Charles Copland, Executor, Dec. 4, 1783."

CHARLES COPLAND AND REBECCA NICOLSON

Regardless of the tentative evidence of Charles Copland's parents, research of genealogist Janice Nicolson Holmes states that "Charles Copland first practiced law in Staunton, VA, 38 miles from Charlottesville, Albemarle County."[28] Another source states that he "was probably a native of Charles City County. Certainly he was living there during the American Revolution, and there he probably began his legal career. Few facts have surfaced to explain Copland's legal training or introduction to the practice of law. However, it is known that by the middle 1780s he was actively practicing in the courts of Williamsburg and the surrounding counties."[29]

In Williamsburg, Copland probably met the successful merchant Robert Nicolson and his family. A York County marriage bond reveals that in February 1786, Copland married Nicolson's youngest daughter, Rebecca. Mrs. Holmes, a third great-niece of Rebecca Nicolson Copland, states in her work, "on December 29, 1788, Charles moved with his 22 yr-old wife and their infant daughter, Mary, from Williamsburg to Richmond, where he continued his law practice." The couple's first-born daughter, Mary Copland, would become the mother of Margaret Copland Brown Wight in 1809.

From his new residence, Charles Copland continued to attend court in Charles City County and served as deputy commonwealth attorney. Gradually, he transferred the bulk of his legal practice to Richmond, the new capital city, relocated from Williamsburg in 1780. Margaret's grandfather qualified in 1790 to practice in Wythe's High Court of Chancery and in the U.S. District Court. Within two years he was also appearing before the Richmond Hustings Court, the Henrico County Court and the Virginia General Court. Copland's rise in the Richmond legal community was seemingly rapid.[30] One of his notable cases involved Gabriel, slave and blacksmith of Thomas Henry Prosser of Henrico County. Charles Copland served as Gabriel's defense attorney in 1799, a year before the Richmond conspiracy was disclosed. A local neighbor, Absalom Johnson, had accosted Gabriel in an apparent confrontation over a stolen pig and had lost "a considerable part of his left ear" to Gabriel's uneven but effective bite. As a result, the Henrico Court tried the blacksmith for maiming Johnson.[31] A year later, Gabriel took part in the planning of a large-scale slave uprising, an incident referred to as Gabriel's Rebellion, which resulted in trials and executions of many participants, including Garbriel himself.

> As a rising young attorney, Copland purchased a lot in the so-called "Court End" of Richmond near Capitol Square, at the northeast corner of Broad and Eleventh Streets. Sometime before 1796 he built a small one-story cottage facing 11th Street. Later he added a two-story structure facing Broad Street to the original house. This home, built in the vicinity of those of fellow attorneys John Wickham and Edmund Randolph, and of Judge Spencer Roane, remained standing until 1921. For a brief period Margaret's grandfather also dabbled in politics, succeeding to Dr. William Foushee's old seat in the House of Delegates as Richmond's representative in the assemblies of 1799–1800 and 1800–1801.[32]

At the height of his professional career, two tragedies touched the lives of Charles Copland and his family. The first was the death of his wife, Rebecca, in late July of 1800, which left behind nine young children. The second tragedy occurred on the terrible night of the Richmond Theater Fire in 1811. Four of Copland's children were there. According to Copland's diary and other sources, three of his children found their way home to report their sister Elizabeth missing. Copland raced to the burning theater to find his daughter. He could not. Young Elizabeth, along with as many as seventy others, had perished in the fire. When the Monumental Church was built on the site of the burned theater, a crypt, which contained the ashen remains of many of the victims, was placed inside.

Charles Copland kept meticulous records about his business and family. His tendency to record events may have been passed on to his granddaughter Margaret Wight and her son Charles; their personal diaries form the basis for this book. Copland's day books are at the Library of Virginia and portions have been published in several periodicals.

As previously stated, of her four grandparents, Charles Copland would be the only one Margaret Copland Brown Wight would ever personally know. Her paternal grandfather, John Brown, died when she was just a year old. Both of her grandmothers, Nancy Anne Geddy Brown and Rebecca Nicolson Copland, had left their husbands widowers years earlier. Charles Copland died in 1836 but lived long enough to witness Margaret's marriage and the births of several of her children.

John H. Brown and Mary Copland

It is disappointing to have so little to report about Margaret Wight's parents—John H. Brown and Mary (Maria) Copland. Mary Copland (1787–1845) was the oldest daughter of Charles & Rebecca Nicolson Copland and was referred to as both Maria and Mary.[33] She married John H. Brown in Richmond on September 25, 1806. Margaret Copland Brown was born three years later on June 30, 1809. No information has been found to document the occupation of her father, John H. Brown. Other than his will and accounts of his death, the only reference located that mentions his name appears in a probated Chesterfield County will dated September 10, 1810. The text follows: "Trustees Charles Copland & John H. Brown to sell lots in Manchester permitting wife to occupy lots and possess 4 negroes in Richmond." The daybooks of Charles Copland[34] show that on March 19, 1811, his son-in-law John H. Brown "died at Savannah in Georgia…He had gone to Savannah with a hope of improving his health." Brown's death left behind Mary (Maria) Copland Brown, a twenty-four-year-old widow, with an infant daughter, Margaret Copland Brown, whose diary is the basis for this book.

John H. Brown was buried at Colonial Park Cemetery in Chatham County, Georgia. His will was probated May 16, 1811. He named three executors: his father, John Brown (I); father-in-law, Charles Copland; and friend John G. Gamble. John H. Brown left a sizeable estate, which would provide for the well-being of his wife and daughter. Mary never remarried and seems to have continued to live in Richmond near her father. The 1830 Census shows a Maria Brown (age forty to forty-nine) living in Richmond's Madison Ward District with one white female (age twenty to twenty-nine) and four slaves. Some other details about Mary's life can be found by examining insurance policies, as well as her father's account books and will. Mutual Assurance Society policies reveal that as early as 1813, Mary Copland Brown was living in a Richmond house on the corner of I (now Marshall) and Eleventh Streets. Additional policies indicate her continued occupation of that residence at least until 1836. The 1829 insurance policies for Charles Copland show him living in the same block as his daughter. His property consisted of an office, kitchen, servants' dwelling, stable and carriage house. Review of the Charles S. Morgan 1848 map of Richmond divulges that Copland's holdings made up most of the block fronting Broad between Tenth and Eleventh Streets.

Based on available evidence, it seems that Margaret's grandfather was an active participant in her life. Excerpts from some of Charles Copland's records show that he made payments, as his daughter's executor, to Mary for her financial support and that of her daughter, Margaret. Beginning as early as 1822, the account of John H. Brown's estate shows monthly "cash paid to Mary Brown as guardian of Margaret Brown," which continued for several years. In 1827, an entry appears that cash was paid for a *pianoforte*[35] for Margaret Brown.

Margaret's mother, Mary Copland Brown, was alive to witness the birth of eight of her daughter's ten children, three of whom died before their grandmother. As an only child, Mrs. Wight seems to have maintained a relationship with her mother throughout her life. Several personal letters of Ann Eliza Wight, Margaret's sister-in-law, are among the Virginia Historical Society's manuscript collection. Some of her correspondence reveals that Mary Brown accompanied her daughter to Goochland County on various occasions and mentions Mrs. Brown personally. Perhaps her personality is reflected in one of the codicils to her will where Margaret's mother requested a "plain funeral without ostentation as well as a plain tombstone." Maria (Mary) Copland Brown's obituary, printed December 2 in the *Daily Richmond Enquirer,* read: "Died 30 November 1845 Mrs. Maria Brown in her 58th year, funeral at the residence of her son-in-law Mr. John Wight."

Wight Family Heritage

The roots of Margaret Copland Brown Wight's ancestors—the Geddys, Nicolsons, Coplands and Browns—are clearly planted deep in Virginia soil. Quite the opposite is the case when reviewing the heritage of her husband's family. Researcher William Ward Wight created an extensive genealogy of Thomas Wight, whose family immigrated to seventeenth-century New England, specifically Dedham, Massachusetts—part of the Massachusetts Bay Colony. Even though Margaret's husband was born in Virginia, John Wight's early ancestors seem to have lived primarily in the states of Massachusetts and Connecticut.

Jabez Wight (I) and Ruth Swan

John's paternal great-grandfather, Jabez Wight, was born in 1701, probably in Massachusetts. His ancestors were subscribers to the fund that established Harvard College, from which Wight graduated in 1721. In 1723, records show he was a grammar schoolmaster in Medfield, Massachusetts. Three years later, Jabez became the ordained minister of the Fifth Church of Norwich, which was constituted under Reverend Jabez. He was its first and only pastor. After his death in September 1782, no public worship was held and the church was allowed to decay. The inscription on his Connecticut tombstone states that he had been a minister for fifty-six years. It appears he and his wife had six sons and one daughter.[36]

Jabez Wight (II) and Sarah Lord Preston

John Wight's paternal grandfather was also named Jabez. Born in 1730, he married Sarah Lord of Preston, Connecticut, where he lived and his children were born. Specific details of their lives were not found beyond the births of four daughters and four sons. The couple's third son, Hezekiah Lord Wight, would become the father of the John Wight who later married Margaret Copland Brown. Jabez died in 1787, and his widow died the next year at age sixty.[37]

Hezekiah Lord Wight and Nancy Leeds

John Wight's father, Hezekiah, was born in 1765 and left Preston, Connecticut, in early 1791. His final destination became Richmond, Virginia. In 1798, several years after his arrival in Richmond, Hezekiah married Nancy Leeds in Chesterfield County. Nancy was also from Connecticut and may have come to Virginia with her father, Jeremiah Leeds, who left Preston for Richmond in 1791[38] also. Further research is required to establish why the Leeds came to Virginia.

Hezekiah Lord Wight is described in various records as being a tobacco merchant in Richmond and was at times in partnership with his cousin John Fitch Wight and with the latter's son, Jabez Wight.[39] To say simply that Hezekiah was a tobacco merchant seems to discount the dynamics of his business activities. Reading Hezekiah's will and personal papers[40] provide additional information about some of his pursuits. To fully comprehend the extent of his commercial enterprise would require further research. Yet a review of Mutual Assurance Society policies discloses much information about the properties owned and operated by Hezekiah Wight. Careful examination shows just how many buildings were involved in his tobacco operation. For example, in 1836 Hezekiah Lord Wight owned a tobacco factory, worth $4,000, around the old warehouse district in Richmond. The policy shows Wight owning a three-story building on Eighteenth Street between D and E Streets contiguous to five other warehouses. An additional policy in 1836 shows insurance for other properties owned by Wight along the entire block between D and C Streets and Virginia and Fourteenth Streets. The buildings consisted of kitchens, a stable, three counting houses and a dwelling. These policies do not constitute the entirety of Wight's real estate holdings over the years but do provide insight into his business success over time. Census records also reveal a notion of prosperity. In 1820, Hezekiah Wight's Richmond enumeration shows a total of fifty-three persons, forty-seven of whom were slaves. The 1830 Census confirms his move to Goochland, where the record shows a total of twenty-eight people, of whom twenty were slaves.

It is not known how Hezekiah Wight became a wealthy tobacco merchant, but various accounts describe the city's thriving tobacco industry in what is called today Richmond's "Tobacco Row" in Shockoe Bottom.

> The tobacco industry began in the district in the 18th century
> with the establishment of tobacco inspection warehouses, where

farmers bought their hogsheads of tobacco for storage and inspection. Certificates from the warehouses were a medium of exchange with local tobacco merchants. In the early 19th century, the nature of the tobacco business changed from exporting cured tobacco to the North or Europe as a raw product to manufacturing chewing tobacco in Richmond factories…slave workers stemmed tobacco leaves and pressed them into cakes of chewing tobacco. The tobacco industry continued to grow in the late 19th and early 20th centuries.[41]

Many of the early tobacco establishments were consumed in the Evacuation Fire during the Civil War, and the Wights' property was probably included.

Hezekiah Wight and his wife had seven children: Edwin Lord, Calvin, William Leeds, John, Sally Ann, Louisa and Ann Eliza Wight. Various census records show that he and his family lived in Richmond, even after his wife's death in 1813. It seems that Hezekiah never remarried. Margaret's father-in-law would eventually relocate to Goochland County when he became part owner of a prestigious plantation, which is now a historic national landmark.

After engaging in Richmond's tobacco industry for over thirty years, Hezekiah and his son, Edwin purchased the "large estate called 'Tuckahoe' founded by the Randolph family, one of the most outstanding colonial families in Virginia. A numerous clan, the Randolphs had an enormous influence in shaping the habits, customs, and political science of both the colony and the nation."[42] Tuckahoe's historical records also reveal that Thomas Jefferson lived at the plantation as a young boy and received his first education in the one-room schoolhouse that still stands today. On January 12, 1830, Tuckahoe Plantation passed out of the hands of the Randolph family. The Wights purchased 588 acres of land in Henrico and Goochland Counties, including all of Tuckahoe except the family graveyard, for $11,000 at auction from creditors of Thomas Randolph III.[43] When Hezekiah Wight died in 1837, terms of his will stipulated that Edwin become the beneficiary of his father's portion of the plantation.

CHILDREN OF HEZEKIAH LORD AND NANCY LEEDS WIGHT

Edwin Lord Wight (1799–1850), Hezekiah's eldest son, appears to have engaged in the tobacco business with his father. Records show that in 1837 Edwin married Margaret Nicolson Copland, cousin of diarist Margaret Copland Brown Wight. It appears the couple resided at Tuckahoe and had no children. Edwin's obituary in the *Richmond Daily Whig* stated that he died on March 25, 1850, in the city. "His relatives & friends and those of his brothers Dr. William L. Wight & Mr. John Wight are requested to attend his funeral this day at 9½ o'clock from the United Presbyterian Church from whence his remains will be carried to his late residence, Tuckahoe, Goochland." Edwin's widow was named beneficiary of most of her husband's estate. However, less than two months after Edwin's death, Richard B. Haxall as executor and Margaret N. Wight as executrix of Edwin Wight deceased, sold Tuckahoe and the personal estate of Edwin Wight. Goochland County

Tuckahoe Plantation. Built by the Randolph Family of Virginia between 1730 and 1740, this National Landmark was the boyhood home of Thomas Jefferson. Hezekiah Lord Wight and Edwin Leeds Wight owned the property from 1830 until 1850. Several family members including Hezekiah Wight, Nancy Leeds Wight, Edwin Wight, Louisa Wight and Ann Eliza Wight are buried in the family graveyard on the property. Tuckahoe is listed on the National Register of Historic Places. *Tuckahoe Plantation*

Here Lyethe Ye bodyes of Descendants of
THOMAS WIGHT
Selectman of DEDHAM Massachusetts 1635
One of five original founders of
HARVARD COLLEGE 1638
HEZEKIAH LORD WIGHT
Of
TUCK-AH-OE
B. April 14, 1765
D. July 12, 1837
His wife
NANCY LEEDS WIGHT
B. Jan. 1, 1790 — D. Feb. 26, 1812
EDWIN LORD WIGHT
D. Mar. 12, 1799 — D. Mar. 12, 1852
LOUISA WIGHT
B. Aug. 16, 1807 — D. Sep. 29, 1821
ANN ELIZA WIGHT
B. Mar. 16, 1811 — D. Jan. 11, 1869
Restoration 1948

Headstone for Members of the Wight Family. The headstone lies in a fenced area at Tuckahoe Plantation in Virginia. Based on court records and other official documents, the date of death for Edwin Lord Wight is incorrect. It appears that the headstone was refurbished in 1948 and this may account for the error. Edwin Wight died in 1850. *Dale Paige Talley*

court records show that on May 8, 1850, Joseph Allen of Richmond made the purchase for $32,000.

Hezekiah and Nancy Wight's third son, William Leeds Wight (1802–1873), was born in Richmond and graduated from Yale in 1822. He received his medical training at the University of Pennsylvania in Philadelphia and practiced medicine in Goochland County until his death. William married Grace Hughes of New Haven, Connecticut, in 1834. In 1844, the couple purchased Ingleside Plantation, where it appears they lived for much of their married life. Both sons of William and Grace Wight were Confederate soldiers. Their oldest, William Washington, attended the University of Virginia before enlisting on May 1, 1861. Records indicate that Henry Theodore Wight entered the Confederate army on August 12, 1862. Fortunately, both of John Wight's nephews survived the war.

John Wight, husband of Margaret Copland Brown, was born on November 15, 1803, in Richmond. It seems curious that Hezekiah's sons, descendants of Harvard College founders, would attend Yale College. Yet the archives there indicate John Wight graduated in 1823, a year after his brother William Leeds. In 1824, John attended Litchfield Law School in Connecticut. Since students did not graduate or receive diplomas, no graduation records were kept.[44] John Wight married Augusta Maria Huggins in New Haven, Connecticut, on September 18, 1827. Their only child, Julia Leeds, was born there in 1828. Augusta's life was cut short. In 1830 as reported in the *Richmond Daily Whig*: "Died on June 15, 1830 at Tuckahoe Mrs. Augusta M. Wight, consort of John Wight." John Wight's official residence at the time of Augusta's death could not be confirmed, but the 1830 Census shows a John Wight (free white male age twenty to

Children of John and Margaret Wight. This half plate is framed in an embossed leather case. This mounting of several photographs in a single frame was prepared by William A. Pratt of Richmond, Virginia, who pioneered this "medallion" technique. Produced sometime in the 1850s, the photographs represent seven of Margaret Wight's children. Based on their ages, the children are thought to be as follows (from the top center clockwise): Charles Copland Wight, Mary Elizabeth Wight, Emily Cornelia Wight, William Marshall Wight, Virginia Chapman Wight ("Jennie") and Anne Louisa Wight. The center is thought to be John Henry Wight. *Collection of Robert E. Haines.*

twenty-nine) residing in the Monroe Ward District of Richmond. Included in his household was one free white female, age twenty to twenty-nine—the description fits that of his sister, Ann Eliza—and one free white female under age five, who was probably John's daughter, Julia Leeds. The census also shows one colored female, age thirty-six to fifty-four, living there.

John Wight had three younger sisters. The oldest died in 1806 as an infant. His second sister, Louisa Wight, died in 1821 at age fourteen. The last child born of Hezekiah and Nancy was Ann Eliza Wight (1811–1869), who seems never to have married but to have kept a close relationship with her brothers throughout her life. Although minimal details came forth about her personal activities, contents of several of her letters provide some information. For instance, Ann Eliza wrote to her friend Mary Carrington on July 18, 1833, from Tuckahoe, where she commented that she hadn't "seen Margaret [diarist] yet but hope to on Saturday. She will come up the country from all I can hear about the 10th of August." In another letter written from Tuckahoe on January 25, 1837, Ann Eliza states, "Margaret [Brown Wight] has a daughter five weeks old which she calls Ann Louisa. Ann after me & Louisa after my Sister, a very pleasing name to me. She is to be called Ann."[45] It is not known when Ann Eliza Wight became a resident of Richmond, as revealed in Margaret Wight's diary. However, the contents of her father's will show that she inherited a building with three tenements on the corner of D and Virginia Streets in Richmond when Hezekiah died in 1837, and Mutual Assurance Society policies continued fire coverage of Ann Eliza's property through 1858.

John Wight and Margaret Copland Brown

Margaret Brown and John Wight were married on November 31, 1831. The ceremony took place in Richmond. Biographical notes from the Litchfield Historical Society state that John Wight's profession was "business" and that he became a merchant when he returned to Richmond from Litchfield Law School in Connecticut. It is plausible that John was employed in his father's tobacco business, but evidence to support that idea has not been found, although the 1840 Census does indicate that John Wight's occupation was "in commerce."

Margaret and John Wight had ten children. They started their family together with the birth of their first child, Margaret Copland, in October of 1832. She died several months later. Five additional children had been born by 1840. Two of these children, Ellen Augusta and Alice Lester, both died in 1842, just four days apart. When the 1840 Census was taken, it showed John Wight as head of a large Richmond household of thirteen people, including four slaves. By 1850, five additional children had arrived, all of whom reached adulthood. Margaret's husband must have become employed by the city of Richmond some time before the next census. The *1845–1846 Richmond City Directory*, the 1850 Census and the *1852 Richmond City Directory* all show his occupation as "collector of city taxes." By the time the *1855 Richmond City Directory* was issued and the 1860 Census was taken, John Wight did not give an occupation but did list his residence as Charles City County. In that year, his personal property was listed at $7,100, but no value for any real estate was provided.

Julia Leeds, John Wight's daughter by his first wife, left the household in 1848 when she married William Hedges Hubbard Gardner, a wholesale shoe dealer in Richmond.[46] The couple may have relocated at some point, considering their first child, Gertrude Augusta, was born in New Jersey in 1851. However, the family could have returned to Richmond later; records show the birth of their only son, Guy Huggins, occurring in Richmond in April of 1853. Just three years later, Julia's husband died in Richmond, but Julia and her children didn't remain in the city permanently. Evidence shows they moved north at some time, as the 1860 Census reveals Julia living with her two children in New Haven, Connecticut, birthplace of her deceased mother, Augusta Maria Huggins.

Beyond John Wight's employment, details related to living arrangements of the Wight family during the mid-1850s present conflicting information. One source states that "John Wight and family resided in Richmond until 1852. In that year they removed to a plantation, Ball Field [Bullfield], in Charles City County, Va, an estate still in the family but now in ruins."[47] It does appear that the Wights took possession of a farm and probably relocated there in 1854. Charles City court records show that property was purchased on December 30, 1853, using money from Margaret Wight's trust left by her mother, Mary Brown. Margaret's uncle William Copland had acted as trustee. His name appeared on the deed as having purchased the property known as Bullfield. Surprisingly, a review of a Charles City County deed book reveals that William Copland, again acting as trustee, sold Bullfield five years later for $6,500 to Archibald Taylor on August 8, 1859. Assumptions, therefore, that the Wights ever lived at Bullfield or were living there at the start of the Civil War are called into question. Further research is required to fully understand the issue. However, the 1860 Census shows three daughters "at home" with John and Margaret Wight in Charles City County: Ann Louisa, Emily Cornelia and Virginia Chapman.

Their eldest son, John Henry, married Agnes Adams in 1855 and lived in Richmond. The earliest record (1850–51) found for John Henry shows him working as a clerk at 181 Main Street (his father's office was at 161 Main Street). The *1859 Richmond City Directory* listed John Henry as a bookkeeper on Broad between First and Foushee Streets. When the 1860 Census and *1860 Richmond City Directory* were reviewed, he was listed as head of household and as a bookkeeper, respectively. In 1860, John lived on Ninth Street, north of Leigh, with his wife and two sons, John James and Robert Caskie Wight.

The Wights' oldest living daughter, Mary Elizabeth,[48] was not listed as living with the family in Charles City in 1860. A serendipitous discovery in the *1859 Norfolk City Directory* lists a Miss M.H. Wright [*sic*] as an Assistant to the Principal of the Female Department, Norfolk Public Schools.[49] Mary was obviously in Norfolk in December of 1859, as revealed in a letter she wrote to the Virginia Military Institute regarding tuition payment for her brother, Charles Copland Wight. The *1860 Norfolk City Directory* repeats a listing for Mary in the Norfolk Public Schools. But her subsequent activities were unknown until another of her letters from Norfolk to VMI dated February 20, 1861, surfaced. Mary was still in Norfolk, and two months after that letter was written, the Civil War began.

Mary Wight may have decided to leave Norfolk because she no longer had a job. One source suggests that in

> April 1861 our schools were probably closed, because Norfolk was momentarily expecting the frigate Cumberland to bombard the city. Parents are hesitant today about having their children in school during a hurricane or snowstorm…and would have refused to subject them to the hazard of a bombardment. Brawls and barroom fights were not uncommon during the early days of the war, and it would have been unwise for parents living any distance from a school to have sent their children to classes. The streets were filled with troops, many of them arriving daily from other Southern states.[50]

By August of 1861, Margaret's oldest daughter, Mary was in Culpeper, Virginia, at the Smith Hospital where she volunteered as a nurse. Her service there apparently resulted in her untimely death.

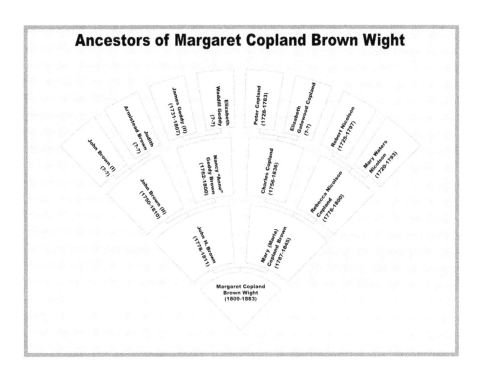

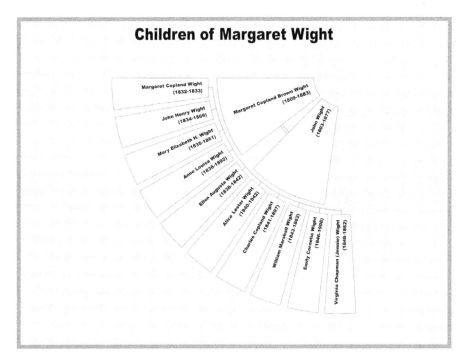

Children of Hezekiah Lord Wight

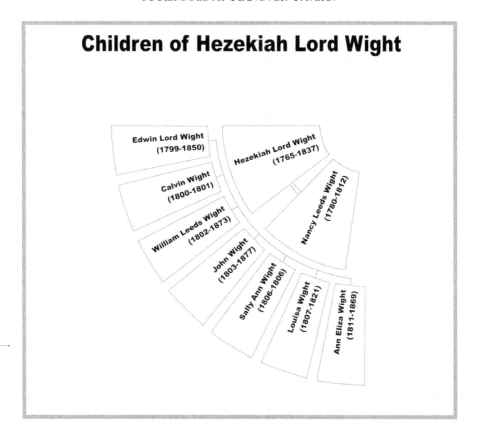

Two other children of John and Margaret Wight were not present for the 1860 Census. Their middle son, Charles Copland, was beginning his third term at VMI in Lexington, Virginia. By virtue of his status as a cadet, Charles went into the Confederate service in April of 1861. His younger brother, William Marshall, was not living in Charles City with his parents, and it is known that he also became a Confederate soldier in 1861.

Throughout the research for this book, a particular issue has remained a puzzle. When and why did the Wights leave their home in Charles City County? Mrs. Wight states on the opening page of her diary that she, her husband and their daughter Emily had been living at the Hanover Tavern for one year. To add further confusion, another entry dated April 11, 1864, reveals that Mrs. Wight disclosed that "all our necessary articles of furniture are in Norfolk which is now in possession of the Yankees." Countless reasons can be constructed concerning the location of the Wight family in 1861, but none have been conclusively proven.

Chapter Two

FRAMEWORK FOR DIARY

PROLOGUE

West Point graduate Edward Porter Alexander would play a leading role as an artillerist in the Confederate forces and was on duty as a second lieutenant of engineers in the United States Army at Fort Steilacoom in the Washington Territory in 1861. When word reached him that his native South had seceded from the Union, he asked for a leave to head east to fight for his new country. In his memoir, Alexander remembered the prophetic words of his commanding officer in response:

> If you must go, I will give the leave of absence…But don't go… This war is not going to be the ninety days affair that papers and politicians are predicting. Both sides are in deadly earnest, and it is going to be fought out to the bitter end. If you go, as an educated soldier, you will be put in the front rank. God only knows what may happen to you individually, but for your cause there can be but one result. It must be lost.
>
> Your whole population is only about eight millions, while the North has twenty millions. Of your eight millions, three millions are slaves who may become an element of danger. You have no army, no navy, no treasury, and practically none of the manufacturers and machine shops necessary for the support of armies, and for war on a large scale. You are but scattered agricultural communities, and you will be cut off from the rest of the world by blockade. Your cause must end in defeat, and the individual risks to you must be great… in a cause foredoomed to failure.[51]

Framework for the Diary

Since its end, thousands upon thousands of pages have been written about the cataclysm that was the Civil War. Military historians have documented offensive and defensive strategies, command structures, strength of force and tactical movements to explain the success or failure of any given unit in any given battle on any given day. Debates about issues such as slavery and states' rights remain the subject of historians' work.[52] Since the 1970s, however, some historians have begun to look beyond these well-documented views "to the almost unparalleled riches of the Civil War era—the extensive collections of official records as well as the letters and diaries often produced by individuals who never would have recorded their experiences for posterity apart from the crisis of war." These resources give insight into "the complexity of the civilian experience, and to the kinds of conflicts that occurred behind the lines."[53]

Without a framework for interpretation, Margaret Wight's diary might seem a cryptic litany of war, work, worry and weather. Yet the diary touches on some of the central themes of the conflict: women as refugees; the frequent blending of home front and battlefront; the role of religion in relation to Southern patriotism; financial crisis; scarcity, shortage and privation; and the stress of grief and loss. For many, the crisis that resulted from the sectional strife was immediate and fundamental. And on a practical, day-to-day basis, such simple tasks as traveling by train or getting accurate news from the wartime press presented new challenges as war presented disruption and destruction. A brief look into some of these topics may lend a deeper understanding of the Wight family during the war.

Refugee Status

Most of the war was fought on Southern soil and nowhere more than in Virginia. Here, the line between home front and battlefront was often blurred, as Mrs. Wight's diary demonstrates. The war brought financial crisis, labor shortages and battles that upset the equilibrium of everyday life. In the South, throughout the war, a new social group emerged—the refugees—families on the move who struggled to find safety and a semblance of normalcy in the midst of crisis. Historian Joan E. Cashin said the war cast women "into the

---

WARTIME RESIDENCES OF JOHN AND MARGARET WIGHT

DATE	LOCATION
January 1862	Hanover Tavern
April 11, 1864	Richmond City with Ann Eliza Wight
May 4, 1864	Hanover County with Dr. Charles E. Thompson (Beaverdam)
May 18, 1864	Hanover County with Mrs. Cora DeJarnette (Hanover Junction)
June 6, 1864	Rented basement room in Richmond
June 22, 1864	Hanover County with Mrs. Cora DeJarnette (Hanover Junction)
March 13, 1865	Hanover Tavern
April 5, 1865	Courtland, home of Mrs. William O. Winston (Hanover Courthouse)
April 28, 1865	Richmond
April 29, 1865	Left Richmond from Rockett's Landing for Charles City County

---

trackless wilderness."[54] In Margaret Wight's case, the "wilderness" may have been more figurative than literal, but the war certainly left her in unfamiliar territory in many respects. Some families made deliberate decisions to leave their homes for safer ground. Others were forced off by marauding armies who trampled fields, seized livestock and carried off provisions, leaving little to sustain those left in the wake. Why the Wights became refugees remains a mystery. However, for Margaret Wight, the hardship of having no home to call her own—at least from 1862 until the end of the war—led to longing and sometime dismay. She wrote in her diary that "this roving life does not suit old people."

The separation from their traditional homes could be especially difficult for women. In the mid-nineteenth century, "women's lives were centered almost exclusively on the household, which was the workplace as well as the dwelling place. The household was not only a physical place but a 'symbol of all they held dear.'"[55] When the war began, Mrs. Wight was a mother and grandmother in her early fifties who, by all rights, should have been enjoying her golden years at her own hearthside surrounded by family. Instead, she, her husband and their youngest daughter moved from home to home (sometimes separately) either as guests or lodgers. Margaret Wight decried her status as a refugee repeatedly in her diary and made plain her longing for stability and a place to gather her family once again.

Added to the emotional upheaval of having to leave her home and the often distressing separation from her children, Mrs. Wight apparently struggled to find a source of income to keep a roof over her family's heads and food on its table. Many of the displaced would find the refugee experience not only disorienting and unpleasant but also financially ruinous. Unless they stayed with family or friends, refugees had little choice but to pay high prices for small, sometimes crowded rooms. By 1862, the Wights chose to live at Hanover Tavern in the small hamlet of Hanover Courthouse. The cost of living there rose over time to an unaffordable level for the family. In her opening diary entry in 1863, Mrs. Wight complained that the price of board already exceeded the family's means. Yet with careful management and by taking on work, the family managed to stay until the spring of the following year. By that time, board had risen threefold, and the Wights sought less expensive lodgings. According to Mrs. Wight, whatever happened, they would make a conscientious effort to stay out of debt. While financial considerations seemed to be the prime motivation for relocation, threatening Federal troops dictated the family's movements from time to time.

"Refugees spent much of their time waiting to hear of the outcome of a battle, the progress of an army, or the migration of relatives, so that they might determine their next move."[56] This assessment is an apt characterization of Mrs. Wight's diary. For those caught in battle lines or about to be, as was often the plight of Mrs. Wight, caution was necessary to stay out of harm's way. Newspaper reports, rumors of impending battles and the warning sounds of musketry and cannon in the immediate vicinity could make a quick decision about relocation necessary. Overall, Mrs. Wight and her husband seemed able to make thoughtful and planned decisions about their lodgings as they moved from Hanover Tavern to Beaverdam and Hanover Junction. But sometimes they moved when immediate circumstances left few choices. When armies threatened, although a course of action may have seemed unclear, the imperative to move was not. They could either stay where they were and be swept up in the chaos of clashing armies, or they could flee. In the final year of the war, from May 1864 through May 1865, Mrs. Wight seems to have been dodging the Union army on a regular basis. Ultimately, the itinerant nature of refugee families proved to be just one among the many "disruptive forces transforming the customary patterns of southern domestic life."[57]

THE PULPIT

"Because the American Civil War was not a war *of* religion, historians have tended to overlook the degree to which it was a religious war."[58] The August 1, 1861 *Richmond Daily Dispatch* illustrates the point in this editorial that read: "Harriet Beecher Stowe proposes that the present struggle between the North and the South shall be designated 'The Religious War.'" The editors continued: "In this we are inclined to agree with the author of *Uncle Tom's Cabin*. It *is* a religious war. It is the Bible and pure Christianity against infidelity and God-dishonoring crimes, and we are glad to see that the churches of the South are alive to their responsibility in this regard."

The United States in the mid-nineteenth century was a deeply religious country. When secession created two separate countries, each side seemed to believe that God's hand would guide them. On both sides, it seems, the moral fiber and the essence of national character were on trial. Victories were interpreted as evidence of His hand on the pure and deserving; defeats were interpreted as a punishment for sins that must be repented.[59] Margaret Wight wrote in August of 1863: "Surely we are now being punished for our great wickedness. O! may the cries that spread...from those who put their trust in God alone be answered in mercy and deliverance given us from our enemies." For many women, including Margaret Wight, religion appeared to be a fundamental source of consolation in the midst of all they had to endure.[60]

From the outset of the Civil War, the Confederacy declared itself a nation that would be established under "the favor and guidance of Almighty God."[61] The Great Seal of the Confederacy bore the motto "Deo Vindice" (roughly translated as "God is our Protector"). Henry Timrod, sometimes called the poet laureate of the Confederacy, proclaimed, "To doubt the end were want of trust in God."[62] Margaret Wight seems to have adopted this notion when she wrote in her diary in 1863, "If GOD is not with us in this unequal contest as to the numbers, vain is the help of man. I cannot but believe that fervent, heartfelt prayers sent up by devoted Christians daily, will be heard and answered—and that we will not be visited according to our sins. If we were we might despair indeed."

Before the war, Virginia theologians, such as Robert Lewis Dabney, and Richmond clerics Reverend Moses Drury Hoge and Reverend Thomas Verner Moore viewed the crisis of secession as a subject to avoid. In 1861, Dabney wrote to Hoge: "My conviction all along has been that we ministers, when acting ministerially, publicly, or any way representatively of God's people as such, should seem to have no politics…there [are] plenty of politicians to make the fire burn hot enough, without my help to blow it."[63] Hoge responded: "Moore and myself do not mean to introduce anything political into our sermons, but wish to direct the minds of the people from man to God."[64] Yet when secession came, all three men became ardent supporters of the Confederacy and offered their full-throated support from the pulpit and in the religious press. Moses Drury Hoge became chaplain to the Confederate Congress and to the soldiers at Camp Lee. Robert Lewis Dabney served as Chief of Staff to Stonewall Jackson. On the occasion of the first Confederate National Fast, Reverend Moore delivered a sermon that was characterized by many as "a fearless, honest and forcible expression of truths essential to our existence and success in the great struggle in which our Confederacy is now engaged."[65]

Some historians believe that "without the clergy's active endorsement of secession and war, there could not have been a Confederate nation and war."[66] Mrs. Wight often attended services in Richmond at the First Presbyterian Church where Reverend Moore preached. Reverend Hoge presided at the Second Presbyterian Church. She may have been referring to men like Dabney, Hoge and Moore when she said, "I was for the Union…but when I saw that so many of our best men thought the Southern cause was a just one and that the Almighty blessed our efforts…all my feelings became enlisted on our own side."

If the Confederate government called for the sacrifice of comfort, homes and even of loved ones to the war effort, the clergy called on citizens to repent their sins to end the war. "By casting the hardship of war into a narrative of punishment, reformation, and deliverance, clergy offered southerners a basis for strength and confidence even amid disaster."[67] In October of 1864, Mrs. Wight wrote: "I have strong faith yet we may have to pass through a fiery ordeal but I pray we may come

God our Refuge and Strength in this War.

A DISCOURSE

BEFORE THE

CONGREGATIONS

OF THE

FIRST AND SECOND PRESBYTERIAN CHURCHES,

ON THE DAY OF

HUMILIATION, FASTING AND PRAYER,

APPOINTED BY

PRESIDENT DAVIS,

FRIDAY, NOV. 15, 1861.

BY REV. T. V. MOORE, D. D.

RICHMOND, VA.
PUBLISHED BY W. HARGRAVE WHITE.
1861.

Fast Day Sermon of Reverend Thomas Verner Moore, D.D., 1861. The Confederacy was supported by an active clergy whose full-throated support of the war was a key influence. This sermon, on a Day of Fasting and Prayer declared by President Davis, demonstrates the confluence of church and state when Reverend Moore said: "Whereas it has pleased Almighty God, the Sovereign Dispenser of events, to protect and defend the Confederate States hitherto, in their conflict with their enemies…and whereas with grateful thanks we recognize His hand, and acknowledge that not unto us, but unto Him belongeth the victory." *Duke University Library* out refined and purified." In this statement, Mrs. Wights seems to reflect a commonly shared idea that prayer, devotion and righteousness alone could win the war.

THE PRESS

According to historian Ted Tunnell, the Civil War era was a period of "intensely personal journalism in which editors freely blurred the distinction between news and opinion."[68] War and rumors of war reverberated in Richmond perhaps as nowhere else in the South. The telegraph office was the receiver and distributor of news dispatches used by the four most important daily papers—the *Daily Richmond Enquirer, Daily Richmond Examiner, Richmond Daily Dispatch* and *Richmond Daily Whig.* Each paper had its own editorial style that, to modern readers, would seem to generate more propaganda than reporting. But "despite differences in style and policy, the Richmond papers set the tone of unflagging patriotism that characterized Virginia's Confederate press throughout the war."[69] Military events in Mrs. Wight's diary seem to reflect the reports and analysis of the *Richmond Daily Dispatch.*

The press served an important function in bolstering Confederate spirits, but the most important job of the Confederate press was to inform the public about the war.[70] Keeping up the flow of accurate information may have been a task easier contemplated than executed. Newspapers struggled to produce daily issues as paper and ink became scarce and as men left their presses for the battlefield. The trains that carried mail and newspapers to communities outside of Richmond were frequently raided and brought to a halt. Mrs. Wight fretted more than once in her diary that the "cars" (railroads) were not running and there was, therefore, no news of the war. Even when presses were in full operation and the trains ran on time, the newspapers faced another difficulty in the release of accurate and timely news. From the beginning of the war until the end, news was censored by officials both military and civilian through monopoly of the telegraph. As a result, Richmond papers often augmented what might otherwise have been sparse daily editions with news from Northern papers.[71] In July of 1864, when her son Charles was marching with General Jubal Anderson Early in the Shenandoah Valley, Mrs. Wight wrote in her diary, "The Northerners afford us our only information."

Northern dispatches did provide information for news-hungry readers. But the newspapers also published as fact what was only rumor. A prime example of this tendency is the coverage of the Battle of Gettysburg. The battle began on July 1 and ended in a Union victory on July 3, 1863. For nearly two weeks after the battle, a series of half-truths and fabrications printed in the Richmond papers kept the public confused. Margaret Wight reported in her diary on July 5, "News has reached us that we have gained a victory at Gettysburg but not official." Her entries continue to show she was not fully informed about the actual outcome of the battle until July 18 when she wrote, "Gettysburg…was the most terrific one of the war and in which our loss in Officers and soldiers was appalling." Indeed, the newspapers struggled to report military losses as they tried to maintain a patriotic and optimistic front. Miliary reversals created a dilemma for the press. Defeats meant that the South could lose the war and were difficult to address when the public also suffered from want and privation. They signified a feared loss of honor and respectability the South struggled to maintain. Having taken on a role as guardians of public opinion, "editors were caught in a trap of their own making. Notwithstanding the ever-lengthening casualty lists, the $125-a-barrel flour and the suffering of tens of thousands, defeat became that which could not be mentioned."[72] In the last days of the war, Margaret Wight remained almost completely in the dark about the imminent fall of Richmond. The Richmond papers seemed to have found the news of an ultimate impending defeat too difficult to print.

Railroads

The importance of the Virginia railroads in the Civil War would be difficult to overestimate.

> When Virginia seceded from the Union in 1861, its railroads were in full operation and ready to perform. Four years later, the state's entire network would be in ruin. Rolling stock would be destroyed or disabled and the miles of track in disarray. The railroads' ultimate failure by 1865 came not from their initial poor condition or operation but rather from the length of the war itself. The longer the war lasted, the more apparent became their fragility and the inability to sustain their success over a long, attritional war.[73]

The problems that plagued the "roads" (as they were known) were multi-faceted and fundamental. A primary weakness lay in the fact that in the mid-nineteenth century, Southern railroads were private, investor-owned businesses. By contrast, when the war started, the United States government nationalized the rail system, giving it coordinated control over transportation networks. The Confederate States' government did not take the same measure. Because owners and investors in railway companies feared giving their competitors any advantage, they were reluctant to share such assets as rolling stock, spare parts and rails. Although some of the owners of the railway lines did make their railroads available to serve the Confederacy, self-interest and squabbling over operational issues, such as troop movement and mail delivery, was a continual problem throughout the war. The Confederate government appealed to companies to consolidate their rolling stock and other resources to no avail. The inability to work together caused delays, confusion, and logistical inefficiency throughout the war.[74]

Independent ownership and lack of coordinated control between railways was only one dilemma. Before secession, Southern railway owners had obtained the lion's share of their locomotives and spare parts from the North. With unfettered access to Northern markets, most company owners had not foreseen any necessity to stockpile crucial supplies that would become essential for the upkeep of the roads in wartime. When secession came, those markets were closed to the South that then had to rely on its own manufacturing facilities. To make matters worse, the small number of Southern supply facilities that were in operation at the start of the war—rolling mills, foundries and repair shops, such as the giant Tredegar Iron Works in Richmond—were converted to produce goods for the military. Those shops and foundries also suffered manpower shortages as men left for war. Dwindling supplies, the lack of manufacturers and absence of men to work the forges presented a serious challenge to Southern railway operations.[75] To add to these manifold challenges, the Union army's frequent raids on railways became perhaps the most seriously destructive force that operated on the railway system. Yet had none of these problems presented themselves, difficulties in maintaining open and efficient railroads would still have persisted—the issue lay in the poor construction of the railway lines themselves.

Virginia railways had been built in the two or three decades before the Civil War, primarily to transport passengers and agricultural products. The builders had not anticipated ever having to haul heavy machinery such as mortars and other artillery pieces over the lines. Nor had they considered

High Trestle Railroad Bridge. One observer wondered about the Virginia rail system, "the single line of rails, the loosely-built road-bed, the frightful trestle-work over deep gorges, the frail wooden bridges thrown across rushing rivers, and the headlong speed at which the train is often urged on its perilous way…a long journey by rail…was as hazardous as picket duty on the Potomac." *Library of Congress*

the strain on the physical infrastructure of moving thousands of men and their equipment to and from battlefields over long distances around the clock. The rail beds that had been laid without adequate ballast were quick to become unstable when heavy rains and resulting floods saturated the ground beneath them. Thin tracks wore out quickly from constant use and the wood could rot, sometimes causing overloaded cars to sink through the tracks and ties to the ground. The pressures on the railroads to perform tasks they were not designed to handle only added to the challenge of keeping the trains running.[76]

Disruptions in train service posed frequent difficulties for John and Margaret Wight and their family who relied on the railroads to travel to and from the homes of family and friends scattered throughout Virginia. In the spring when local rivers and streams flooded tracks, railways might be closed for days. The chief disruption, at least for Margaret Wight and her family, seems to have been the frequent cavalry raids throughout the region. Mrs.

Wight's diary is replete with references to the difficulties of rail travel and of the raids. Although five major railways fed into Richmond from around Virginia, only three played a major role in Mrs. Wight's experience.

The Virginia Central Railroad ran from Richmond northward over the Meadow Bridges to Hanover Courthouse. About a mile southwest of Hanover Tavern, on what is today Depot Road, the Hanover Depot of this railway served as a passenger and mail stop as well as a storage facility for the railway and the Confederate army. Mrs. Wight witnessed the complete destruction of the facility in 1863. The railroad stretched from Hanover Courthouse in a northwesterly direction to Hanover Junction just over the South Anna River. From the junction, it continued to Beaverdam and continued as far west as Jackson River.[77] John and Margaret Wight used this railway system to travel to and from Richmond and from time to time, to points west, such as Staunton. In Richmond, it would be necessary to transfer to the Richmond and York River Railroad to reach their daughter Annie's home in Charles City County.

The Richmond and York River Railroad provided the essential connection for Mr. and Mrs. Wight and their family between Richmond and Charles City County and the home of their daughter Annie Waddill. To travel there from Hanover County, Mrs. Wight would likely have used the Virginia Central Railroad from one of its several depots to travel to its terminal at Broad and Seventeenth Streets. From there, she would have made her way to the Richmond and York River line on the docks at Twenty-Second Street. The railroad's full length took it to West Point,[78] although at least once, Mrs. Wight indicated that she got off at Tunstall Station, crossed the Pamunkey River by boat and rode in a wagon across the twenty-plus miles to Annie's home in Charles City. This particular railroad was especially vulnerable to flood, as it passed through low-lying areas along the Pamunkey River as it headed east. Mrs. Wight reported its disruption more than once in her diary.

The Richmond, Fredericksburg & Potomac Railroad (RF&P) left from its terminal at Broad and Eighth Streets in Richmond and traveled north to its depot in Ashland. From there, it headed farther north over its bridges at the South and North Anna Rivers and continued to Fredericksburg. Another frequent target, the RF&P withstood repeated assaults during the war. From time to time, however, it remained operational when the Virginia Central Railroad did not and provided an alternate route for Mrs. Wight. She said in July of 1863 that "we have had no cars since the Yankee raid. Had to send to Ashland for our Mail."

The railroads remained a vital and vulnerable link for both civilians and military personnel throughout the war, and despite efforts to keep trains running, the network was often rendered useless. Yet, considering the issues that troubled the railroads for the duration of the war, "the Virginia railroads maintained a surprising amount of success…primarily due to the skill and dedication of the railroad owners themselves. The administration of those companies found ways to make the best of the situation presented them in order to get people and cargo moved, and above all, to keep trains running."[79]

SHORTAGES

Margaret Wight began her diary with a running report of escalating prices and a declaration: "It is difficult to imagine how we are to carry it on another year or how we are to live." If she was monitoring the prices in the *Richmond Daily Dispatch* on January 7, 1863, she would have noticed a statement that represented the collective voice of the merchants: "A scarcity in the market, owing partly to a lack of the facilities of transportation, tends to keep up the buying and selling rates." There was much more to the story.

The shortages of nearly everything necessary for daily life plagued Mrs. Wight, along with almost the entire Southern population, for the entirety of the war. In the days and weeks following secession, the Union naval blockade of Atlantic seaports closed nearly all traditional markets to the Confederacy. The blockade remained in effect for the duration, resulting in scarcity in the consumer markets of such basic products as coffee, tea, sugar and cloth. The absence of products for sale appears to have invoked the time-honored rule of "supply and demand," and so what products were available for sale were offered at a premium price. While the closing of ports certainly contributed to scarcity, other factors were present to exacerbate the problem. The Confederate government seemed to have little control over monetary policy and had not developed adequate methods of funding the war. Throughout the war, the Confederate government tried but failed to develop effective policies to correct these weaknesses. "The result was inflation that neared 700 percent in the first two years. By the end of the war, prices in some cases were 9,000 percent higher than those of 1860."[80] Mrs. Wight speaks clearly and often of shortages and ever-escalating prices in her diary. In October of 1863 she wondered at the

Escalating Prices

1860			1863		
Bacon, 10 lbs. at 12½c	$1.25		Bacon, 10 lbs. at $1.00	$10.00	
Flour, 30 lbs. at 5c	$1.50		Flour, 30 lbs. at 12½c	$3.75	
Sugar, 5 lbs. at 8c	$.40		Sugar, 5 lbs. at $1.15	$5.75	
Coffee, 4 lbs. at 12½c	$.50		Coffee, 4 lbs. at $5	$20.00	
Tea (green), ½ lb. at $1	$.50		Tea (green), ½ lb. at $16	$8.00	
Lard, 4 lbs. at 12½c	$.50		Lard, 4 lbs. at $1.00	$4.00	
Butter, 3 lbs. at 25c	$.75		Butter, 3 lbs. at $1 75	$5.25	
Meal, 1 pk. at 25c	$.25		Meal, 1 pk. at $1.00	$1.00	
Candles, 2 lbs. at 15c	$.30		Candles, 2 lbs. at $1.25	$2.50	
Soap, 5 lbs. at 10c	$.50		Soap, 5 lbs. at $1.10	$5.50	

Escalating Prices in Richmond. Civil War diarist John Beauchamp Jones listed price hikes in the Confederate capital from 1860 to 1863 in his well-known work, *A Rebel War Clerk's Diary at the Confederate States Capital* in 1866. The information is likely derived from Richmond newspapers. In 1863, as his list shows, the price of bacon had risen ten-fold since 1860. Prices continued to climb so precipitously that by 1864 most papers stopped publishing the information. By then, some prices had risen 9,000 percent above pre-war levels. *Graphic produced by the Hanover Tavern Foundation*

conditions that then prevailed as war and privation continued: "starvation we must have if the present prices continue. $125 a Bar. for flour, $16 a Bus. for meal $35 a load for Wood $30, for coal giving everything in proportion. Ladies shoes $50 and $60, children's not to be had. Cotton $6 a yard, gloves $20. Bonnets from $150 to 250!! and no prospect of peace so what are we coming to?"

If scarcity, inflation and privation were the enemy without, greed became the enemy within. Hoarders, speculators and "extortionists" were responsible for much of the suffering of the Confederate population during the war. And when it came to fixing blame for the misery, a collective finger was pointed more directly at hoarders than even the reviled Yankees or the Confederate government. Mrs. Wight railed against the speculators, profiteers and blockade runners repeatedly in her diary. Other voices echoed her scorn. The large number of speculators and black marketeers led one newspaper to state bluntly: "Every man in the community is swindling everybody else, and everybody else is swindling him."[81]

WOMEN AT WORK

At the start of the war, in the South, many middle and upper-class families had enough capital and income from investments to stave off poverty. But no matter the method chosen to preserve their holdings and assets, by the last years and months of the war, a large number had exhausted their reserves, and even many of the South's so-called "best families" would find themselves in dire straits.[82] When Margaret Wight began her diary in 1863, the family seemed to have had limited means of support. To cope with an ever-growing need for money for basic necessities as prices continued to climb, Confederate women like Margaret Wight, who might never have considered working outside of their homes for wages, had to come to grips with the idea that they would have to earn their own support.[83] Need aside, age and position in society had much to do with attitudes and approach to working outside the home. Younger women, like Emily Wight, seemed to embrace the challenge more easily than their elders. Some Southern women could not bring themselves to accept the challenge on any terms. Noted Civil War diarist Mary Boykin Chesnut, wife of a prominent South Carolina politician, was a war refugee who certainly needed money. Yet she was horrified by the notion of women working in public, "outside the 'rooftree' of the prescribed domestic sphere…We will live at home with our families and starve in a body."[84]

At least four female members of the Wight family—Margaret, Emily, Ann Eliza Wight and Margaret Wight's cousin, Margaret Cabell Brown Loughborough (who was in Richmond for most of the war)—sought and found supplemental sources of income. Fortunately for Emily and Margaret Loughborough, employment was available that was suitable to their status in society. In a break with tradition, the Confederate government hired women. With men vacating official positions for the battlefield, the Confederate government struggled to conduct routine administrative tasks, especially in the departments of Treasury, Quartermaster, the Post Office and the Commissary in Richmond. It seems the jobs were doled out as political patronages.

> The salary scale for female clerks reveals their social location and influence…Privates in the Confederate army were paid $11 a month. In 1862 and 1863, by contrast, female clerks received $65. By 1864 the annual salary of women holding Treasury posts had risen to $3,300 in the South's depreciated currency. These women

were seen to be worth more than the Confederacy's ordinary fighting men and to have needs and expectations for special treatment that the Confederacy did not wish to gainsay. Clearly, too, they were regarded differently from most other females in national service.[85]

According to Mrs. Wight's diary, by late 1864, Emily Wight obtained a post through family friend Richard H. Catlett. She was to work in the office of General James L. Kemper, who was commander of Virginia's Reserve Forces. Her salary (and that of Margaret Cabell Brown Loughborough, who also worked in a government department) soared to astronomical levels. Astonishingly, even with an elevated income, women struggled yet to make ends meet. Loughborough explained in her diary: "I got a room, as I could not board…then got a salary of $1000 a year, temporarily increased to $4000 a month [This may be an error of the diary's transcriptionist. It is more likely that female government clerks received that amount annually, ed.] That amount paid my room rent, gas, and washing and the cooking of two meals a day, generally composed of biscuits made of flour and water, sometimes potatoes and some sort of tea. In buying material for these sumptuous feasts, I hadn't a cent left."[86]

Mrs. Wight fretted over finding a way to augment her family's resources of cash. She said she wanted to help "make a support" for her family. She was willing to work but perhaps, like Mary Chesnut, not in one of the Richmond departments. John Wight solved her problem. He entered into a contract with the Confederate government to produce a large quantity of plain and "official" envelopes. In early 1863, in what Mrs. Wight called "an experiment," she began what became an almost full-time occupation until early 1865. She manufactured the envelopes by hand, and although getting enough paper to complete the work was sometimes problematic, Mrs. Wight could do the work in the privacy of her residence—wherever it happened to be. Based on records in the National Archives, it appears that in all, she made more than thirty thousand envelopes either on her own or with the help of ladies she enlisted in the enterprise.

In October of 1863, John Wight, with the help of his son John Henry, secured a civilian position with the Quartermaster's Department. For his services, which seemed to have related to supply deliveries and shipments to and from Virginia Central Railroad depots in Hanover County, Margaret's husband received $75 per month, plus monthly rations worth $100. The Wights could and did sell the rations for cash on the open market at least once. With the envelope business and John Wight's income, Mrs. Wight said they could "meet our board and have a little over." Based on receipts from the Confederate government, John Wight received as much as $1790 for the sale of envelopes made by his wife.[87] The family's financial picture was also made brighter on two occasions by unexpected infusions of cash. In 1864, John Wight received a windfall of $7,000 when the will of his former sister-in-law, Margaret Copland Wight Munford, was probated. In that same year, a protracted negotiation over the purchase of land John Wight had begun before the war resulted in a settlement of $2,500 paid directly to him in 1864. The Wights were by no means destitute, but, like most, found their reserves stretched by inflation. While Margaret Wight made frequent complaints in her diary about prices, the family seemed to find a way to pay their way by moving to less expensive lodgings and by finding sources of income with the envelope business, as well as John's position in the Quartermaster's Department. Added to the inheritance and settlement of the real estate transaction, they seemed to fare reasonably well throughout the war. However, in May of 1865, Margaret Wight said that her husband used the last money they had—$125—to pay for a train ticket from Hanover to Charles City County. And in her last wartime entry, she indicated they were not alone in their penury when she wrote, "No one has any money."

Adapting to Shortage

Almost every aspect of daily life touched by want and scarcity met with creativity and ingenuity on the part of women in the wartime South. When paper became scarce, women wrote letters on pages from old ledgers, family albums, books and even wallpaper. Pokeberry or persimmon juice, with a rusty nail used to darken the color, produced a passable ink. Glue for sealing a letter could be made by mixing peach gum with cornstarch. Lard mixed with peanut oil could make lantern fuel, and sorghum became a suitable substitute for sugar.[88] Margaret Wight tried an experiment using Chinese sugar cane to produce a substitute for molasses, which was becoming too expensive to buy. She found it passable. Late in the war, Mrs. Wight went on forages for blackberries "that were hardly noticed before the war but now sell for $3 a quart." She gathered walnuts that would fetch $1 per dozen on the market. In the fall of 1864, Mrs. Wight purchased a single pound of tea for $50 that she hoped would net some cash through resale. Perhaps she had caught a little of the "speculation fever" herself. She said she planned to use the proceeds from the sale of tea to buy a new dress to replenish a wardrobe on which she said she had spent only $50 in two years.

Mrs. Wight's reference to clothes calls up the question of mourning dress. During the Civil War, nearly every woman in the South grieved for a loved one. American women generally observed the elaborate Victorian practice of mourning with its rigidly prescribed code of dress and seclusion from society. Tradition dictated that widows wear black for anywhere from eighteen months up to two and a half years. The death of a child required at least nine months in full mourning dress that could include wearing black from head to toe and covering the face with a black veil.[89] Having lost three children in the span of fifteen months during 1861 and 1862, according to custom, Mrs. Wight would have been in mourning dress. Yet women were often compelled to abandon the ritual for lack of money or supply of cloth. In her historically important work *Diary of a Southern Refugee During the War*, Judith Brockenbrough McGuire noted: "One sad young girl sits near me, whose two brothers have fallen on the field, but she is too poor to buy mourning."[90] Unless she had a store of mourning clothes already in her possession, Mrs. Wight may not have spent scarce money on the expensive attire. Perhaps she, like so many others, put aside the ritual out of necessity.

Mourning aside, getting dressed in the 1860s was a complex process. Writer Bill Bryson humorously describes women of the period as virtually "imbedded in their clothing."[91] The custom was to wear (1) drawers or pantalettes, followed by (2) a chemise that was a sort of loose-fitting shift that stretched from shoulder to knee to protect the corset from oils on the skin. Next (3) a corset was added over the chemise. Then (4) a camisole was worn over the corset. Then (5) a crinoline or hoop that gave skirts their shape was added, and over the crinoline, (6) petticoats offered a smooth surface on which the fabric of the skirt could lay. Dresses also came in layers: bodice, skirt, sleeves and separate collar and cuffs.[92]

Accessories were not whimsical adjuncts to the wardrobe. For Southern women during the Civil War, a respectable and properly dressed lady needed stockings, gloves, handkerchiefs, a bonnet and shoes. Throughout her diary, Mrs. Wight recorded the ever-rising prices for these essentials, which were almost obliterated from the market (except at exorbitant prices) from the first days of the war. But even "making do" had limitations. The blockade seems to have prevented a reliable supply of such essentials as fabric, linen, buttons, ribbons, trimming, pins, needles and bonnets. Hoop skirts would be nearly unobtainable after the first year of war. Finally, shoes and hats occupied attentions of ladies of the South as prices for these basic articles of clothing soared. Judith McGuire reported making her own shoes from the resurrected canvas sails of a ship that had been sunk in the James River. She and her circle of ladies made their own bootblack and fashioned their own gloves.[93] Margaret Cabell Brown Loughborough's husband bought her a pair from a sutler's wagon at Gettysburg (see below). On January 21, 1864, Margaret Wight said in her diary that her husband bought a pair of shoes for Emily "on speculation." In September 1864, Mrs. Wight joined thousands of Southern ladies who fought "bonnet inflation" by making their own hats. "Almost every girl plaits her own hat, and that of her father, brother and lover, if she has the bad taste to have a lover out of the army, which no girl of spirit would do unless he is incapacitated by sickness or wounds. But these hats are so beautifully plaited, of rye straw, and the ladies' hats are shaped so becomingly…our Confederate girls look fresh and lovely in them."[94] Mrs. Wight corroborated Mrs. McGuire's note in her own diary entry in 1864. "Almost every lady in the country [Confederacy] is braiding straw to make Hats and Bonnets. I have finished one for Emily."

Perhaps the inventiveness of women is perfectly illustrated in this diary entry from Margaret Cabell Brown Loughborough. At the end of the war, she painted a comic, but resourceful picture of the ensemble she wore when she traveled from Richmond to Baltimore:

> A homemade flannel underskirt, woven on the plantation, home knit white stockings, shoes my husband brought from a sutler's wagon at Gettysburg, cost him $250.00, unwillingly taken in Confederate money, a hoop skirt cost $150.00, a coarse black alpaca dress, a silk girdle from my grandmother's scrap bag. The dress was trimmed with three rows of worsted skirt braid which I had re-dyed with pokeberry juice. The dress reached the ground all around, made from a pattern out of the Ark, a black embroidered lace veil, a bonnet with cape crown and strings…a very old India Cashmere shawl, hair pins made of locust thorns with sealing wax heads, and a point lace collar yellow with age—handkerchief made of old tablecloth.[95]

Chapter Three

THE LAY OF THE LAND

If geography is destiny, then Virginia is a prime example of how location can dictate events. The Confederate capital was in the center of the state. Federal attempts to capture the city brought battles to much of the territory in Virginia that provided access to Richmond. In one estimate, nearly one-quarter of the Civil War's battles occurred in Virginia in the Union army's attempt to gain Richmond. Four strategic points presented access to Richmond and became frequent scenes of battle. First, the Lower Peninsula of Virginia between the James and the York Rivers provided an approach to Richmond through the lowland between Fort Monroe and the capital. Second, the open country of western Virginia could have allowed the Federals to sweep in from the Shenandoah Valley. The third and fourth points were the two Northern approaches into Virginia from Maryland and from Washington, D.C.[96] Taken one by one, the strategic importance of these regions becomes apparent.

At the tip of the Lower Peninsula, just ninety miles from Richmond, Fort Monroe represented a Union stronghold impregnable to assault by land and easily provisioned and garrisoned by sea. From its walls, Union forces could move up the peninsula using both captured Confederate railways and the navigable waters of the James and York Rivers that flank the finger of land. For much of the war, especially 1862 forward, Union forces tried again and again to take Richmond from this point.[97]

From the west and northwest, the lower end of the Shenandoah Valley around Harpers Ferry and Manassas Gap served as the backdoor to

Washington for Confederate armies, as well as a direct line into Maryland. For Union forces, it served as gateway to the resource-rich valley and the western approaches to Richmond. Control of the valley was of considerable value to either side and, according to one source, "The guns seldom fell silent in the Shenandoah Valley during the Civil War. The official records tell of 326 armed conflicts in the Valley…but even that lengthy list does not include many of the raids, ambushes, and partisan actions that were a constant companion of life in the Valley during those years."[98]

Finally, the Northern approach to Richmond is a ninety-mile stretch from the Union capital in Washington, D.C., in a nearly straight line that eventually passes through Hanover County and into Richmond. History demonstrates that Union commanders and Federal forces expended considerable energy and left significant destruction as they attempted to cross the natural defenses of the Rappahannock, Rapidan, North Anna, South Anna, Pamunkey, James, York and Chickahominy Rivers to overtake Richmond. The counties along the banks of these rivers were often scenes of battles. In Hanover County, the North and South Anna, Chickahominy and Pamunkey Rivers were contributing factors to its "unusually crowded Civil War record. From 1862 until the close of the war, Union armies marched on river crossings to destroy rail bridges and render railways useless. Hanover would see more action by 1865 than any other county in Virginia, except perhaps Spotsylvania and Dinwiddie."[99] Margaret and John Wight chose at least three different residences in Hanover during the war (at Hanover Tavern, Beaverdam and Hanover Junction). They would be caught between the lines more than once before war's end.

RICHMOND AT WAR

Soon after Virginia seceded from the Union in April of 1861, the Confederate government relocated its provisional capital from Montgomery, Alabama, to Richmond. Thomas Cooper De Leon, a noted journalist of his day, traveled with the government to Richmond and wrote his first impression of the capital on his arrival: "The city was thoroughly jammed—its ordinary population of forty thousand swelled to three times that number by the sudden pressure. Of course, all the Government, with its thousand employees, had come on; and in addition, all the loose population along the railroad over which it had passed seemed to have

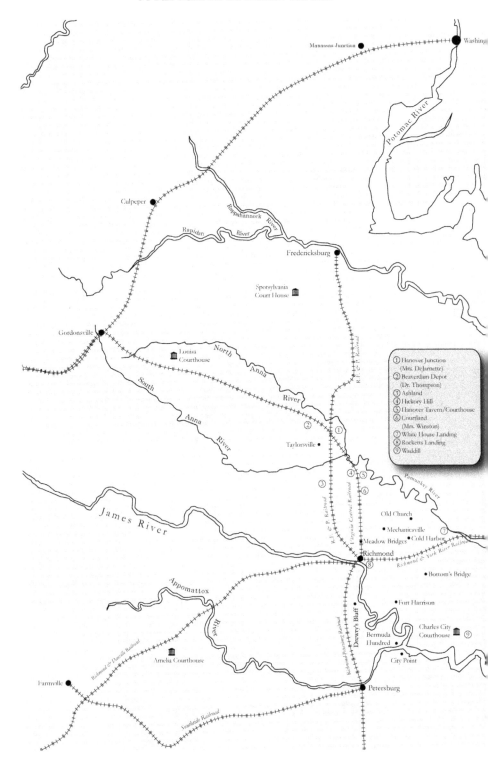

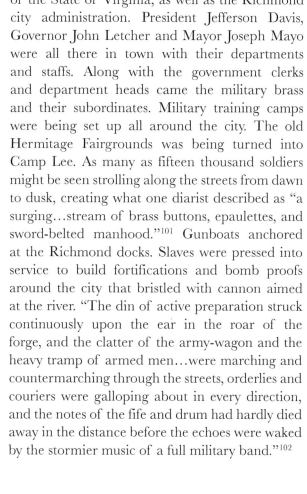

clung to and been rolled into Richmond with it."[100] Now, as the capital of the Confederacy and its symbolic heart, Richmond became "ground zero" in the war effort.

Home to the government of the new Confederate States of America, it was also the seat of the State of Virginia, as well as the Richmond city administration. President Jefferson Davis, Governor John Letcher and Mayor Joseph Mayo were all there in town with their departments and staffs. Along with the government clerks and department heads came the military brass and their subordinates. Military training camps were being set up all around the city. The old Hermitage Fairgrounds was being turned into Camp Lee. As many as fifteen thousand soldiers might be seen strolling along the streets from dawn to dusk, creating what one diarist described as "a surging…stream of brass buttons, epaulettes, and sword-belted manhood."[101] Gunboats anchored at the Richmond docks. Slaves were pressed into service to build fortifications and bomb proofs around the city that bristled with cannon aimed at the river. "The din of active preparation struck continuously upon the ear in the roar of the forge, and the clatter of the army-wagon and the heavy tramp of armed men…were marching and countermarching through the streets, orderlies and couriers were galloping about in every direction, and the notes of the fife and drum had hardly died away in the distance before the echoes were waked by the stormier music of a full military band."[102]

Lay of the Land. This (incomplete) map of Virginia represents the principal rivers, railroad routes, towns and residences mentioned in Mrs. Wight's diary. It is not to scale. *Hanover Tavern Foundation*

All over the city, residences and public buildings were being repurposed. Pre-war Richmond had only two hospitals—Bellevue (for whites) and Main Street (for slaves). By the summer of 1861, after the seminal First Battle of Manassas, the five railways that rumbled into the terminals began to grind to a steamy halt loaded with wounded, sick and dying soldiers in need of food and clothing and a place to rest and recuperate. When a *Stranger's Guide*[103] to Richmond was published in 1863, the number of hospitals had swelled to more than thirty main facilities. The sight of so many wounded men became a daily grim reminder of war. Mrs. Wight's cousin, Margaret Cabell Brown Loughborough, the then-Treasury Department clerk, said, "The hospitals were so crowded that as soon as the breath was out of a patient's body, he was taken to the dead room so as to make room for a live man as soon as a coffin could be knocked together."[104]

The trains that did not bear Confederate soldiers in and out of the city brought Union prisoners. Privates and non-commissioned officers were herded into the open-air stockade on Belle Isle. Union officers were crowded into the infamous Libby Prison in Shockoe Bottom. Castle Thunder housed a collection of Confederate prisoners, criminals, deserters and recaptured slaves.

As territories were captured and taken behind Union lines, a burgeoning population of refugees crowded into the city. Again, journalist De Leon paints a vivid picture: "Private boarding-houses sprang up like mushrooms on every block; bereaved relics [*sic*] and ambitious spinsterhood equally clutching the chance to turn an honest penny…Discomfort of the hotels was great enough; but life [in the boardinghouses] became simply unendurable. In this strait many private families were induced to open their doors to the better class of strangers; and gradually the whole dense population settled down, wedged into comparative quiet."[105] The quiet may have been gained in part by the declaration of martial law enacted to help ease tensions between members of an otherwise unlikely mix of society crammed together in a city that seemed ready to burst.

John Henry Wight and his family would remain in town. Emily Wight would eventually move into the city when she secured a job with General James L. Kemper. Ann Eliza Wight likely rented out her property (although no records could be found to indicate the lessee) and stayed in Richmond for the duration. Apparently John and Margaret Wight did not wish to be continually in the crush of wartime Richmond and found a home in Hanover County, a few miles north of the city, at the old Hanover Tavern.

Hanover Tavern

Today, the Hanover Courthouse and the old stone jail, clerk's office and Hanover Tavern are listed on the National Register of Historic Places. In 1862, when Margaret Wight and members of her family chose the Tavern as their residence, the venerable old hotel was already more than one hundred years old. There had been a tavern at Hanover Courthouse serving courthouse users, residents, travelers and stagecoach passengers since 1733. The oldest part of the current building was constructed in 1791 with additions in 1822, 1832 and the late twentieth century. When Margaret Wight arrived, the Tavern contained twelve thousand square feet configured in twenty-seven rooms with more than fourteen fireplaces.[106] Broad, covered verandas on both the east and west façades of the building could offer a

Hanover Tavern (circa 1880). There has been a tavern at Hanover Courthouse since 1733. The oldest part of the current building was constructed in 1791 with additions in 1822, 1832 and the late twentieth century. When Margaret Wight and her family arrived in 1862, the tavern contained twelve thousand square feet configured in twenty-seven rooms with more than fourteen fireplaces. Although restored, the Tavern remains with generally the same exterior and interior configuration as existed during the Civil War. Today, Hanover Tavern is listed on the National Register of Historic Landmarks. *Hanover Tavern Foundation*

Hanover County Courthouse. It is the third-oldest courthouse still in use in the United States. Some local historians cited the Courthouse as built in 1735, but the state historical society notes it was built between 1737 and 1742. Today, it is a census-designated place and the county seat of Hanover County, Virginia. While historically and technically known as Hanover Courthouse, the Census Bureau and the community's post office and residents refer to it today as Hanover. *Hanover Tavern Foundation*

shady haven against the grueling summer heat when temperatures could soar to one hundred degrees Fahrenheit. Inside, the large rooms with their cozy fireplaces would have made the home snug and warm when winter saw temperatures drop as low as zero.

In 1861, Catherine and Philip H. Winston, friends of Margaret Wight, owned Hanover Tavern and the surrounding land totaling approximately 626 acres. In January of that year, they sold 262-plus acres along with the hotel to Cleavers S. Chisholm and his wife, Amizela. Supporting the operation of the hotel and farm were a kitchen, stable, barn, icehouse, smokehouse and slave quarters. The surrounding acreage was a working farm. According to slave schedules in 1860, Chisholm owned thirteen slaves who would have seen to cooking and cleaning for the family and residents of the Tavern.[107] The Chisholms would be the Wights' landlords and companions from 1862 until May of 1864.

The Tavern, Courthouse and a few other buildings along with the depot constituted a small local hamlet concentrated along an old north–south stage road that ran from Richmond to Fredericksburg. In the surrounding countryside, families like the Winstons, Wickhams, Wingfields and Prices had their homes. Mrs. Wight knew of them all and wrote about them in her diary. Mrs. Wight said that Catherine and Philip Winston were old friends. In the last days of the war, Margaret and John Wight went to live at the home of the widow of William O. Winston, who had been clerk of the court at Hanover. Her home known as Courtland was almost within sight of the Tavern. General Williams Carter Wickham owned the nearly four-thousand-acre Hickory Hill Plantation, about five miles northwest of the Tavern. Mrs. Wight reported the capture of General Robert E. Lee's son "Rooney," who was recuperating there in 1863. Captain Henry Wyatt Wingfield, from Marl Ridge Plantation close to Hanover Courthouse, was the captain of Charles Wight's company in the Fifty-Eighth Infantry Regiment. In 1864, Mrs. Wight reported that Dr. Lucien Price's Dundee had been troubled by Union troopers. In fact, they had set up their headquarters before the 1864 battle at Hanover Courthouse during the Overland Campaign.[108] From the Tavern, the banks of the Pamunkey River could be reached by traveling approximately two miles north. The summer resort of Ashland, where the RF&P Railroad ran through the center of town to the bridges over the South and North Ann Rivers, was just five miles to the west. A few miles northwest of Hanover Courthouse on the other side of the South Anna River, was the Hanover Junction of the Virginia Central Railroad. Beaverdam Depot on the same railway was about twenty miles west of Hanover Courthouse.

Mrs. Wight said that the hotel had a "home feel." Although research did not reveal specific details about the furnishings of the Tavern in 1863, historian Martha McCartney found evidence that the Winstons and Chisholms were certainly members of the upper echelon of Hanover society.[109] During the war, at least from time to time, a probable list of boarders includes as many as fifteen people: Margaret, John and Emily Wight; Cleavers Chisholm and Amizela; the Chisholm sons, William and Julian; the Chisholm daughters: Conway Chisholm Mitchell, along with her two children—Charles and Alma—Conway's sister Sally Chisholm Cralle and her two children, Bessie S. and Conway J. Cralle; Susan Campbell (a friend); and Mrs. Charles S. Anderson, wife of a Virginia Central Railroad engineer. The size of the group could wax and wane. In 1863, Emily Wight was enrolled in the Farmville Female College in Farmville,

Virginia, and left the Tavern for at least the winter term that year. When not in school, Emily spent much of her time in Richmond, Charles City County or Goochland with relatives. The Chisholm boys went off to the Confederate army. Mrs. Wight often noted that members of her family had come to visit her at Hanover Tavern. John Henry Wight sometimes brought his children to see their grandparents. Charles would have one long furlough and a leave during which he visited his mother and father at Hanover Tavern. Together, this small mass of humanity weathered the storm of the Civil War in Hanover County.

Chapter Four

1861

Mrs. Wight's first diary entry is on January 1, 1863. Yet the first two years preceding her record of the war were pivotal in her life and of her family. In the two years before the diary began, Mrs. Wight lost three of her children. Two daughters—first, eldest daughter Mary Elizabeth, then youngest daughter Virginia ("Jennie") Chapman—died between August of 1861 and April of 1862. All three of her sons would eventually serve in the Confederate army, but only two would survive the first years of the ordeal. Youngest son William Marshall died in battle in 1862. Each member of the Wight family had a different imperative as dislocation, military service, hardship, disease and even death entered their worlds. Their stories may be generally typical of the wartime experience of countless Southern soldiers and civilians. Yet each of the experiences of Margaret Wight's family is uniquely defined by gender, location, age and the hand of fate. Here are the stories of Mary Elizabeth, Virginia Chapman, Charles and William Marshall Wight before the diary began.

MARY WIGHT, 1861: "A MORAL HEROINE"

The genealogical research on the family showed that twenty-four-year-old Mary Wight was working in the Norfolk City Public Schools as early as 1859. However, by 1861, with schools in Norfolk likely closed, Mary would have been out of work. She chose to enter the Smith Hospital in Culpeper, Virginia, to nurse wounded soldiers. In making this choice, Mary Wight seems to have put aside Southern notions of propriety that had, before the war, kept women out of public hospitals. Traditionally, Southern women had cared for the sick exclusively in their own homes or in those of family and friends. Public nursing was regarded as inappropriate, except for members of the lower classes, and nearly always only for men. When military service propelled most men to the battlefront, there was a critical shortage of nurses. Women would be called upon to fill the void, but overcoming long-held ideas about the subject became a challenge for not only the women but also the Confederate government and military officials who so needed their help. Confederate women "who offered their labor in the South's military hospitals undertook perhaps their most dramatic and frightening departure from traditional female roles. It did after all involve some level of intimacy with male bodies."[110] Although their daily activities would be defined largely by the supervision and preparation of food, administration of medicines and helping soldiers to write letters home, old social guidelines seemed to pose a barrier for many in taking up the challenge. Resistance to public nursing was also rooted in the irrational but pervasive idea that women were too fragile to bear such harsh realities as would prevail in the crowded, ill-equipped hospitals. Phoebe Yates Pember, chief matron in Division No. 2 of Chimborazo Hospital in Richmond, spoke directly of this misplaced opinion. "The natural idea that such a life would be injurious to the delicacy and refinement of a lady—that her nature would become deteriorated and her sensibilities blunted, was rather appalling."[111]

The Confederate government well understood the need to convince women to defy convention. It used its allies in the press to print editorials and reports that cast hospital nursing as not only respectable but also the essence of the sacrifice required of patriotic women. An unintentional aid in the recruitment of women was the widely read *Notes on Nursing* by Florence Nightingale, which had been published in the United States in 1860. Her writing demonstrated that a woman whose social status was beyond reproach could make a marked difference in the care of the wounded, ill and dying.[112] Whether Mary Wight was concerned about notions of respectability when she volunteered is beyond knowing. Margaret Wight explained in her postwar diary that her daughter said her great desire in volunteering was that "if her brothers should be wounded she would be there to nurse them." Mrs. Wight described her daughter as selfless. If she was, she was also brave. Civil War hospitals could be nearly as dangerous as battlefields. Ill-equipped and with medical personnel lacking a clear understanding of the transmission of the microorganisms, hospitals were perfect vectors for widespread outbreaks of infectious diseases.

The *Richmond Daily Dispatch* continued to impress upon the public the heroic and what it chose to call "fashionable" aspects of volunteer nursing by extolling, for example, the virtues of Mrs. Maggie Haley at the Smith Hospital. On August 13, 1861, the *Dispatch* published an accolade for Mrs. Haley: "She was one of, if not the very first to volunteer her services…she was still the leader…in that path of usefulness that has now become…so very fashionable. There are several other good ladies at that Hospital…[but] she supervises the care of Yankee and Southerner alike." Just two days later, Maggie Haley published her own tribute[113] to one of the young ladies who had given her life caring for the soldiers there. It was for Mary Wight.

Although written in "flowery" Victorian prose, Mrs. Haley's remarkable tribute to Mary Wight illustrated precisely the ideal devotion and selflessness that the Confederate press had attempted to define. Mrs. Haley seemed to speak through clenched teeth as she alluded to those whose delicacy prevented them from manifesting the virtues that seemed to distinguish Mary Wight. The tribute, published in the *Richmond Daily Dispatch* on August 15, 1861 read:

A Moral Heroine's Reward.

Her death was as much martyrdom to some of the South's brave defenders as though she had by the process of transfusion, given the last of her precious blood unto their veins for the preservation of their lives—the necessary destruction of her own.

Leaving her business, the source of her support…Norfolk… she came…not as the curious come, to see, to speak an idle word or two of intended comfort, to administer, perchance, for form's sake, with dissembled yet not hidden distaste, some slight material comfort to the sick soldiers…Her ministrations were not those of form, but were those of deed—deeds not intermittent or transient; but continuous and enduring. She sat not selfishly or prudishly aloof from her patients until their manly forbearance, overcome by their swelling anguish, called timidly for relief; but she stayed, whether waking or dozing, by their sides, anticipating their every want.

Had this been only to the undiseased wounded, she would have merited praise; and had she in this died only from exhaustion, she would have deserved a golden monument of memory in the heart of her country; but when, as was the case, these ministrations were to the sick—the infectiously diseased, from whom she died… Let those now recovered soldiers upon the tented field, and those convalescents now amid the endearments of home, whose renewed lives are parts of her life given them; let their parents, relatives and friends; let her grateful country and an appreciating world, say what shall be her reward. For, unlike the manly soldier, she ventured not within the gates of death under the sustaining influence of martial music, of enthusiastic multitudes, and the surety of glory's reward—nor yet, for a pecuniary consideration; but she visited the charnel precincts from a religiously patriotic sense of duty.

Beside those solemn portals I made her cheerful acquaintance…I feel that I knew her well, and can well say that no purer, sweeter soul dew drop was ever from the Hermon of virtue absorbed into Heaven by the sun-ray of duty performed.

Mary Wight died of typhoid fever in Staunton, Virginia, on August 6, 1861. The *Richmond Daily Dispatch* posted the death notice on August 9 and called friends and family to her funeral at Second Presbyterian Church in Richmond, where Dr. Moses Drury Hoge would conduct the service at five o'clock. Mary would be the first of Margaret Wight's children to die in wartime.

Sons at War

Both of John and Margaret Wight's younger sons, William Marshall and Charles Copland, entered the Confederate army almost immediately after secession in April of 1861. Barely eighteen, William Marshall Wight said he was a farmer when he enlisted on May 4, 1861, in Company H of the First Virginia Regiment in Richmond.[114] His twenty-year-old brother, Charles Copland Wight, was a student in his last year at Virginia Military Institute in Lexington.[115] By April 20, Charles was officially in the army by virtue of his status as cadet. Eldest son, John Henry Wight, was married and living in Richmond with his wife, Agnes, and two small sons. He worked as a clerk in the Quartermaster's Department in Richmond. In 1863, military necessity forced the clerks and Richmond's other male noncombatants into military organizations. John Henry served in Company E, Third Virginia Battalion, Local Defense Troops,[116] a unit that periodically took the field in response to Union threats around Richmond.

Each brother would have a different experience of the war based on his age and status. Young William Marshall appears to have been an enlisted private with no military training. Charles Wight was a VMI cadet with nearly three years of military instruction under his belt. These two brothers found themselves on the same battlegrounds on the same day three times during the war. Both were on the field at the First Battle of Manassas in 1861 and again at Gaines' Mill in 1862. The third time the brothers would fight together was on August 30, 1862, at the Second Battle of Manassas. During that engagement, William Marshall was killed in action.

Charles Copland Wight, 1861: VMI Cadet Goes to War

When secession was announced, all regular academic classes for the cadets at the VMI were suspended immediately with the exception of infantry and artillery drills and instruction in strategy and tactics. Those cadets in their last year of classes, including Charles Wight, would never return to regular sessions at the VMI. On December 12, the Board of Visitors decided not to require the Class of 1862 to return for its final year's studies and declared its thirty-two members graduated as of that date. Charles Wight was third in his class.[117] Apparently, Charles Wight kept a diary beginning just before secession that he used to prepare a postwar memoir that is today among the records of the Virginia Historical Society. The details of his early war experience traveling with General Thomas Jonathan Jackson provided much of the detail for this section.

On April 20, by Order No. 62, the body of the Corps of Cadets were ordered to Richmond to act as drillmasters for the thousands of raw recruits massing at the military camps around the town.[118] Then-major Thomas Jonathan Jackson (later called "Stonewall") was to command the departing troops. On the appointed day, the 176 boys selected to go with Jackson

Virginia Military Cadet, circa 1861.
Unidentified cadet in uniform holding
a U.S. Springfield rifled musket. *Virginia
Military Institute Archives*

were called to attention at the parade grounds at Lexington. They were instructed to face east and moved out smartly when Jackson commanded, "By file left! March!" Stagecoaches waited to transport the cadets to Staunton and then on to the Virginia Central Railroad and Richmond.[119] For the cadets, the war had begun.

The same order sending the Corps to Richmond to become drill masters exempted Charles Wight and forty-six other cadets. Among those who stayed behind was young Charles R. Norris, a sixteen-year-old freshman cadet. Wight, Norris and those who had not gone to Richmond were to remain in Lexington on guard detail protecting the arsenal, remaining ammunition and weaponry at the Institute. Probably disappointed in his assignment, Charles Wight might have been tempted from discouragement by an almost instant promotion to first sergeant in the Thirteenth Virginia Infantry. On April 22, newly-minted Sergeant Wight and nine other cadets, Charles Norris among them, were ordered from Lexington to escort an ammunition wagon train being sent to reinforce new Confederate recruits at Harpers Ferry.[120] Charles Wight wrote: "We were in the full enjoyment of the excitement and novelty of war without any of the hardships or suffering."[121] By mid-1864, Charles Wight would be a veteran who would have had plenty of suffering and hardship. Fortunately, he would live to tell his children about it all.

According to his diary, Charles was made a drillmaster for the new recruits at Harpers Ferry under General Kenton Harper (the name is an interesting coincidence). Soon the men were reorganized into the Twenty-seventh Virginia Infantry under General Jackson, who had returned from his duties in Richmond. In late May, the men would leave Harpers Ferry. As a final gesture before departure, the Confederates took the precaution of destroying factory buildings and blowing the bridge across the Potomac River at the ferry to deny its usefulness to Union troops. Charles made note of his first impressions of war. "I was horrified at seeing all those valuable houses burned and it struck me that was a cruel thing."[122]

Until now, what Charles Wight and his fellow cadets knew about war was found between the pages of textbooks and the drilling fields of Lexington. When the men moved out of Harpers Ferry, Charles wrote in his diary: "I was glad for I was just then very tired of playing soldier." When told they were going to fight with General Pierre Gustave Toutant Beauregard, Charles Wight explained, "The men were urged to do their best but there was no necessity for this; the wildest enthusiasm prevailed."

Charles Wight's description of the First Battle of Manassas on Sunday morning, July 21, 1861 renders a most vivid picture of a young soldier's first battle:

> Now I see the body of the first Federal soldier I had passed… It was a boy of 17 or 18…He was lying on his back…the blood was oozing from his temple…Just at this time I noticed a caisson which had been abandoned the horses having been killed and I directed my steps to it thinking that it would serve as a partial protection where I could shoot with greater advantage myself. Before reaching this, however, I stopped to fire and as I did so felt something had happened. I could not tell what. I saw the sky and thought there was something wrong…it flashed upon me that I was wounded.[123]

Wight was only grazed.

The next day, in a field that the rain had turned to sludge, squads of men struggled to bury those who had fallen the day before. Among the dead was young Cadet Charles R. Norris. Witnesses said that during the battle, the freshman cadet had taken command of his company in the absence of its captain. He had rallied his men with the cry, "Come, on, boys! Quick and we can whip them!" As he uttered these words, he fell senseless to the ground. [124] When he was discovered among the dead in the aftermath, he was wearing a VMI coatee. A rend in the upper left shoulder bore witness to the fatal bullet's entry. Inside the collar of the jacket was a handwritten, handsewn label with the name "Wight."[125]

If Charles Wight knew that the freshman Norris wore his coatee that day, he made no note of it in his memoir. The official newspaper of the

Charles Norris VMI Coatee. Cadet Charles R. Norris was found among the dead on the field after the First Battle of Manassas. A handsewn label inside the collar bore the name "Wight." It is speculated that when Charles Wight was promoted to first sergeant in April of 1861, he exchanged this garment for a long frock coat befitting a Confederate officer. Norris may have been given this garment by his classmate Charles Wight. Today, the coatee, with its telling bullet hole in the left shoulder, is on display at Manassas National Battlefield Park. *Family of Charles R. Norris*

VMI, *The Cadet,* published a memorial on November 19, 1913, to three young first-year cadets who died that July day at Manassas. The article may lend some insight. "Charles Norris [was one of] several hundred cadets who found their way to the momentous field of Manassas but most of these had already won commissions in the army and had changed the natty coatee for the long frock coat of a Confederate officer." As the cadets had moved from Lexington to Harpers Ferry, Charles Wight had been promoted to first sergeant. He would likely have been issued a frock coat befitting his promotion. Perhaps he offered his coatee, with his name sewn inside collar, to his young classmate and fellow soldier.[126] July 21, 1861, saw so many young boys, including the VMI cadets, give their lives for the Confederacy and the Union. Of the battle, Charles Wight wrote: "It has been thought that our victory here was easily won…This is very far, however from being the case. For several hours this was as hardly contested as any field of the war."

WILLIAM MARSHALL WIGHT, 1861: "OLD BOREY"

John and Margaret Wight's youngest son, William Marshall, "Willie" as his family called him, joined Company H of the First Virginia Regiment on May 4, 1861.[127] He was not yet eighteen. In just over two weeks, Willie and the First Virginia had all the drill they would receive from the VMI drillmasters at Camp Lee and moved out rather more smartly than when they arrived for Manassas Junction. Like his brother, Willie must have had a sense of anticipation and imagined himself on the battlefield. These were still the heady days of war. Martial music drifted over columns of troops and as they left camp, "hundreds of relatives and friends were at the fairgrounds to see the regiments off on the Richmond and Potomac Railroad…bands from the camp were on hand, and they all played mostly 'Dixie' and the 'Marseillaise'…Every musket, it seemed, was adorned with bouquets of flowers. Finally, the engine gave a whistle and the train pulled out amid the music from the bands and the cheering of those left behind. All along the route, ladies were assembled at the various stations, Ashland, Frederick Hall, Tolersville and Louisa Court House to hand out flowers, cakes, and other tokens…From Hanover Junction, the regiment traveled on the Virginia Central Railroad to Gordonsville. On May 26, they reached Manassas Junction."[128]

At Manassas, Willie Wight and the First Virginia Regiment were to join with other forces, including Charles Wight and the Fifty-eighth Regiment, to bolster General Beauregard in the upcoming battle against the Union army there. To pass the time before the battle, the First Virginia continued its practice of holding regimental dress parades. According to First Virginia historian Charles Loehr, their performance was unequalled. At camp, Willie Wight had grown so fond of drilling and marching that his friends in the regiment nick-named him "Old Borey"—a term frequently employed for General Beauregard. At the dress parades, the First Virginia often had spectators, among them General Beauregard himself.[129] It must have pleased Willie to demonstrate his prowess at drilling in full sight of his appreciative namesake.

On July 21, 1861, the first battle in the Civil War on the plains of Manassas began. No one alive today knows if the Wight brothers saw each other or knew the location of the other's unit on the field that day. But when the battle ended, both Willie and his brother Charles, who was slightly wounded, were among those who had gained an important victory for the South. The conflict in Manassas brought significant military action in Virginia to a halt for the remainder of the year. Charles and Willie would spend the winter of 1861 and early 1862 in winter camp with their units at Centreville, Virginia. By most accounts, Christmas in the Confederacy in 1861 was a happy holiday. Perhaps for the family of John and Margaret Wight, the season was less merry. A little over two weeks after the battle at Manassas, their eldest daughter Mary Wight died of tyhpoid fever contracted while attending wounded soldiers.

Chapter Five

1862

In this second year of the war, three events would alter the history of the Wight family. Two of them were tragedies. As the year began, Charles and William Wight were in camp with their regiments around Centreville, Virginia. Whether they were able to visit with each other is unknown. According to her diary, John and Margaret Wight were living at Hanover Tavern. Mrs. Wight indicates in her diary that began in 1863 that the family was living at Hanover Tavern for the full year of 1862. She gives little detail as to which family members were among the boarders. It would seem likely that John, Margaret, Emily, Annie and Jennie were together in Hanover, but there is nothing to prove it conclusively. On April 13, 1862, John and Margaret Wight's youngest living daughter, Virginia Chapman Wight, whom the family called "Jennie," died in Charles City County. Jennie had just turned fourteen. Why and how their child died in Charles City County when Mrs. Wight said the family had been living in Hanover remains a mystery, despite attempts during this project to discover the facts.

In April of 1862, a happier event took place. The Wight's now eldest daughter, Ann Louisa—"Annie"—married Edmund Waddill, clerk of the court of Charles City County. Almost instantly, Annie, who was twenty years younger than her husband, took on the responsibility of the six children in the household of the former widower. The new Mrs. Waddill was the only child of Margaret Wight and John Wight to stay in Charles City County during the war. The fact that Annie was in an area that saw frequent military action was a continual source of anxiety for Mrs. Wight for all the years of her Civil War diary. A typical entry about Annie reads: "What is to become of my poor child. I don't know and I am perfectly miserable about her."

On August 30, 1862, John and Margaret Wight lost a second child in the same year and the third to die since 1861. Their youngest son, William Marshall, was killed at the Second Battle of Manassas. Mrs. Wight never mentioned the deaths of Mary Elizabeth or Jennie in her diary until the epilogue thirteen years after the end of the war. Throughout her Civil War diary, she made frequent mention of Willie on his birthday, for example, or when she expressed gratitude that her remaining soldier sons, John Henry and Charles, had been spared after a battle and not been "sacrificed" (her word), like Willie.

In 1862, war planners would focus on two objectives: the national capitals in Washington and Richmond. Union general George Brinton McClellan had assembled an army estimated to be 120,000 strong at Fort Monroe. From there, he planned to move his army up the peninsula to capture Richmond and end the war. His plan depended on reinforcements that were to have arrived from around Fredericksburg. Early in 1862, General Robert E. Lee assumed the role of advisor to President Davis. His chief objective was to devise a plan to stop McClellan's advance. Lee advocated a "simple" plan. He would prevent the reinforcements from reaching Richmond by mounting an offensive against Washington through the Shenandoah Valley. He hoped to use General Jackson's army already in the region to clear it of Union troops to provide uncontested access through the valley and on to Washington.

In the Shenandoah Valley, Northern forces outnumbered Jackson's troops three to one. Yet between May 8 and June 9 of 1862, General Jackson prevailed in one of the most stunning campaigns of the war. Charles Wight and Captain Wingfield—a fellow Hanoverian from Marl Ridge plantation—were with the brigade every step of the way. "In the forty-eight days" of the storied "Valley Campaign" in the spring of 1862, "the largely inexperienced Confederate army had marched 676 miles—an average of fourteen miles per day for each day of the campaign. Jackson's 'foot cavalry' fought five battles and six skirmishes and had brushed with the enemy almost daily for a month."[130] Jackson's performance in the valley kept the reinforcements from linking up with McClellan before Richmond. It did not, however, eradicate the mounting threat to Richmond from McClellan's forces on the Peninsula. "The vast army of M'Clellan hovered upon the northern and eastern skirts of the city…his camp-fires could even be seen by night, and his balloons of observation, hanging like oranges in the sky, were clearly discernible in the afternoon. It was plain enough that an attack of the enemy in heavy force was expected at any moment."[131]

McClellan's Peninsula Campaign of 1862, known collectively as the Seven Days' Battles, would see Charles and William Wight in the middle of the action. The first of these engagements began on May 5 at the Battle of Williamsburg. William Marshall Wight was there, along with the First Virginia and the rest of the troops under General James Longstreet. In the middle of the Seven Days' Battles, on May 27, McClellan sent forces to attack the Confederate position near Hanover Courthouse. Their objective was to cut the railroad and to open the Telegraph Road for Union reinforcements. Confederates, attempting to prevent this maneuver, were defeated just south of Hanover Courthouse. Michael C. Hardy, who has produced the only full-length account of the action, observed: "The battles that whirled around the Kinney's Farm and Peake's turnout were just the beginning of military action in Hanover County."[132] A few days after the engagement, the *New York Times* published a vivid battle description, including the detail that a twelve-pounder howitzer was taken during the encounter. Mrs. Wight would likely have seen that piece of artillery from her vantage point at Hanover Tavern had she looked across the road.

Meanwhile, the Peninsula Campaign continued. For two days—May 31 and June 1—at Seven Pines, William Wight fought with his regiment along the Chickahominy River. From June 25 until July 1, Union and Confederate forces clashed at Beaverdam Creek, Gaines' Mill, Glendale and Malvern Hill. Both Charles and William Wight were on the battlefield at the third of the Seven Days' battles at Gaines' Mill. Captain Wingfield of the Fifty-Eighth Infantry wrote in his diary of the engagement: "This surpasses any battle for the severity of musketry that I have witnessed. Adjutant Charles C. Wight…[was] wounded." For a second time, Charles and his brother William escaped serious injury in a major battle.

The importance of these battles would be difficult to underestimate for the Confederacy. When the Seven Days' battles ended, against all odds, General Lee had turned what began as a Confederate retreat from Yorktown into an offensive action that drove McClellan and his army back to Fortress Monroe. General Lee and his army had probably saved Richmond for the Confederacy in 1862.

Just before the Seven Days' battles, Lee asked General J.E.B. Stuart to conduct a reconnaissance mission to estimate the strength and position of the Union forces then in Virginia. On June 12, Stuart, along with 1,500

Battle of Hanover Courthouse, 1862. During the battle, this twelve-pounder Howitzer was captured by the Seventeenth New York and Twelfth Maine Regiments on May 27, 1862. Mrs. Wight would likely have seen the artillery piece from her vantage point at Hanover Tavern had she looked across the road. *Library of Congress*

cavalrymen mounted up and set off on a three-day sprint around McClellan's army that has become the stuff of legend.

After the ride, General Stuart and his cavalry set up camp at Hanover Courthouse. Heros von Borcke, a Prussian cavalryman who came to fight for Confederate forces during the war and who spent much of his time with General Stuart, described the scene.

> On the 21st July we received orders again to remove our encampment, and the spot chosen for it was in the immediate

neighbourhood of the Court house of the county of Hanover...
It is a small building of red brick, pleasantly situated on a hill
commanding a pretty view, several miles in extent, of fertile fields
and dark-green woods, and a clear stream, which winds like a
silvery thread through the distant valley. The Court-house and
several offices belonging to it are surrounded by a shady enclosed
grove of locust and plantain trees, about five acres in area...The
cavalry regiments and horse-artillery were encamped in full view
all around us—nearly 8000 men, with their grazing horses, white
tents, and waving battle-flags—an animated panorama of active
military life.[133]

From the veranda of Hanover Tavern, or through an open window, the
strains of military music may have wafted across the fields to reach Mrs.
Wight and the other boarders.

Union Army Massing before Richmond, 1862. Confederate general J.E.B. Stuart left
Richmond on June 12, 1862, to make a daring ride abound McClellan's forces that were
massing for an attack on Richmond. On a three-day ride completely around the Union
Army of the Potomac, Stuart was able to supply Robert E. Lee with critical intelligence.
Stuart's men camped at Hanover Courthouse shortly after the raid. These forces were at
Cumberland Landing on the Pamunkey River. *Library of Congress*

The men would not be long at the Courthouse. No sooner had McClellan been thwarted in his attempts to gain Richmond than a new threat posed itself in the form of Union general John Pope, who began operating in the vicinity of Warrenton, Virginia. To meet the threat, General Lee incrementally transferred his army in that direction. General Stonewall Jackson marched around Pope in the last week of August, capturing Manassas Junction. This action against Pope precipitated the Second Battle of Manassas. Both Wight brothers made their separate ways, along with their units, in the direction of Manassas for the second time in just over a year.

The fighting began on August 28 and lasted through August 30. As part of Jackson's command, Charles Wight and the Fifty-eighth Infantry fought mostly on August 29 along what is known as the "The Unfinished Railroad." William Wight and the First Virginia were traveling with General Longstreet who arrived on the evening of August 29 and took part in the fighting on the following day. Despite their staggered arrivals, Charles and William were likely within a mile of each other during the battle on August 30, though it is extremely unlikely that they actually saw each other on that day. At some point during the battle, the First Virginia famously attacked a Union battery on Chinn Ridge, about a mile south of "The Unfinished Railroad." When the combat ceased and the dust settled, the officer in charge of the First Virginia entered in his official report: "William M. Wight, a private in Tyssinger's Company, was killed when he tried to capture a flag which flew above a battery still being served by the bluecoats."[134] Margaret Wight's youngest son's death notice was printed in the September 13 edition of the *Richmond Daily Dispatch:*

This devoted young soldier volunteered in his sixteenth year,[135] at the first call for troops, and became a member of Company H, 1st regiment Virginia Volunteers. He fought bravely in the battles of Bull Run and Manassas of 1861, Williamsburg, Seven Pines, and the Seven days battles before Richmond, passing through all these terrible conflicts unscathed although the Spartan First Virginia was reduced to the mere skeleton of thirty-four men. When our army moved against Pope, young Wight followed the flag he had so often fearlessly followed before, and was engaged in the second great battle of Manassas. His regiment, with another had charged a battery, and, as he reached forward to haul down the Yankee ensign of tyranny, he was shot through the body. He died on the field, with the shout of victory in his ears and a flush of triumph on his face. The devoted patriotism of this noble youth was conspicuous in the silent endurance of cold and want at Centreville, last winter, and in his great punctuality, obedience, and faithfulness in discharging the duties of camp, as in his conspicuous courage in action. He has left to his superiors an example for imitation, to his sorrowing relatives an honorable name, and to his country noble efforts to secure its independence. None knew him but to love him, None spoke of him but in praise.

For Charles Wight, there was little time to grieve or to rest after the battle at Manassas. General Lee pressed his advantage almost immediately by marching his Army of Northern Virginia into Northern territory for the first time. The Fifty-eighth Regiment was part of the plan. Less than two weeks after Manassas, on September 12, Lee's army was headed for the banks of Antietam Creek and the Maryland town of Sharpsburg. His men were growing weary. Just before the battle, Captain Wingfield wrote in his diary: "Many of the men are giving out from excessive fatigue."[136] The Battle of Antietam on September 17, 1862, was a horrific scene of carnage for both sides and a defeat for General Lee's Army of Northern Virginia. It is estimated that one in every three of Lee's soldiers was killed or injured. [137] Luckily, Charles Wight again escaped injury. Lee's Army returned to Virginia and as fall faded to winter that year, Charles must have been exhausted—and grief-stricken. Since the beginning of the war, he had lost two of his sisters and his younger brother. He had been in the hard fighting that year in General Jackson's Valley Campaign, the Seven Days' Battles, the Second Battle of Manassas and, less than a month after his brother's death, was thrust into the Battle of Antietam. Still, there would be little time for reflection, grief or even for rest. On December 13, Charles Wight was a part of the Battle of Fredericksburg—a last-ditch attempt by Union forces to gain a victory in Virginia that year. They did not succeed.

Chapter Six

1863

On January 1, 1863, Margaret Wight made her first diary entry.

> I only regret that I did not commence this earlier in life, as it might
> have afforded some gratification to my children and grandchildren,
> to read at some future day a record of the past. I shall not confine
> myself to family matters, but notice briefly the principal events
> that may occur in this most unhappy contest, which is now at its
> height, between the two sections of our once happy country. It is
> difficult to imagine how we are to carry it on another year or how
> we are to live.

In this first entry, financial woes seemed to be uppermost on her mind
as she lists the prices of staples that seemed to have risen precipitously.
Although her main concern seems to be money, the strain of mounting grief
and trial brought to the Wight family since 1861 must have been apparent
to at least one family member. From his home at Ingleside Plantation in
Goochland, brother-in-law Dr. William Leeds Wight took it upon himself
on April 18, 1863, to write to James Seddon, Confederate Secretary of War,
with an appeal for aid for the family. He was quite specific in his request (see
letter on following page).

No change in the military service of Charles Wight appears to have
resulted from the appeal. Margaret and John Wight would continue to have
cause to worry about their son who would remain in the Army of Northern

Dear Sir.

I am not willing to presume upon your time but a deep feeling of interest in a nephew compels me to do so. I write to ask if any appointments are now being made in the Regular Army and if so, to commend this nephew to your favorable consideration. A lieutenancy would be a situation that would greatly please him and for which I think him qualified, but for qualifications, I would refer you to Col. Preston...When the war broke out, he was holding a high position as Cadet at Lexington—was sent from there to Harpers Ferry. And as soon as he arrived he was ordered to act as Drill Master. His present position is that of 1st Lieutenant and Adjutant in the 58th Virginia Regiment, General Early's division, an appointment he obtained through the highest testimonials from Gen[eral]s. Jackson and Smith, Col[onel]s. Crutchfield and Preston and ex-President Tyler. Since that time he has been in all of Gen. Jackson's hard-fought battles and been twice wounded...If no such appointments as above are being made, could he obtain a situation in the Camps of Instruction? My brother's family has been so severely afflicted since the war, that in this...our hopes are centered.

Very respectfully, your friend, William Leeds Wight[138]

Virginia in near continuous combat until July of 1864 when he was captured and taken to Camp Chase Prison in Ohio.

Mrs. Wight began the chronicle of her war experiences with the news on January 2, 1863, that Charles would be home for a visit. "We were surprised and delighted to receive a visit from Charles who has been fighting in Gen Lee's army, General Jackson's Corps, now stationed at Port Royal. He has been in seven pitched battles, and slightly wounded twice. We have deep cause for gratitude that he has been spared and not sacrificed like our precious Willie who fell while bravely assisting his Reg (the 1st Va) to take a battery[,] offering up his life to his Country's [Confederacy's] cause."

As she followed events in Virginia throughout 1863, Mrs. Wight also monitored news from what she called the "south" and "west"—events in Charleston, South Carolina, and Vicksburg, Mississippi. Charleston seemed to have a symbolic significance for the Confederacy. South Carolina had been the first state to secede on December 20, 1860. The war began in earnest when Confederate forces fired on Union Fort Sumter in Charleston Harbor on April 12, 1861. Throughout the war, the city, its harbors and forts suffered bombardment and eventual siege. Margaret Wight wrote frequent and simple entries in her diary like "Charleston still holds." She did the same for Vicksburg. Margaret Wight cheered each victory around Charleston and Vicksburg and worried at each defeat.

The year began with an alarming event. On January 9, Mrs. Wight wrote of an apparent case of smallpox that agitated the residents of the Tavern—and with good reason. Diseases like smallpox, diphtheria, measles and typhoid were serial killers in the mid-nineteenth century. In December of 1862, details of an outbreak in Richmond's smallpox hospital had been widely publicized. Of the 250 patients admitted during the week of December 12, 110 died—a rate of 44 percent. Mrs. Wight did not say who had been infected or indicate the final outcome for the victim of smallpox at the Tavern.

Margaret Wight's note describing the infamous Bread Riot in Richmond on April 2, 1863, is an illustration of the power of newspapers in shaping public opinion. There are countless renditions of the actual event. Each one seems to differ from the other in tone and in fact. Mrs. Wight reported that a "mob of women" marched "on the pretense of seizing the necessities of life for which they were starving…but it proved to be a wholesale robbery." Her version of the story mirrors the tone of several of the Richmond newspapers' reports. The actual events of the incident can be described as a group of women—pushed to the breaking point between hunger and inability to pay the high prices for food in Richmond—pressed Governor Letcher for help. Relief was not forthcoming. Out of desperation, they began a march to Main Street with the intent of taking the food they required. Along the way, a band of stragglers joined them, eager to see where it all ended. A riot ensued that saw President Davis and troops in the street to restore order. At least sixty people were arrested.

The idea that women were rioting for food in the streets posed a problem for the press and the government alike. They had a public relations headache on their hands. They did not wish to see headlines in local papers that people in the city were close enough to starvation that they would resort to anarchy to get enough to eat. The government tried to suppress the story, but it was too late. The Northern press had already gotten wind of the story. Some printer's ink would have to be used to address the issue. The *Daily Richmond Examiner*'s opinion on April 4, 1863 was that the crowd was managed by "a handful of prostitutes, professional thieves, Irish and Yankee hags, gallows-birds from all lands but our own…with a woman huckster at their head." In Mrs. Wight's mind, the incident would serve to "injure us more in the eyes of the Yankees than anything that has occurred." She chalked it all up to "men of the worst character" who had somehow goaded the women into it. Mrs. Wight added a final comment about the Bread Riot: "The worthy women among our poorer class had no concern in it. This is but one of the disgraceful attendants upon this unholy and in my opinion unnecessary war." It appears there was a chink in Mrs. Wight's patriotic armor.

In late March and early April of 1863, Mrs. Wight would be distracted from war news. Annie was ready to deliver her first child in Charles City County and she may have wanted her mother with her. The best route available to Mrs. Wight was the Richmond and York River Railroad from Richmond. By this time, the heavy winter snows and spring rains had caused freshets, or floods, in local rivers and streams that completely swamped the railroad. Unable to learn if the railroads were running without actually going to the terminal in Richmond, Margaret Wight made several trips to town to try to board the railway. Each time, she was thwarted. When she was finally able to reach Charles City County on April 6, it was too late to offer Annie any help during the delivery. William Marshall Waddill, whom his grandmother named after her fallen soldier boy, was born on April 5, 1863.

Grandmother, grandson and mother spent a few weeks together in Charles City County. While she was there, Margaret Wight reported that her son John Henry Wight had been conscripted into service along with the other clerks. She prayed, for the sake of his family, that he would not be taken. By May 2, she was back in Richmond with John Henry. John Wight had come to town from Hanover to be with her. A report in the *Richmond Daily Dispatch* on May 2, 1863 gave them pause—"It is more than probable that one of the severest conflicts of the whole war will take place to-day or to-morrow…in the neighborhood of Chancellorsville." The information prompted John and Margaret to reconsider their return to Hanover Tavern, and they remained with John Henry. As events unfolded, it seems the Wights were wise to stay where there were.

On the morning of May 3, at the very moment the armies were locked in combat fifty miles north of Richmond at Chancellorsville, thousands of cavalry men arrived in the Richmond environs to wreck railroads and to sever lines of communications. General George Stoneman's command had pulled away from the Army of the Potomac before the battle began and arrived on the outskirts of Richmond. His men fanned out in smaller groups to ruin the Meadow Bridges over the Chickahominy River and the Hungary Station on the RF&P. At Ashland, some of the troopers tore up tracks and then surprised a train full of Confederate wounded passing through from the Chancellorsville fighting. When they arrived at Hanover Courthouse, Union raiders burned wagons loaded with supplies and demolished the railroad equipment, including the depot. In a postwar memoir, Virginia Central Railroad engineer Charles S. Anderson, whose wife was among the boarders at Hanover Tavern, described what had happened there:

> The raiders…completely destroyed the depot and several cars full of army supplies. James D. Christian was the railroad agent at the Hanover depot and lived in a company owned house about 50 yards from the depot with his wife and five young daughters. At the sound of horses moving close by, Mr. Christian looked out of the window and saw the whole depot yard full of Federal cavalry. He knew what was going to happen. He instructed his family to carry everything they could outside the house and into the garden. Soon furniture, clothing and several frightened women and children huddled in the yard. Mr. Christian humbly approached the officer in charge and begged him not to destroy the building. The cavalry officer reported that he had orders to burn all the railroad buildings. When the officer turned his gaze from the burning depot to speak to Mr. Christian, he caught sight of his fearful family and all their belongings. The federals did not burn the house. The man in charge said to Mr. Christian, "If I could truthfully reproduce this picture and carry it north, there would be no more war." In half an hour, every soldier had gone and nothing but the huge pile of smoking embers, casting their weird light against the sky, was left to speak of their visit.[139]

The raid kept the Wights in Richmond for a few more days. On May 5, 1863, Mrs. Wight said, "They have now gone back and the panic is somewhat over. We cannot get home as portions of the Railroad have been destroyed." By the next day, however, she said she returned to Hanover Courthouse and reported that the depot had been "entirely destroyed—no injury done to private property except to take away all the horses and many of the servants…The raiders still going through this part of the country at their pleasure. It is too bad."

Chancellorsville was a stunning victory for the South. But victory had a high price. General Stonewall Jackson was mortally wounded on the evening of May 2. His death on Sunday, May 10, came as a demoralizing blow for the Confederacy. Mrs. Wight received a letter from Charles "telling us about the battle 'out of our hundred and sixty' the number in his Regiment, they lost sixty in killed, wounded and missing, but every thing is now swallowed in grief at the loss of the greatest and best General the world has ever seen. Gen Thomas J Jackson. The idol of the army, the Nation. But God permits no people to look to any man as the giver of Victory. He alone is the God of battles and he saw best to summon this Christian warrior from the field of strife to a haven of rest."

After Chancellorsville, Margaret Wight made a cryptic entry in her diary. "June 4—heard Gen. Lee has gone with a portion of his army toward Culpeper." In fact, Lee once again pressed the advantage after a signal victory and began a move into Maryland that would result in the seminal Battle of Gettysburg. Based on a letter from Charles on June 4, Mrs. Wight believed that he was headed there with General Lee's army. On June 11, she wrote of a "great cavalry fight at Culpeper." While Lee's army was moving toward Pennsylvania, the Federal cavalry struck a part of a Confederate encampment at Brandy Station near Culpeper. One of the injured at Brandy Station was General William Henry Fitzhugh (Rooney) Lee. General Lee's son was hit by a ball that passed through his thigh. He was taken behind the lines by his brother, Lieutenant Robert Edward Lee Jr., and transported to Hickory Hill plantation in Hanover—the large estate of his uncle General Williams Carter Wickham.[140]

After Brandy Station, Lee's forces continued their march through the Shenandoah Valley, reaching Winchester on their way north. From June 13 through 15, there would be a fight at the town that ended in the Confederates' favor. No one in Charles Wight's unit was reported wounded, but three thousand Union prisoners were taken. Captain Henry Wyatt Wingfield and Adjutant Charles Wight (among others) were placed in charge of a unit that would take the captured officers to Libby Prison in Richmond. After having seen to his charges in Richmond, Charles was able to make a visit to the Tavern to spend a few hours with Mrs. Wight. She seemed surprised to see him stroll through the doors of Hanover Tavern unannounced on June 22. As he left to rejoin his regiment, his mother said, "He looks well and is very cheerful, seems to have perfect confidence in the success of Gen Lee's army wherever he may go." News reached Mrs. Wight on July 1 that General Lee was headed into Maryland. Based on her diary, she assumed Charles was marching with him toward Gettysburg.

Life on the home front carried on even in the midst of war. The constant worry for her children and for the progress of the war did not stop the necessity to earn some money. In June, Mrs. Wight began to manufacture the envelopes that would provide a supplementary source of income to the family for the remainder of the war. The work would net needed cash but may also have provided some opportunity to be distracted from worry about her family. From time to time, neighbors and friends called on Mrs. Wight to help with family members who were ill. On June 18, Margaret Wight went to the home of her friend Catherine Winston. Although the term is a modern one, it seems that she provided what amounted to hospice care to Catherine's husband, forty-six-year-old Philip H. Winston, as just five days later, the *Richmond Daily Dispatch* printed his obituary (June 23, 1863).

Yet, however she may have wanted to escape the war, the battlefront and home front would collide again as Colonel Samuel P. Spear mounted a Union cavalry raid that disrupted the residents at Hanover Tavern and around the local counties. On June 26, Mrs. Wight wrote in her diary:

> We were all sitting quietly at our work when about two thousand Yankee Cavalry came upon us like a perfect hurricane. The whole household were in commotion hiding all the silver and valuables. They had orders not to disturb private property so we began to breathe rather more freely[,] but they spread themselves all around us and in every direction taking all the Government Stores at the Depot and destroying them—every mule and horse they could find, tearing up a portion of the Railroad. They then went up to the Junction but were stopped at the Bridge by about eighty of our soldiers who defended it bravely and did not surrender until they lost eight or nine men. Hearing we had troops above they were afraid to proceed further. They soon returned bringing their prisoners, killed and wounded and some of ours as well as Negroes, wagons &c [etc.] in abundance. In addition to all this they went to Mr Wickham's and took Gen Fitzhugh Lee (who was badly wounded at the fight at Kelly's Ford) out of his bed and brought him by in a carriage as prisoner and carried him on to the White House (his old home) where their camp now is. After

remaining here four or five hours they retired with horses, mules, negroes and all their plunder.

Casualties of this brief raid were slight, and the effect was more psychological than material. Once again, Brigadier General W.H.F. "Rooney" Lee figured in the action. Spear's men knew the general was at Hickory Hill. They found and captured him there and hustled him off to the supply depot at the White House on the Pamunkey in New Kent County. From there he was taken to the Union prison at Fortress Monroe.[141]

Mrs. Wight reported on July 4 that they had "another visit from the Yankees." Apparently Colonel Spear's raid failed to accomplish the goals of Union commanders. On June 28, a total of sixteen thousand men composed of both cavalry and infantry under General George W. Getty were sent to complete the destruction of the bridges along the North Anna River. On July 3, Union pickets were stationed at Hanover Courthouse and the bridge to give the raiders unimpeded access to the railroads. They destroyed the

White House Landing on the Pamunkey River, as Union Supply Depot.
Originally the home of Martha Dandridge Custis, who would marry George Washington, the plantation home was burned by McClellan's forces in 1862. At the time, it was owned by Mary Custis Lee, wife of General Robert E. Lee. Thereafter and for the duration of the Civil War, the area served as a critical Union supply depot. General Lee's son, William Henry Fitzhugh Lee, was taken from Hickory Hill Plantation in Hanover County to White House as a prisoner in 1863 and transported from there to Fortress Monroe.
Library of Congress

station house at Ashland and then marched up the Richmond and Potomac Road to the bridge over the North Anna. The Confederate forces there were able to fend off the invaders who went back to the White House from whence they had sprung, setting fire to the Littlepage's Bridge over the Pamunkey along their lines of retreat. The two attacks on the railroad bridges left the Virginia Central Railroad incapacitated, but the RF&P line in Ashland remained open. Mrs. Wight reported in her diary that she had to send to Ashland for her mail until the end of July when the railroads were repaired.

Mrs. Wight said only this in her diary on the day the Battle of Gettysburg began on July 1: "We hear that Lee's Army had gone into Maryland." The fighting at Gettysburg that began on July 1 and ended on July 3 received short shrift in the daily newspapers. Mrs. Wight, like most of the newspaper-consuming public, did not learn there had been a defeat until days later. On July 18, she received a letter from Charles. When she learned that her son had not been at Gettysburg, her prayers offered up on the Willie's birthday on June 29 seem to have been answered. "God grant I may not be called to mourn the loss of another son before this dreadful war ends." The lucky event of having to transport prisoners to Richmond after the fighting at Winchester had kept Charles from rejoining Lee's forces in time for the invasion. An earlier letter on the sixteenth of July informed her that Charles was headed into Maryland. As she could not get details from the newspapers she did not realize that he was going there not to fight but to help Lee's retreating army make its way back to Virginia. The wagon train that bore the Army of Northern Virginia home from Gettysburg was said to have been more than fifteen miles long. Charles Wight was with the Fifty-eighth Regiment as it was sent forward to help guard the men and provisions as they crossed the Potomac back into Virginia. At Hagerstown, the Union cavalry tried to cut off part of the retreat. When they attacked, the Fifty-eighth Regiment drove them back. After Gettysburg, there were no more large battles in Virginia for the remainder of 1863, though two more campaigns would involve Charles Wight before the year was over.

The defeat at Gettysburg was not only shocking to the South, but it also caused deep reflection on the part of General Robert E. Lee. Mrs. Wight heard a rumor on July 28, that he had resigned. Her diary entry to this effect was written well in advance of the official date of Lee's tendered resignation (a fact that speaks to her tendency to reorder events in her diary). Official records show that on August 8, the general's letter to President Davis read in part:

The general remedy for the want of success in a military commander is his removal. This is natural, and in many instances, proper. For, no matter what may be the ability of the officer, if he loses the confidence of his troops disaster must sooner or later ensue. I have been prompted by these reflections more than once since my return from Pennsylvania to propose to Your Excellency the propriety of selecting another commander for this army.[142]

Three days later, on August 11, President Davis replied: "To ask me to substitute you by someone…more fit to command, or who would possess more of the confidence of the army…is to demand an impossibility."[143]

Mrs. Wight's August 7 entry records a rumor about a new "proclamation" from Abraham Lincoln that, according to her, would allow "for every negro taken in battle by us and executed, he [Lincoln] will kill two of our Southern soldiers so that will compel us to shoot them all instead of taking them prisoners." It is difficult to comprehend Mrs. Wight's understanding of this rumor. Abraham Lincoln issued sixteen proclamations in 1863—none in August and certainly none along the lines of Mrs. Wight's description.

In the midst of turmoil, church services seemed to offer Mrs. Wight some comfort and an opportunity to meet with members of the community. When she could not get to town to the Presbyterian services, she seems to have attended whatever church was close at hand. St. Paul's Episcopal Church was within walking distance, just a few hundred yards from the front doors of Hanover Tavern.[144] In the western part of the county, she went to the old Fork Church to hear the sermons of Parson Horace Stringfellow. From time to time, she visited the Baptist church at Taylorsville a mile or two north of Ashland.

During the searing summer of 1863, a deadly outbreak of diphtheria came to Hanover Tavern. By the time it was over, Mrs. Wight reported that the disease sickened ten and claimed the lives of two. Perhaps the patients who survived did so because of Margaret Wight's care. By her own admission, she did not fear the disease, although she was certainly not without risk. The first death reported in the diary was on August 16 when a "little child" died apparently within the space of twenty-four hours of the onset of symptoms. On August 21, another boarder—a Miss Campbell—was stricken. She died eight days later after what Mrs. Wight described as "much suffering." By August 26, three new cases kept Mrs. Wight fully occupied. The "home" (as Margaret referred to Hanover Tavern) was virtually quarantined as "the neighbors are afraid to come near us. I don't wonder at it for it is truly alarming. The physicians say they consider it worse than small pox." Death by diphtheria, as in the case of Susan Campbell, meant literally choking to death.[145]

In the middle of nursing diphtheria patients at Hanover Tavern, Mrs. Wight had begun the process of finding a school for her youngest daughter, Emily. On September 5, Margaret wrote to friend Frank Watkins who served on the Board of Trustees of the Farmville Female College (now Longwood College) in the town of the same name. She asked him to help find a suitable school for Emily for the fall and winter term. Apparently, Watkins assured the family that Emily would be well-served by the curriculum at Farmville Female College, seventy-five miles southwest of Richmond. While most colleges for men had closed with the advent of war as professors and students alike headed for the battlefield, female schools apparently overflowed with students. According to the school's president, French-born E.A. Preot, parents were urged to apply for admission early to guarantee board. Tuition was to be paid in advance without exception. Also according to the school bulletin, Emily Wight was expected to furnish her own lights (lamps and candles), napkins, towels and toiletries. Board was fixed at $250 and included fuel and laundry (limited to one dozen pieces per week). The English Department classes would cost $40; Ancient and Modern Languages, $20; and piano or guitar, $40, including a usage fee of $8 for the piano. Incidental charges would total $3.[146] At the end of September, Mrs. Wight reported that she and Emily traveled to Farmville after weeks of preparation. At the college, Mrs. Wight said she paid Mr. Preot $450 for the October to February session. She bade her daughter farewell and returned by train to Hanover Tavern.

Having returned from her trip to Farmville in early October, Margaret Wight continued to monitor events in the various theaters of war. From July until September 7, operations around Fort Wagner and Morris Island in South Carolina had been in the news. Now it would seem, after a long siege, the fort was abandoned by the Confederate army. In the west, Chattanooga and Knoxville, Tennessee, seemed to be a frequent topic in the newspapers and in entries from Mrs. Wight's pen. Throughout the summer and into the fall, contesting armies there traded victories and defeats that seemed to elicit worried entries in Mrs. Wight's diary. The trend of victories in 1861 and 1862 was shifting in 1863 to more defeats and loss of territory for the Confederacy. In Virginia, the Battle of Culpeper Court House took place on September 13, resulting in the Union army routing the Confederate hold on the train depot on the Orange and Alexandria Road. A good example of Mrs. Wight's predisposition to interpret events of the war by conflating religion and patriotism followed her entry of this battle. "It is hard to think that the wickedness of our people will cause us to be sabotaged. The South is divided into two classes, the Patriots and extortionists and I begin to fear the last are greatly in the majority."

According to Mrs. Wight, the family decided to spend time together beginning on October 5, in Charles City County at the home of Annie and Edmund Waddill. Apparently the diversions of life in the country with Annie and her new grandson did not provide opportunity or motivation for Margaret to keep up her diary. It does not begin again until December 1, 1863, when Mrs. Wight offered a recap of military events that she had not reported before she left for Charles City County. Before year's end, Charles and the Fifty-eighth Regiment would take part in two more campaigns: Bristoe Station on October 24 and the Mine Run Campaign that took place from November 26 through December 1, 1863. Christmas in 1863 would be the last time that the family would spend together during the war. Only Charles was absent, as Mrs. Wight reported he could not get a furlough to join the family. John, Margaret, Emily, Annie and John Henry all gathered together at the Tavern on Christmas Eve to celebrate. The year had been a trying one by all accounts, both at home and on the battlefield.

Chapter Seven

1864

Lincoln would have to face re-election in November of this year. Without a clear victory to end the war, the Northern population began to clamor for negotiations to bring it to a close. Lincoln's second term was not guaranteed. As a hedge against his opposition, by the end of 1863, Lincoln sought ways to find a path to military victory. In his opinion, the solution lay in the utter defeat of the vaunted Army of Northern Virginia under the command of General Robert E. Lee.

To accomplish the goal, Lincoln appointed General Ulysses S. Grant to take command of all forces in the United States in early 1864. Grant's successes in the western theater of war the previous year convinced Lincoln that this general, unlike the many before him, had the will and strategy to do what was necessary to stop the fighting and end the war. Mrs. Wight and her family would be entangled in nearly every aspect of Grant's efforts to crush the Confederate armed forces and to take Richmond in this year and the next.

The miserably cold weather in the winter of 1864 was slow to leave. At Hanover Tavern, Mrs. Wight continued to make envelopes. Charles was in winter camp with General Lee's forces. In this year, Mrs. Wight would report that Union troops would raid Annie and Edmund Waddill's property and take their food and livestock. On November 10, Edmund would be captured and taken behind Union lines, leaving Annie and their many children alone in Charles City County. Emily Wight had returned from Farmville Female College at Christmas in 1863, but in January contracted measles followed by chicken pox. Her recovery apparently lasted long enough that she did not return to school to finish the term. John Henry continued his work with the clerks in Richmond and would be called out from time to time on military duty around the Richmond defenses.

The war news seemed bleak on many fronts in early 1864. The resolve of the Confederacy was plain, but long years of war and the resulting attrition sapped Southern armies who were now struggling mightily to replenish both men and materiel. Inflation and shortages continued to plague the country and make life on the home front difficult at best. Mrs. Wight complained, "Every thing seems to be swallowed up…in the worthlessness of the money and difficulty of getting provisions which gets worse and worse." Yet one bright spot would have a cheering effect on Mrs. Wight. On February 16, Charles Wight was able to get a twenty-day furlough to spend time visiting the scattered members of his family in Richmond, Charles City, Goochland and Hanover. In late February, just before he was to return to camp around Orange Courthouse, Virginia, Mrs. Wight described another nerve-racking cavalry raid that brought Union troops again to her doorstep. "Wakened up about 2 o'clock in the night by a courier telling us the Yankees were between this place and at Ashland and we made Charles go into some place of safety until we could find out the truth of it."

The raid was a part of a now-familiar tactic to those who lived around Richmond and in Hanover County. With the bulk of armed forces, both Union and Confederate, massed near Fredericksburg, Union general Hugh Judson Kilpatrick and Colonel Ulric Dahlgren seized an opportunity to make a run for Richmond to try and take the capital. Their elaborate plan was to split their forces and make a two-pronged attack on the city. One column would rip up rails and cut communications lines along the Virginia Central Railroad. The other would advance to Richmond and free the Union prisoners on Belle Isle. With the prisoners adding force to their army, the men planned to take Richmond and assassinate President Davis and his cabinet. A series of mishaps and stiff resistance by some companies of the Local Defense Troops, including John Henry Wight and Mrs. Wight's sixty-two-year-old uncle, Robert Copland, who was visiting Richmond from New Orleans, met Kilpatrick's men around Richmond and helped to drive them off. Colonel Dahlgren was met with an odd mixture of stray Confederates, including some local troops, in King and Queen County, where he was killed. The newspapers reported that documents found on his body described the audacious plan of the raid. Whether Dahlgren had crafted the raid's strategy himself or whether it had been developed by Union authorities is still the subject of debate. At the time, however, the "uncivilized" aim of the raid outraged the Southern population. Mrs. Wight's description of the raid was peppered with indignant exclamation points.

Soon after the raid, Charles returned to camp—again. It is not hard to imagine the trepidation Margaret Wight must have felt each time she bade farewell to her war-weary young son, who had been fighting nearly constantly since the early days of 1861. Added to the tension of constant combat, soldiers were hungry and worn. Even so, Mrs. Wight said he was assured of victories in the coming season as he left her once again for the battlefields of Virginia.

At the Tavern, on March 10, Margaret lamented the death of a "young and beautiful widow." The woman appears to have been Conway Chisholm Mitchell, daughter of Cleavers and Amizela Chisholm, owners of Hanover Tavern. In a postwar statement, given in support of a claim against the United States government, seeking reimbursement for provender and livestock confiscated from the Chisholms by the Union army,[147] Mrs. Chisholm stated that her daughter Conway Chisholm Mitchell died on March 10, 1864, leaving behind two children, Charles and Alma Mitchell. It is of interest to note that in his book *The Majors and Their Marriages*, James Branch Cabell indicates that Alma Conway Mitchell eventually married one of Edmund Waddill's sons by his first marriage. (Alma Mitchell and young Edmund Waddill were married in 1878.)[148]

On March 20, 1864, Mrs. Wight learned further details about the disposition of the estate of her cousin Margaret Wight Munford, whose death she had learned of in August of 1863. Apparently, Mrs. Munford's will had been probated in the interval. Final distributions under the terms of the will resulted in a windfall to the Wight siblings. The story is a complex one. John Wight's brother, Edwin Lord Wight, married Margaret Nicolson Copland in 1837, a cousin of Margaret Wight's. Interestingly, for a period of thirteen years, *two* Margaret Wights were both cousins and sisters-in-law. When Edwin died in 1850, his will stipulated that his estate, including Tuckahoe plantation, would pass to his wife, Margaret Nicolson (Copland) Wight for her use during her lifetime (after a specific bequest of property to his niece and John Wight's daughter, Julia Leeds Wight). There were caveats. The one applicable to the Wight family was the statement in Edwin's will that after the death of his wife, whatever was left of his estate was to be bequeathed to Mrs. Octavia Haxall. Edwin Wight appointed Richard B. Haxall, principal in the important Haxall Mills in Richmond,[149] as his executor. Sometime after Edwin's death, Margaret Nicolson Copland Wight sold Tuckahoe. She remarried, becoming Margaret Munford. By August 8, 1863, Mrs. Munford died. Based on her diary entry at the time, Mrs. Wight clearly expected that Edwin's will would be carried out as originally written and that the estate would pass to Octavia Haxall. Somehow it did not. Therefore, in March of 1864, each of the Wight siblings, Ann Eliza, Dr. William Leeds and John Wight received (according to Mrs. Wight) $7,000 each. To put the sum in perspective for John and Margaret Wight, the 1860 census showed their *total* personal property valued at $7,100. Inheritance notwithstanding, by March 29, the Wights decided to find less expensive lodgings and would soon leave the Hanover Tavern.

On May 3, John and Margaret Wight left the Hanover Tavern and relocated to the household of local physician Dr. Charles E. Thompson near the depot at Beaverdam. Almost on arrival, Mrs. Wight was made aware that the "mistress" of the household (probably Edith Potty, widowed sister of the Thompson brothers) was not amenable to guests in their home. For women accustomed to running their own households, it could be a strain on even the most gracious of hostesses to accept strangers into their homes. It must have been equally stressful to the strangers. Although she said she would never have a "home feel" at Dr. Thompson's, upcoming events would make the stay memorable.

A report in the *Richmond Daily Dispatch* from Orange Courthouse near Culpeper in northern Virginia on May 2 dispatched ominous news: "Scouts report that the enemy have struck their tents in Culpeper, and that the Yankee army is moving." On the following day, the dispatch from the same area read, "Ample preparations are going on to meet the enemy, and the week can hardly close without a desperate general engagement. Our troops are eager and confident. Grant is reported to have a very large force." Two days later on May 5, the opening battle of Grant's Overland Campaign, was fought in the dense woods known as "the Wilderness" near Fredericksburg. Mrs. Wight had been following the news and heard from some soldiers arriving from that direction that the fighting had begun. She was well aware that her son Charles would be in the thick of it and felt anxious about his safety. "My poor Charles what a time of anxiety for us and we can't hear from him for days."

By May 7, the Battle of the Wilderness ended in a tactical draw. In the past, Union generals had retreated after an inconclusive battle and heavy losses such as took place at the Wilderness. General Grant simply disengaged his forces and moved toward the area to the south of the Wilderness at Spotsylvania Courthouse. He was drawing closer to Hanover County and

Richmond. Over the following days and weeks, Mrs. Wight reported other activities in the Shenandoah Valley and around Richmond and Petersburg, but events that followed the Battle of the Wilderness seemed to consume all of her attention. She was about to experience what she would call, "the most exciting scene I ever witnessed"—a cavalry chase right before her eyes. From May 9–11, her diary contained detailed description of General Philip Henry Sheridan's cavalry raid around Richmond. During the raid, Mrs. Wight saw the flames consume the Beaverdam depot not far from where she lived. She and the household at Dr. Thompson's were subjected to Union soldiers searching the house and threatening to burn it down when a pistol was found. The soldiers left them unmolested and eventually moved on. She observed with dismay the wounded and dead soldiers who fell in the raid: "They left some twenty wounded and dead not far from us. Most of the former were taken into homes but one or two were allowed to lie on the ground exposed to the inclement weather for days before any one had humanity enough to give them a shelter. We need not talk so much of Yankee cruelty when we allow wounded and dying men to suffer, altho' they are our enemies." She was further saddened to write of the death of General J.E.B. Stuart on May 12 at Yellow Tavern in Henrico County. The raid had deprived the South of another of its most beloved generals.

In her diary, Mrs. Wight said she felt unwelcome in the Thompson household. On May 18, within a fortnight of their arrival at Dr. Thompson's, John Wight seems to have accommodated his wife's sensibilities and secured new lodging for the couple at the home of Mrs. Cora DeJarnette at Hanover Junction on the Virginia Central Railroad. Mrs. DeJarnette's demeanor proved a happier match for Margaret Wight, and the couple would remain there until the last days of the war. On the same day, John Wight arrived at Mrs. DeJarnette's with news of a raid in Charles City County that greatly heightened Mrs. Wight's continual anxiety over Annie and the children there. Over the next few weeks and months, information and rumor would continue to drift in from Charles City that made Annie's situation there seem grave indeed. On May 21, 1864, the *Richmond Daily Dispatch* gave a report:

> On Monday last (May 16), a party of negro Yankee cavalry committed a most diabolical murder in Charles City County, Va. The victim was Mr. J.L. Wilcox, residing thirteen miles from the Court-House, on the Lower Chickahominy. The negroes, under the direction of a white officer, first burned his dwelling, out-houses, and everything upon the place. Mr. Wilcox was...shot

through the head. It is said that the Yankees have also certainly hung Robt Ely, a painter, living in Charles City.

The newspaper accounts were probably exaggerated in fine points, but the "African Brigade" of Brigadier General Edward A. Wild, stationed at Fort Pocahontas near the Waddill home in Charles City County had been dashing in and out of the area for some weeks, freely harassing the local population. Mrs. Wight was relieved when on June 4, she received word from Emily, who had been with Annie, and her family in Charles City County. "She writes that the Yankees (black) have never been on the place at all altho' every one around them has suffered, some have been killed, homes burned and nearly all the gentlemen taken prisoners."

During this busy fighting season, while Grant and Butler were moving ever closer to Richmond, Major General Franz Sigel of the Union army was deployed to the Shenandoah Valley. His mission was to ruin the railroad and canal at Lynchburg. At Newmarket, Sigel was thwarted by a smaller Confederate force. In the assault were 247 cadets from VMI. Victorious, the VMI cadets returned to Lexington having captured the only battle flag ever taken by a body of college students.[150] Sigel was relieved of command after this battle and replaced by General David Hunter. Perhaps there was some satisfaction and pride in this news of VMI for former cadet Charles Wight.

Just as after the Wilderness, General Grant moved on after several inconclusive battles at Spotsylvania. He still pressed to get himself between Lee and Richmond. Beginning on May 21, until nearly the end of May, Lee's forces poured into Hanover County from Spotsylvania Courthouse, once again just ahead of Union troops who moved to the North Anna River at the location of the RF&P Bridge. In the wake of the army, the railroad was occupied by Union troops and destroyed as far back as possible. Grant's men twisted the rails by heating them to near molten state over burning railroad ties. Bent ties could be reformed and reused; twisted ties could not. The Union army was in no mood to leave material behind that could be recycled. Mrs. Wight began to report seeing troops moving in, and she said she could hear firing in the distance. The battles of the Overland Campaign were about to be upon her.

Just as Lee's army began arriving in Hanover, Charles Wight arrived at Mrs. DeJarnette's on May 22, ill and on the verge of exhaustion after having been in constant fighting since the first days of May at the battle of the Wilderness. Mrs. Wight said he got a certificate from his surgeon indicating he was "unfit for duty." He remained out of commission until June 7, when

Left: **Confederate Redoubt at Chesterfield Bridge Overlooking the North Anna River.** The bridge was captured by Union troops on May 23, 1864. The gun is in position, and soldiers sit in front of shelter tents. *Library of Congress*

Below: **Union Troops Crossing at Jericho Mills, May 1864.** No bridge existed at this crossing. Union troops built their own pontoons to gain access to the south side of the North Anna River. *Library of Congress*

Right: **General Grant's Army Ruins RF&P Bridge over North Anna River, 1864.** The Richmond, Fredericksburg and Potomac Bridge was destroyed by Union troops on May 25, 1864, as part of General Ulysses S. Grant's Overland Campaign and the series of battles collectively known as the Battle of North Anna. *Library of Congress*

Below: **Chesterfield Bridge Crossing on the Telegraph Road, May 1864.** One of the avenues for Union troops to cross the river from Caroline County into Hanover County during the Battle of North Anna. *Library of Congress*

he returned to his regiment. Mrs. Wight said she was worried because he seemed so tired and exhausted. It is no wonder. The now veteran soldier had been in the line of battle for more than fifteen days during this campaign. He stayed for a time with his family at Hanover Junction but soon ventured to Richmond, apparently to seek his surgeon at a hospital.

The end of May was a blur of blue and gray in Hanover County and around Richmond. On May 23, Mrs. Wight said:

> Our whole army is on the move finding the Yankees were pushing in this direction. Thousands are coming in. Gen Lee has arrived and has been riding around all day so we may have a fight about here after all…A division of our troops…are on the march. I have been in the woods with Mrs. DeJarnette to see them pass. They are all so cheerful and confident of whipping Grant yet. The firing this evening is constant. We hear it is near the railroad bridge over North Anna River.

From May 23 until May 26 a number of small battles that came to be known as the Battle of North Anna sputtered along the river and its bridges at Chesterfield, Jericho Mills and Ox Ford. General Lee's forces out-defended and out-maneuvered much larger Union forces. But again, no clear victory could be claimed on either side, and the armies continued to pour in. As she watched them coming, Mrs. Wight exclaimed, "What a time of anxiety and suspense about children and country."

On May 24, Mrs. Wight said, "Gen Gordon rode here for an hour this evening to see his wife who came this morning." The general advised the ladies to move to Ashland, about five miles south of the junction. According to Mrs. Wight, many of the ladies in the neighborhood had left, but she elected to "wait awhile to see what is to be done." By the next day, however, she said, "The whole of our army is extended along our central road. In front of our windows, it is a busy and novel scene cutting down trees, making breastworks planting their cannon around the top of the hill on which this home stands." Margaret Wight observed that Mrs. DeJarnette's property had suffered from the presence of troops and that her fields had been ruined and her livestock killed. She also said that the patriotic landlady was "willing to bear it all if Grant can only be whipped." As Mrs. Wight watched the troops and pondered her next move, a battle in Charles City County would take place in the territory close to Annie and Edmund Waddill.

In Charles City County on May 24, in an effort to put a stop to General Edward A. Wild's marauding around the wharves in Charles City, General Fitzhugh Lee's cavalrymen, totaling around three thousand men, attacked Wild's two regiments with only half that number at the Battle of Wilson's Wharf. Union forces carried the day in a battle that gained some notoriety because of the presence of black troops defeating front line soldiers from the Army of Northern Virginia.[151] Mrs. Wight did not learn of the battle until she received a letter from Annie in early June in which she learned that the Waddill's had suffered less than their neighbors during the attack. She said it was because of Mr. Waddill's "great kindness and likeability to all classes." Yet, in the fall, Waddill would be captured and taken behind Union lines. In the interim, Emily remained in Charles City County with her sister.

On May 28, operating on the intelligence that Charles, who had left Hanover Junction days earlier, was now in a hospital in Richmond, the Wights decided it was time to depart Hanover Junction. As no trains were available, John and Margaret packed what they could carry in their satchels and traveled by shank's mare about a mile and a half south to Taylorsville, where they could take the cars to Ashland and then Richmond on the RF&P. Along the way, Mrs. Wight said, "Just [as] we reached the main road we found ourselves in the midst of Gen Ewell's Corps who were on their way to meet some of the enemy...It does me good to be with and talk to our brave and veteran troops."

Mrs. Wight reported that they reached John Henry's home in Richmond that afternoon and found Charles there. He had remained quite ill since they had seen him last but now was on the mend. The Wights may have planned their departure from the junction at just the right time. On the day of their arrival in Richmond, General Lee's forces were massed from Atlee's Station on the Virginia Central Railroad south and east to the Mechanicsville Turnpike. Union troops were along the Shady Grove Road, extending to the Mechanicsville Turnpike (Route 360) and about three miles south of the Totopotomoy Creek. They extended all the way back to Hanover Courthouse. The Virginia Central Railroad had been destroyed as far back as possible by Union forces.[152] The stage was set for the rest of the battles of the Overland Campaign to explode. Mrs. Wight's entry from John Henry's home in Richmond on May 31 belies that fact. "Every thing is quiet here. No one would suppose that an army of one hundred thousand Yankees were within a few miles aiming to burn and destroy this devoted city." The battles of the Overland Campaign that had begun at North Anna and Wilson's

Wharf would continue in rapid succession in Hanover—Haw's Shop (May 28), Totopotomy Creek (May 28–June 1), Matadequin Creek (also called the Battle of Old Church) (May 30), Bethesda Church (May 30), Hanover Courthouse (May 31) and the Battle of Cold Harbor (May 31–June 12). Just before the battles commenced, the area around Hanover Junction was surrounded by Confederate and Union forces. On May 31, Union troops made concerted efforts around Hanover Courthouse and Ashland, not without success. Ashland became a center of activity as the Federals moved to ruin the two railroad bridges over the South Anna for the fourth time during the war. Union cavalry were also advancing along River Road toward Hanover Courthouse. They set up headquarters at the home of Dr. Lucien Price at nearby Dundee. A battle began there and spun northwest toward Hanover Courthouse. Confederate defenders brought cavalry and artillery onto the high ground there and set up a strong line of defense. Some of the heaviest fighting took place at the Virginia Central Depot, close to Hanover Tavern. In the end, Union forces managed to dislodge Confederate soldiers, and the Union prevailed in clearing the way for advancing Union troops to make a direct assault on the bridges over the South Anna.[153] Mrs. Wight reported that she had heard of Union soldiers at Dr. Price's and also at Courtland (the home of Mrs. William O. Winston) about a quarter of a mile southeast of the Tavern. Apparently, dismounted cavalry had entered the Tavern and broken up all of Mr. Chisholm's furniture.

On June 2, Mrs. Wight's report that "the fighting has finally commenced" was a few days late. The battles in Hanover had been raging for several days. Although Charles remained on medical leave, according to Captain Wingfield who remained with the unit, his Fifty-eighth Regiment withstood the fighting around Old Church with heavy losses.[154] Wingfield also said a few days later that Union troops had been to his home at Marl Ridge. In her diary, Mrs. Wight reported her gratitude that Charles had escaped the fighting as his brigade had "suffered terribly." The beleaguered Fifty-eighth Regiment, without the services of its adjutant, manned the breastworks at Cold Harbor over the next week in a battle that echoes still in history's memory as one of the worst of the war.

As the railroads had been cut, the family could not return to Hanover Junction. Mrs. Wight reported that she and her husband would rent a room in Richmond until it became clearer when and how they could leave for their home at Mrs. DeJarnette's. On June 4, John Henry's company was called out to Bottom's Bridge to fend off Union threats there. On June 7, Charles Wight rejoined his regiment somewhere in the vicinity of Cold Harbor.

Several days later, the Fifty-eighth moved out for the Shenandoah Valley.[155] Mrs. Wight could do little but watch and wait.

The course of the war had changed drastically since the Wilderness. The thirty-two thousand losses borne by Lee's army since then comprised nearly half of his force. A third of his generals had been killed or wounded, and the troops who remained were exhausted as the armies realigned themselves along the Petersburg line. "Grant's forces were soon so well entrenched that Lee could not possibly dislodge them. Worst of all for Lee, what was beginning at Petersburg was a major siege—something Grant had used to smashing success at Vicksburg the previous summer. Siege warfare was a static contest which Lee could not win."[156] For now, the Army of the Potomac and the Army of Northern Virginia remained stalled in front of Richmond and Petersburg. (Margaret Wight referred to Petersburg by its nickname, "Cockade City"—a term coined during the War of 1812 in a nod to the rosettes residents wore in their caps).

In the valley, both sides swapped victories and defeats with regularity. In the South and West, Sherman continued his march to Savannah. In Richmond and Petersburg, a siege began.

General Grant well understood the advantage of depriving his enemy of resources and redoubled his effort in that regard. He gave orders to his commanders in the field to lay waste to stores and provisions whenever and wherever possible. The move was calculated to demoralize the population into surrender. Already the food supply for both civilians and armies was below what could be described as meager. It would get worse. As an example of conditions that now prevailed around Richmond, the *Richmond Daily Dispatch* printed an article on June 15:

> *Suffering in Hanover:* "At the residence of one of the Justices of that county there are now twenty four women and children, entirely destitute the savages having destroyed the house of some, and the food and raiment of all of them. In their behalf we have received a contribution of $50…In the neighborhood of Haw's Shop… many families have been stripped of every comfort of life, and unless immediate relief is given the women and children, many of them may perish for want of food. The Yankees swept the neighborhood of corn, bacon, and cattle of every description, besides ruining the growing crops. Until other arrangements are made, contributions may be left at the counting room of the *Dispatch* for these suffering people.

Despite conditions that seemed to worsen with each passing day, for Margaret Wight, hope sprang eternal. On June 27, she wrote: "They will be baffled yet. We have provisions in Richmond to last months for the army and Grant has a good deal more to do before his famous siege commences." Nothing could have been further from the truth.

Siege warfare generates little daily activity. Rumor and conjecture filled the newspapers and Mrs. Wight's diary, as skirmishes and battles along the siege lines continued with regularity. By June 20 enemy activity north of Richmond had quieted enough for John and Margaret Wight to return to Mrs. DeJarnette's and Hanover Junction. A few days earlier, Mrs. Wight had written: "We hear that Gen Early's Corps has gone on some secret expedition so Charles with it. We shall no doubt hear of it in the right place." Defense of the valley (or its capture) was viewed by both sides as vital. Around June 9, Grant learned that General David Hunter had taken Staunton. Capitalizing on the victory, he launched a renewed effort to close the valley to the Confederate forces once and for all. General Lee responded by sending General Jubal Anderson Early to the valley after them. Charles Wight, reunited with his regiment, was marching with Early toward Lynchburg and Liberty where the Confederate troops would overtake and defeat General Hunter.[157]

On July 8, Mrs. Wight reported that all she could learn about General Early's army (and Charles's whereabouts) in the valley came from the Northern papers. According to this *New York Herald* article on July 8, 1864, "Confederate forces [are] contemplating an invasion of Maryland and Pennsylvania. The true object and extent of the whole movement is yet a mystery." Early's "13,000 mostly barefooted men marched down the valley and crossed the Potomac. They brushed aside a small force at Monocacy, Md., on July 9 and two days later were in battle line on the northwestern outskirts of Washington."[158] His force was of insufficient strength to do more than worry the population of Washington for two days. But the fact that Confederate troops had gotten so near to the capital must have sent waves of fear through the town. Charles had been in Early's expedition.

It is perhaps noteworthy that on what would have been a lively, national celebration in the old Union—July 4—Mrs. Wight made no mention of a celebration of any sort on that day in 1864. In 1863, defeats at both Gettysburg and Vicksburg had offered little cause to mark the holiday. One public mention of the Independence Day appeared in the *Richmond Daily Dispatch* on July 4, that forecast "a heavy attack upon our lines to-day. This is predicated upon the supposition that Grant will essay to celebrate the 4th of

Camp Chase Prison. Charles Wight was captured at the Battle of Rutherford's Farm on July 20, 1864, and taken to the prisoner of war camp in Ohio. At capacity, the prison should have accommodated 8,000 prisoners. By the end of the war, 26,000 were interned at the facility. According to camp records, 2,229 soldiers had died at Camp Chase by July 5, 1865, when it officially closed. Wight survived his imprisonment and was exchanged in early 1865. *National Archives*

July and the capitulation of Vicksburg by an attempt to capture Petersburg; but he will find the latter a somewhat harder road to travel than the one he walked over a year ago."

General Stephen Dodson Ramseur, now in command of Early's old division in the valley, learned that a small force of Union cavalry was advancing toward Martinsburg. Ramseur apparently had not given full credence to the report as his division was ambushed by General William Averell's division and was overrun.[159] On July 20, at Rutherford's Farm, Captain Wingfield made two notes in his diary: "my friend Adj. Wight missing, supposed killed." Four days later, on July 24, Wingfield made another note: "Heard from C.C. Wight; unhurt, is a prisoner."[160] Mrs. Wight had written in her diary earlier in the week that she was unusually anxious about her son. On the day he was captured, she was gathering baskets of blackberries that grew wild along the Virginia Central Railroad tracks in Hanover. She would not learn of her son's capture until July 29, when she received "the distressing intelligence that our dear Charles is a prisoner. It was a great shock but we had so much cause for gratitude that his life had been spared. We hear he has probably been sent off to Camp Chase in Ohio. We can form no idea when our poor child will be returned to us again but he will be spared the dangers of the battlefield for awhile."

The family began to take what little action they could to have Charles exchanged and to get money and clothing to him in Ohio. On August 3, John Wight put an ad in the *Daily Richmond Enquirer*. "I hope my poor boy may see it, and send us word where and how he is." They tried on several occasions to send clothing and money but were, according to Margaret, not entirely successful. From now until March of 1865, Charles Wight would remain at Camp Chase prison in Ohio. Despite newly constructed barracks in 1864, which raised the prison capacity to eight thousand men, by the end of the war, Camp Chase held twenty-six thousand of all thirty-six thousand Confederate POWs retained in Ohio military prisons.[161] According to his mother, Charles Wight suffered from want of food during his capture but was otherwise warm and comfortable enough though the time went by slowly.

On the same day Charles was captured, Mrs. Wight read news of the first battle of the Atlanta Campaign. Sherman's March to the Sea had begun. On August 1, she became aware of the explosion of an enormous mine under Petersburg. For weeks, news stories had begun to build a sense of terror in Petersburg as details of the construction of the mine underneath the city came to light. Wild reports had instilled the belief that the whole city was to be fired in one huge conflagration. In fact, the mine was exploded under a Confederate fort, but the infantry onslaught that followed was poorly executed, and in the end Confederates drove out the Union forces, leaving the siege line intact. Thus began the Battle of the Crater.[162]

On July 21, Mrs. Wight paid a visit to Mrs. Chisholm at Hanover Tavern. She said that all the boarders had left and described the place as "sad and lonely." To add to the melancholy aspect, it is likely that her visit was a sympathy call. The Chisholms' daughter, Sally Chisholm Cralle, died in July of 1864 (according to a postwar deposition given by Amizela Chisholm).[163] Sally Cralle left behind two children, Bessie S. and Conway J. Cralle.

By the middle of September, there was indeed little good news from any front. Mrs. Wight said, "There seems to be a gloom cast over everyone just now, even the most hopeful. It certainly seems to be the darkest period of the War. Altho' a perfect calm it certainly precedes a dreadful storm. Nothing but the mercy of GOD can save us. Grant is collecting an overwhelming force for the last grand onslaught." To add to the despondency, on November 10, in Charles City County, Edmund Waddill, along with his brother Samuel and several others, was captured and taken behind Union lines, leaving Annie and the children to fend for themselves. Mrs. Wight had reported that several raids had left the farm bereft of foodstuffs and livestock. On November 18, James H. Christian, the Waddill's brother-in-law, wrote to General Benjamin F. Butler requesting the release of the two Waddill brothers. The letter read in part: "Mr. Edmund Waddill has been opposed to this war from the beginning. Both are brothers of my wife. Mr. Waddill has a wife and 7 small children, the oldest only 14 years; he has been deprived of most of his personal property 3 times…all his cows and horses were [taken] off and some of his household goods."[164] The diary shows that Edmund Waddill would not be released until January of the following year.

On November 15, John and Margaret Wight returned to Hanover Junction and Mrs. DeJarnette's. Worry for her children remained high. "Can't hear from Annie except that she has made two attempts to get into the enemies lines to see about her husband and without success. My poor child I think of her night and day and I can't help her." Based on diary entries, Charles remained a prisoner in Ohio. John Henry Wight was called out from time to time with the defense troops to ward off attack and reinforce defenses around Richmond. Emily was in the office of General Kemper where she had secured a job. For the remainder of the year, no major operations in any theater of war resulted in a significant Confederate victory. Throughout the remainder of the year in Richmond, siege warfare whittled away at men, material and morale.

On Christmas Day of 1864, Margaret Wight described her state of mind: "It is the first time since we were blessed with children that all, or some of them were not with us, but not one now…All I can do is to leave them in the hands of the One who knows what is best for me and them." On New Year's Day, she expressed the likely thoughts of many in the South: "What sad reminiscences it brings up. Who would tear aside the veil to look into the future? I would not if I could. GOD is merciful in hiding from us the sorrows that may be in store for us."

Chapter Eight

1865

The end was near. In her first diary entry of 1865, Mrs. Wight prayed: "May our Heavenly Father in his infinite mercy bring peace once more to our troubled country and bring us all to look to Him for of ourselves alone we can do nothing." Worry over her children occupied her mind. The first bright spot for Margaret Wight came at the end of January when she reported that her son-in-law, Edmund Waddill, was released by the Union army and was able to return home to Annie and the children. The second came in February when the family learned that Charles would be released. For the remainder of the war, these two events would be the only glad tidings for Margaret Wight and her family. Mrs. Wight reported that in January of 1865, Emily was with Annie in Charles City County. John Henry had been detached with an ammunition wagon to go to the Northern Neck.

In the North, Lincoln's reelection had spawned renewed calls for an end to the war. After months of political wrangling over a meeting to discuss peace, representatives of both governments finally met to discuss terms on February 3 aboard the Union steamer *River Queen* at Hampton Roads. The talks were doomed from the start. The South wanted an armistice; the North demanded surrender. Mrs. Wight's comprehension of the work of the "Peace Commissioners" was this: "All we can do now is for every man to shoulder his Musket, look to GOD for help and fight for his liberty or be a slave. We must be a unit now there is hope of nothing but a conquered truce."

On the battlefront, there was almost no good news to report for the Confederacy. The last open Southern port at Wilmington was finally closed. Sherman's army had reached Savannah and began its northward march through the Carolinas in the opening days of February. By mid-month Columbia, South Carolina was in Union hands. After years of bombardment and valiant defense, Charleston was finally evacuated on February 18. To the south and west, nothing but blue uniforms and captured territory as Southern cities began to fall to the Union. In the Shenandoah Valley, General Sheridan controlled the territory where he continued to spend considerable effort destroying as much of value as possible. And now, he was moving his forces closer to Richmond, leaving an even wider trail of destruction behind from Staunton through Charlottesville to Gordonsville. By March, he was in the counties around Richmond. Truly, there was little left that Confederate forces could do to defend against the overwhelming force mounted against them. Yet, people like Margaret Wight clung to every whisper of Southern victory and brushed aside defeats as temporary. When she heard of Sherman's movements through South Carolina, Mrs. Wight said, "I feel confident he will be whipped before he gets much further, although at this time a gloom has spread over us all." Slowly, however, the truth was beginning to dawn, as this entry in mid-February reveals: "All is gloom and sadness. Sherman has taken Charleston and Columbia and is marching steadily on cutting our Railroads as he advances. But scanty supplies for our army from any quarter, of course they are on very short rations and where are we to get any? Richmond may have to be evacuated unless we can whip them shortly." As she tried to sort out events in the last days of the Civil War, a marked weariness seems to have taken over. "I have gotten to that state now that nothing good or bad seems to move me." In the waning days of the war, Margaret Wight tried to sort fact from fiction. But if all the news she received came from the papers, she would find the task difficult. What follows are examples of news reporting as the war drew to a close.

March 2, *Richmond Daily Dispatch*: "We stated on yesterday that the enemy, in heavy force, believed to be mostly cavalry, were advancing up the valley towards Staunton. As yet we have received no official information on the subject of their advance." And in a later dispatch that same day, "We hear nothing from Sherman, Schofield or Schimmelfenning [moving through the Carolinas]. It is believed that bottomless and impassable mud surrounds them all."

The Northern newspapers were more forthcoming, at least in dire predictions. On March 4, the *New York Herald* reported:

The destruction of the armed force of the Confederacy being now the great specific object of the combinations of our generals, it necessarily involves the forcing of its main army into a central position, from which escape, in case of defeat, is impossible… This war has shown that armies of sixty thousand men, though frequently defeated, cannot be destroyed in a single battle. Antietam, Chancellorsville, Chickamauga, Gettysburg, all illustrate this fact. The material of which our armies on both sides is composed, their long experience of war, the great advantages which the defensive always possesses, render a decisive victory over either Grant or Sherman, under any circumstances whatever, impossible for Lee…How can he replace troops lost in battle? He has no territory from which to draw troops or arms, except that which has already been exhausted by the most violent combats of this war.

If Margaret were to write a comment on this article, it may have been her diary entry on March 10: "Never did a people need more the help of an Almighty hand altho' [although] we deserve not the least of all his mercies. We can only pray for pardon and deliverance from our oppression and that he make us his own people."

By March 13, John and Margaret Wight decided to leave Hanover Junction for the last time. She expressed her fear in her diary. "Still they come on and we don't know what to do. The Bridges will be destroyed and we shall be cut off from Richmond if we remain here." She said they got as far as the old Hanover Tavern. Almost no place seemed to offer safety now. Some of General Sheridan's forces came to the Tavern two days later and began searching all the rooms inside. Mrs. Wight said she called for a guard and the soldiers in blue were soon evicted from the hotel. Mrs. Wight reported that Sheridan's men were headed back to Hanover Junction to burn the depot there and destroy the tracks. In the middle of the confusion, on March 18 Charles arrived at the Tavern from Camp Chase. His mother reported he was a bit thin and worn but otherwise fit. The family came from Richmond to reunite with Charles. Within the space of just over two weeks, the war would end.

The *Richmond Daily Dispatch* continued to report. March 20: "Further intelligence from General Sheridan reports that, on last Monday, a portion of his cavalry was engaged in tearing up the railroad between Richmond and Hanover Junction, while the main body was pushing on towards the

White House, on the Pamunkey River, where it was expected that supplies would reach him, to enable him to continue his work."

On Tuesday morning, March 21, the *Richmond Daily Dispatch* captured the mood of the populations both North and South, as they waited for the next shoe to drop.

> Every moment is protracted into an hour—every hour apparently grows into a week—weeks become years, and years seem expanded to ages.

Also on March 21, the *Dispatch* reported:

> Sheridan has made his hasty raid from Staunton to the White House, passing through the counties of Augusta, Albemarle, Nelson, Fluvanna, Goochland, Louisa, Hanover and New Kent, and leaving some desolation in his track. It is reported that he destroyed a large quantity of subsistence in his route...on the Petersburg lines, about daylight on Saturday morning. The firing was begun by our troops. The results, if any, are unknown.

The *Richmond Daily Dispatch* published this news on March 22, "On Monday night, the enemy...drove in our pickets posted near Old Church, in the lower end of Hanover County...We had apprehended that Sheridan would soon be at work on our lines of communication south of Richmond but from what we learn of the condition of his command, men and beasts, some considerable time must elapse before it will again be fit for field operations."

March 24, the *Dispatch* printed a "Letter from the North." The *New York Times* wrote of Sheridan's raid and the damage done to the farmers along the route, railroads and canals: "...every bridge, nearly every culvert, and scores of miles of the rail itself have been completely destroyed. On Thursday last, General Sheridan moved eastward, crossing the Fredericksburg railroad at Chesterfield Station, and at Mangohick Church. Longstreet, on the same night, encamped at Hanovertown, both armies picketing the Pamunkey." Mrs. Wight said she could see the campfires of the pickets of both armies at night.

When Richmond fell on April 2, Mrs. Wight said that it had been "so unexpected." The news organizations certainly had not prepared her for the evacuation of the city. In its last edition during the Civil War, on April 1,

1865, the *Richmond Daily Dispatch* reported this: "The enemy have pushed a heavy column beyond our right, southwest of Petersburg, but we have heard nothing from that quarter that we can rely upon as authentic since General Lee's report of Thursday [published yesterday], in which he says 'there was skirmishing near Dinwiddie Courthouse yesterday [Wednesday], without decisive result.'"

In reality, on April 1, after a defeat at the Battle of Five Forks, General Lee realized that the city of Richmond would have to be abandoned. It would be the *Richmond Daily Whig* that on April 4, 1865, reprinted a dispatch from the *New York Herald* reporting the fall of Richmond:

> The New York Herald April 4 1865
> CITY POINT, April 3 - 11 A.M.
> Hon. EDWIN M. STANTON, Secretary of War:-
> General Weitzel telegraphs as follows: -
> We took Richmond at a quarter past eight this morning. I captured many guns. The enemy left in great haste. The city is on fire in one place. Am making every effort to put it out. The people received us with enthusiastic expressions of joy. General Grant started early this morning with the army towards the Danville road, to cut off Lee's retreating army if possible.
> President Lincoln has gone to the front.

The diary entry made by Mrs. Wight when she learned that Grant had been placed in charge of all Union forces in early 1864 is recalled now. "Grant has been put in command of the Army of the Potomac but they do not fear him. From the Northern papers an immense army is to be concentrated for this next grand effort to take Richmond. But I hear no one express any fear as to the result." The comment by Mrs. Wight in early 1864 seems now a distant echo of the confidence that buoyed a nation just a year before. It is made all the more apparent by this sentence printed in the *Richmond Daily Whig* on April 4, 1865, just as the Evacuation Fires were consuming the commercial district of Richmond. "It does not seem to have been generally remembered that today is the anniversary of Lieutenant General Grant's taking command of the army in person, at Culpepper [*sic*] Court House, Va."

Pandemonium is the best word to describe Richmond over the next few days, and Mrs. Wight's diary takes on a sort of general panic as she struggled to learn the whereabouts of her children and to calculate her next move.

If she had to rely solely on the newspapers to help her uncover options, she would probably have been perplexed. The *Richmond Daily Dispatch* had ceased printing its newspaper when Richmond fell. On April 4, 1865, the *Richmond Daily Whig* continued to offer graphic detail of the Evacuation Fires that raged in Richmond:

> The evacuation of Richmond commenced in earnest Sunday night, closed at daylight on Monday morning with a terrific conflagration, which was kindled by the Confederate authorities, wantonly and recklessly applying the torch to Shockoe warehouse and other buildings in which was stored a large quantity of tobacco. The fire spread rapidly, and it was some time before the Fire Brigade could be gotten to work. A fresh breeze was blowing from the South, and the fire swept over great space in an incredible short space of time. By noon the flames had transformed into a desert waste that portion of the city bounded between 7th and 15th streets, from Main street to the river, comprising the main business portion. We can form no estimate at this moment of the number of houses destroyed, but public and private they will certainly number 600 to 800.

The paper gave a detailed account of the actual buildings and blocks destroyed by the fire. By its account, the property owned by Ann Eliza Wight, valued at $12,500, was destroyed.

Though Union troops had taken Richmond on April 3, Mrs. Wight seemed unable to accept that the end had come. On April 5, 1865, she said: "Kept in a constant state of anxiety by not being able to hear any thing reliable. Some tell us that Gen Lee is whipped which we won't believe." In the same entry she talked about a recent offer the family received to come to live with Sarah Winston, widow of William O. Winston at Courtland farm. Also at Courtland would be Bettie Winston Rosser, wife of General Thomas Lafayette Rosser, lately of Richmond defense lines. "We have no reason for declining and shall accept. As our Confederate money is utterly worthless now and we have nothing else, our situation is very unpleasant. Nor can we get either to Richmond or to Annie's. Mrs Chisholm was very kind and altho' she knew we had nothing to pay board said as long as she had any thing she would share it with us. My husband is so unwell I constantly fear he will be laid up. How blest those are who have a home." They moved to Mrs. Winston's

Charred Remains of Richmond. Panoramic view of ruins of Richmond after the Evacuation Fire in 1865. *Library of Congress*

Courtland where the respite was welcome. Courtland was a Hanover estate of nearly nine hundred acres that Mrs. Wight said "has less the appearance of <u>war</u> times than any place I have been."

While passing the time with the Winstons, Mrs. Wight yet waited for news of the war. When the city fell on April 3, General Lee had moved quickly west to salvage what he could of his army. Grant pursued. The two armies tangled with each other heading toward the area around Appomattox Courthouse. Beginning on April 7, Lee and Grant began a series of communications to each other through the lines discussing the idea of surrender. Finally, on April 9, Lee penned this note to General Grant: "I received your note of this

morning on the picket-line, whither I had come to meet you and ascertain definitely what terms were embraced in your proposal of yesterday with reference to the surrender of this army. I now ask an interview, in accordance with the offer contained in your letter of yesterday, for that purpose. R.E. Lee, General."[165]

"On April 9, 1865 after four years of Civil War and approximately 630,000 deaths and over 1 million casualties, General Robert E. Lee surrendered the Confederate Army of Northern Virginia to Lieutenant General Ulysses S. Grant, at the home of Wilmer and Virginia McLean in the rural town of Appomattox Court House, Virginia. General Lee arrived at the McLean home shortly after 1:00 p.m. followed a half hour later by General Grant. The meeting lasted approximately an hour and a half."[166]

Three days later, Mrs. Wight reported the "rumor" that General Lee had surrendered. She was incredulous, angry and fearful when she wrote:

> After four years of bloodshed, horror and misery we are compelled…to succumb to our bitter enemies. Whether this war aught [sic] not to have been commenced by the South or whether for the sins of our people (which are grievous) we have suffered these great afflictions we cannot tell perhaps both We have certainly been thro' [through] a furnace of fire. I shall ever think we had not sufficient provocation for breaking up our once glorious Union. What is our condition now? Virginia particularly. Lands laid waste and desolate. Mills, barns burnt and dwelling homes. Servants gone nearly all the horses taken. Confederate money nothing but waste paper and but one in a hundred with specie. No prospect of making any thing or going any where and all this for nothing, nothing.

Her lament continued on the following day: "If we had only remained as we once were, we should have been saved all this humiliation and distress."

Her children, as ever, occupied most of Margaret Wight's thoughts now along with worries about what was to become of them in what she called a "conquered truce." Her diary says that Emily remained in Richmond until April 16 when she asked for and received a parole from General Godfrey Weitzel, military commander in charge of occupied Richmond, to go the Charles City. It seems now that Annie's home would be the rally point for the soon to be reunited family. On the day that Richmond fell, Mrs. Wight said, "Charles, poor fellow got his horse and went off he knew not where for he is on parole still of course could not join his regiment. We had no spare to give him and he went without overcoat or any thing to protect him from the weather. His sad face at parting haunts me still." By April 15, Mrs. Wight reported that he had returned, "mortified and depressed…he had reached Campbell Co with the train when he heard of the surrender. He is unwilling to take the Oath [swear allegiance to the United States] if he can possibly avoid it. He has his parole as a prisoner and on that has gone to Charles City to see his sister." During early 1865, Mrs. Wight made no mention of John Henry Wight apart from his taking charge of a wagon train in January.

On April 18, Mrs. Wight chronicled the assassination of Abraham Lincoln and the attempted assassination of Secretary of State William H. Seward and his son. She feared the South would be blamed for it although, according to Mrs. Wight, "it was no doubt the work of a few desperate characters."

On April 27, after weeks of deliberations about their next move, John Wight bought a train ticket for $125. Mrs. Wight said it was the last money, the Wights had in their possession. He ventured to Charles City Courthouse leaving his wife at Courtland. Although he had feared having to take the Oath, he was not compelled to do so and managed to reunite with the family in Charles City County. Mrs. Wight followed him on April 28. She arrived in Richmond to prepare for the trip that would take her to Charles City County. On April 29, at daybreak, she walked down to Rockett's Landing on the James River.

> To walk through those once familiar streets and see nothing but charred and blackened ruins was indeed a sad sight. I could not tell where I was...When we reached the Steamboat we found crowds of other "rebel" passengers but all subjected to a rigid examination of papers before we were allowed to go on board. It is very hard to keep quiet under such rule but we must bear it as best we can. The river is filled with vessels of every size and description. We were detained hours at Bermuda Hundred and City Point and then again at Fort Powhatan from which place we crossed over in a row boat manned by Yankees to Weyanoke.

A friend of the family, Major Robert Douthat, provided lodging for the night at his Weyanoke Plantation. On the following morning, Mrs. Wight was provided transportation to Annie's home. She saw Annie standing in the yard to greet her. For the Wight family, the war had finally ended.

Chapter Nine

THE WIGHTS AFTER THE WAR

CHARLES CITY COMMUNITY

The collapse of the Southern Confederacy in April of 1865 seemed at first to signal the end of a way of life not only in Charles City County, but everywhere in the South, and indeed the Civil War produced profound change. From 1865 until 1870, Virginia endured a period of "Reconstruction" at the hands of the federal government. The Civil War exacted a terrible economic toll in Charles City County. The passing armies had left the county with miles of mangled roads, torn fences, ravaged fields, and virtually no livestock. Severe debt burdened even the richest of pre-war farms. For most large planters, the shortage of labor in the first years after the war made it impossible to plant large crops and thereby escape the debt cycle. Cash was short, and only a few had the capital to operate profitably.[167]

Along with so many others, the Wights must have struggled to resume their lives after the war as rural residents. As previously stated, Mrs. Wight again gives no clues as to where she and her family are living in Charles City County after the war. The 1870 Census shows John, age sixty-six, as a farmer with real estate valued at $5,000 and personal property of $3,000. Only wife Margaret, age sixty, and daughter Emily, age twenty-five, were shown living in the Wight household. Court records also reveal that Bullfield was sold at public auction in January of 1870, and John Wight purchased the farm for $4,000. It is not known if the family actually resided at Bullfield considering the description of the property as advertised December 28, 1869 in the *Richmond Daily Whig*:

> Valuable Real Estate in Charles City County, Va., For Sale—By virtue of a decree rendered in the circuit court of Charles City County...we will...offer for sale to the highest bidder...a valuable TRACT OF LAND...called Bullfield...containing about seven hundred and ten acres; three hundred and thirty are cleared, and the balance in woods...The buildings consist of a dwelling with four rooms, which, with the barn and other buildings, needs some repairs. The farm will be sold as a whole or divided to suit purchasers.

RICHMOND RESIDENTS

It is unknown how Margaret's sister-in-law Ann Eliza Wight reacted to postwar Richmond. But Margaret clearly establishes Ann Eliza's presence in the worn-torn city during the war. Her diary entries reveal Ann Eliza traveling from Richmond to Hanover Tavern during Christmas in 1863. Margaret describes her sister-in-law's residence in Richmond as being "a little attic room" where she and Emily visited during 1864. One diary entry in June of 1864 states that John and Margaret Wight rented a basement room in the same house where Ann Eliza was living and mentions that she had to work for her living. Evidence suggests property Ann Eliza had inherited from her father was among those of the city's 1865 Burnt District. And Margaret notes in her diary that the fire that destroyed businesses on Main and Cary Streets included Ann's, who had used their rent for her support. An article in the *Richmond Daily Whig* on April 4, 1865, corroborates Margaret's entry; it showed that Ann Eliza Wight's burned property was worth $12,500. It is not known if John's sister remained in Richmond after the war, but records do show that she died at the residence of her nephew William Washington Wight in Goochland County on June 17, 1869.[168]

The Wights' oldest son, John Henry, remained in Richmond with his wife and children after the war. In May of 1865, Margaret Wight wrote in her diary that John Henry was offered a job as a clerk "by a Yankee" if he would take the Oath. He told his mother he had not made up his mind, and her June 1865 entry stated that John Henry was unemployed. A Richmond City Directory does show John Henry as having a job in 1866 at 6 West Grace Street, where he would have witnessed the rebuilding of the city. However, he and his family did not remain in Virginia. By 1867, John Henry Wight is listed in the City Directory of Baltimore, Maryland, indicating his relocation. Apparently since the 1860 Census, John and Agnes had three additional children: Charles Selden, William Lee and Margaret. John Henry died in 1869, the year after the birth of his only daughter. It appears his widow remained in Baltimore as she is listed in the *1871 Baltimore City Directory*, along with several other Wight families.

Bounty in Baltimore

At war's end, Margaret said that Charles "thinks he must teach for a living" and events of his life seem unsettled for a while. John and Margaret's youngest living son, Charles Copland Wight, went to Rappahannock County, Virginia, "where he conducted a school one year and then taught two years in Orange County, Virginia."[169] Letters in the VMI Archives show that Wight petitioned Colonel William Smith and family friend R.H. Catlett to help him find a position at his former school, VMI. Although tentative offers were made, Charles did not accept the post. He did accept a position as principal of a grammar school in Baltimore, Maryland. Charles returned to Virginia to marry Juliet Fauntleroy in Middlesex County on April 16, 1875. In the same year, he was elected professor of history and English literature at Baltimore City College, a chair he held until his death in June of 1897. His obituary was printed in the *New York Times*:

> Charles Copeland [*sic*] Wight, a well-known educator of Baltimore, died suddenly of heart disease at his home in that city yesterday. He was born in Richmond, Va., in September, 1841. His parents were Mr. and Mrs. John Wight, who belonged to one of the best-known families in Virginia. He was educated at private schools in Richmond and at the Virginia Military Institute, where he was graduated with high honors just as the war broke out. He enlisted in Jackson's brigade and served on the staff of that

General during the valley campaign. Immediately after the close of the war, he went to Baltimore, teaching in a private school. Shortly after he became connected with the public schools, and at the time of his death was at the head of the department of English literature in the Baltimore City College. A widow, the daughter of Col Fauntleroy of Middlesex County, Va., and two daughters survive Prof. Wight.

Letters in the VMI Archives corroborate the details of the obituary. Additional information from the City Directories list Charles Copland Wight as a Baltimore resident from 1870 through 1896. The 1880 Census shows Margaret C. Wight, age seventy-three, as a boarder in his household, along with his sister-in-law Isabell [*sic*] Fauntleroy. It appears that Juliet F. Wight, his widow remained at the Baltimore residence after his death in 1897.

John and Margaret's youngest daughter, Emily Cornelia would leave her parents' Charles City household when she married William Baker Graves in October of 1874. How Emily and William became acquainted is not known. There were many residents of Charles City County with the Graves surname, but evidence of any relation to Emily's husband has not been found. In fact, not much is known about the personal life of Emily's husband except that he was a commission merchant and the son of John J. Graves.[170] Census records show that William and his mother were both born in Maryland. As early as 1867, William B. Graves is listed as employed in Baltimore. The Baltimore City Directories show him working in consecutive years through 1899. The 1880 Census indicates William was a grain merchant; in his household are his wife, Emily, and two daughters, as well as a nephew and niece. The 1900 Census reveals a possible change in lifestyle for William, as it states his occupation as farmer at age sixty-five, with Emily and three daughters: Anna Melissa, Emily E. and Margaret C. Graves. Emily's tombstone at St. Thomas Episcopal in Owings Mills, Maryland, reveals that she died in 1908, which explains the absence of her name from the 1910 Census.

Epilogue

The Wight's only child to remain in Virginia was Ann Louisa or "Annie," who, over the course of her life in Charles City, gave birth to six children: William Marshall, Charles Christian, Margaret Virginia, Emily Gertrude,

Wight Family Obelisk at Hollywood Cemetery. The focal point of Lot 22 in Section 5 of Richmond's Hollywood Cemetery. There is symmetry in the method used to inscribe the Wight family names on the obelisk that was raised on the plot of a hill overlooking the James River. On the southern façade of the base are the names of the four sisters who all died before they reached adulthood: Margaret C., Ellen A., Alice L. and Virginia C. Wight. On the northern side are the names of Mary E., William M. and John H., siblings whose lives were directly affected by the Civil War. *Shirley A. Haas*

Julia Leeds and Leonora Wight Waddill. The 1870 Census shows Edmund Waddill as head of household with Annie "keeping house," which included nine additional persons; six of those appear to be Edmund's children from his first marriage. Annie had given birth to the other three children enumerated: William, Margaret and Charles. When this census was taken, the Waddills had apparently relocated. Records show that Edmund purchased fifty acres in 1867 and at some time took up residence at Millford. The 1880 Census shows the Waddill household with ten family members and two servants. Three of Annie's step-daughters were shown as living at the house, and all of them were listed as school teachers. Neither Annie or Edmund would appear in the 1900 Census; Edmund died in 1890, and Annie followed two years later in 1892.

Two deaths in 1877 added to the sorrows of Margaret Wight. While living in New Jersey as a widow, her step-daughter Julia Gardner died in May of 1877. Less than four months later, John Wight took his last breath on September 1. In his will, dated August 24, 1877, John left his property in trust to his wife, during her lifetime. He appointed his son-in-law, Edmund Waddill, as trustee and executor of the will. John Wight stipulated that the estate was to pass to his daughter, Mrs. Annie L. Waddill, as a separate estate

John and Margaret Wight (Detail from Obelisk). According to cemetery records, on August 1, 1883, John Wight was disinterred from Charles City County to be reunited with his wife at Hollywood Cemetery. It is not known when the Wight obelisk was actually erected, but the lot on which Margaret and John Wight are buried was purchased by their son, Charles C. Wight on August 2, 1883 for $147. *Shirley A. Haas*

for Annie's use and that of her children, unencumbered by any debts or contracts of her husband.

The last volume of Margaret Wight's diary (1878–1879) was written during her waning years. It describes a variety of events, scattered among the shadows of her expressed sorrows. She still referred to Charles City as home, while she traveled to visit friends and relatives in Virginia as well as family in Baltimore, all of which provide some insight into Margaret's personal life several years prior to her death.

Even though Margaret Copland Brown Wight was living in Baltimore during the 1880 Census enumeration, she did return to Virginia. Records show she died on July 31, 1883, in Charles City County. According to Hollywood Cemetery records, arrangements were made by her son to procure an appropriate resting place in Richmond for both his parents, even though Margaret states in her diary in a January 1878 entry that John Wight "made all earthly arrangements even who was to officiate at his funeral & where he should be buried until I died and then both to be carried to the family burial ground in Richmond which my dear Annie can carry out or not as she chooses." Based on this comment by Margaret, it appears that John Wight had chosen a Richmond "burial ground" before he died in 1877. It is not known if Hollywood Cemetery was his choice, or that of other family members.

> By 1860, Richmond's white cemeteries had come to represent a complex social hierarchy that regulated a person's status even after death. Hollywood, which became both socially and symbolically the most important of Richmond's postwar cemeteries, was located in rolling country just west of the city, overlooking the James. It was established in the 1840s by a group of prominent Richmonders who desired a rural cemetery. Initially, there had been enormous opposition to Hollywood. It blocked the city's westward expansion and occupied desirable real estate on the river, and because of these and other objections, the General Assembly did not charter the cemetery company until 1856. Lots sold slowly, as Richmonders did not believe Hollywood would be permanent, and not until the Civil War did the grounds begin to fill. In 1858 the body of James Monroe was reinterred in Hollywood, and John Tyler was buried there four years later. Their graves and Hollywood's beautiful landscaped grounds assured the future success and

social prominence of the cemetery, which became one of the most exclusive spots in postwar Richmond, the resting place for the city's heroes and heroines.[171]

Cemetery records confirm that Charles Copland Wight arranged for his father to be disinterred from Charles City County and was reunited with his wife at Hollywood. They were both buried on a hill overlooking the James River on August 1, 1883.

An obelisk, commemorating members of the Wight family, remains as the focal point of Lot 22 in Section 5 of Hollywood Cemetery. Margaret Wight's grave rests among thousands of people from all walks of life who have been buried in Hollywood, now on the National Register of Historic Places. President Jefferson Davis, leader of the Confederacy, and more than twenty Confederate generals are among approximately eighty thousand people buried in the famous Richmond cemetery. Fittingly, there is a ninety-foot tall pyramid, assembled from stone quarried at the James, honoring eighteen thousand Confederate soldiers buried nearby.[172]

As the chapter closes on the life of Margaret Copland Brown Wight and her family, it seems fitting to recognize the significance of their heritage to Virginia history and to applaud the insightfulness of her family members who ensured preservation of her diaries, as well as the daybooks of her grandfather, Charles Copland, and diary of her son Charles Copland Wight. Production of this book was made possible thanks to the efforts of Margaret Wight and family members who must have appreciated the significance of the written word.

Chapter Ten

MARGARET WIGHT DIARY IN THREE VOLUMES

NOTES REGARDING TRANSCRIPTION OF MANUSCRIPT

The text of Margaret Wight's memoirs is contained in three bound notebooks, which were donated to the Virginia Historical Society on June 14, 1957 by Mary Copland Wight of Baltimore, Maryland. The first volume is distinctive by its leather cover, which is embossed in gold with "DISTRICT NO. 4. SECOND FEMALE DEPARTMENT." This volume is 10.5 inches long and 7.5 inches wide with forty-six leaves (ninety-six pages). Several pages were cut out of the notebook before the text begins on January 1, 1863. The second volume measures the same as the first, but has a plain leather cover with only twenty-five leaves (fifty pages). The last notebook only has seventeen leaves (thirty-four pages) and ends in May 1878.

Transcription of Mrs. Wight's handwritten manuscript was undertaken to give a concise representation of what she actually wrote and make the

Opposite, left: **Cover of Margaret Wight Diary (First Volume).** The text of Margaret Wight's memoirs is contained in three bound notebooks, which were donated to the Virginia Historical Society on June 14, 1957, by Mary Wight of Baltimore, Maryland. The first volume is distinctive by its leather cover, which is embossed in gold with "DISTRICT NO. 4. SECOND FEMALE DEPARTMENT." The first page also has an embossed oval revealing the words "NORFOLK, VA." This volume is 10.5 inches long and 7.5 inches wide with 48 leaves (96 pages). *Virginia Historical Society*

Opposite, right: **Margaret Wight's Handwriting.** First page of Volume 1 of Margaret Copland Brown Wight's diary. *Virginia Historical Society*

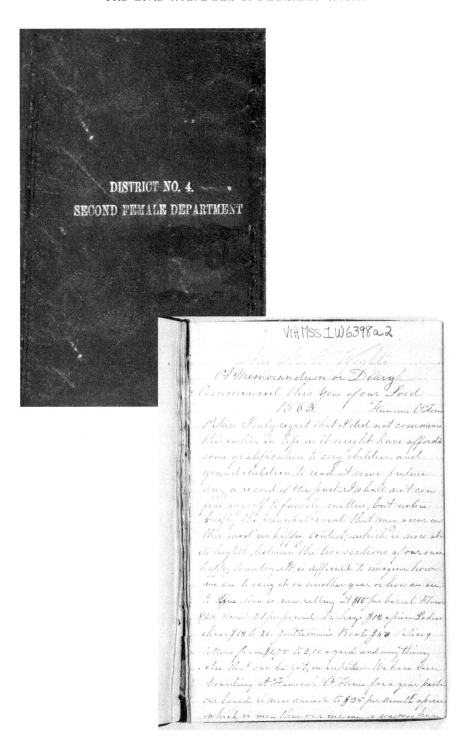

printed copy easy for the reader to comprehend. In an effort to maintain the integrity of the original document, transcription was done adhering as closely as possible to the diary's original format, spelling and overall presentation. Therefore, the text as published appears largely as it does in the manuscript except for spelling of proper names, which have been corrected. Other spelling errors were left without correction. Transcribing standards used for Mrs. Wight's memoirs were obtained from the Association for Documentary Editing, information available online at http://documentaryediting.org/resources/about/index.html and the Minnesota Historical Society's "Transcribing Manuscripts," also online at www.mnhs.org/about/departments/processing/transcribing_manuscripts.pdf.

Margaret Wight rarely used commas in her writing. Most often the dash was used for all types of punctuation, even at the end of a sentence. Therefore, her style of using dashes was continued, except at the end of a sentence (when clearly identified with a capital letter). In these cases, a dash has been replaced with a period. Punctuation has been altered only where it was thought necessary for clarity. Words omitted in the original document have been inserted in square brackets. Uncertain but probable guesses regarding words and phrases are followed by a question mark. Where the manuscript was unable to be interpreted, a notation in the text was made with [*MS. illegible*].

Notes Regarding Frequent, Recurring Abbreviations in the Diaries

In her writings, Margaret Wight usually referred to her husband as "Mr W." This abbreviated format was continued in the transcribed text.

The name of Margaret's daughter Emily is used somewhat inconsistently in the diary; sometimes her full name was noted, whereas other entries are *Em* and *E*. The format was continued in the text without explanation.

Charles Copland Wight is sometimes referred to as "Charlie."

A Memorandum or Diary
Commenced this year of our Lord
1863 Hanover Ct House

1ˢᵗ Jan I only regret that I did not commence this earlier in life as it might have afforded some gratification to my children and grandchildren to read at some future day a record of the past. I shall not confine myself to family matters, but notice briefly the principal events that may occur in this most unhappy contest, which is now at its highth, between the two sections of our once happy Country. It is difficult to imagine how we are to carry it on another year or how we are to live. Corn is now selling at $15 per barrel Flour $25. Hams $1 per pound Turkeys $12 a piece Ladies shoes $18 to 20. Gentleman's Boots $50. Calico & cottons from $1.75 to 2.50 a yard and anything else that can be got, in proportion. We have been boarding at Hanover Ct [*Court*] House for a year past our board is now raised to $35 per month apiece which is more than our income so we may have to look out for other quarters.

Jan 2 We were surprised & delighted to receive a visit from Charles who has been fighting in Gen Lee's Army. Gen Jackson's Corps now stationed at Port Royal. He has been in eleven pitched battles & slightly wounded twice. We have deep cause for gratitude that he has been spared and not sacrificed like our precious Willie, who fell (while bravely assisting[*?*] his Reg (the 1ˢᵗ Va) to take a battery. Offering up his life to his Country's cause.

5 John & his aunt came up this morning to see Charles.

9ᵗʰ A case of Varioloid broke out. One of the boarders–which accasion great alarm in the house & neighborhood.

14ᵗʰ News has reached us that we have gained a great victory at Vicksburg.

19ᵗʰ Charles leaves us to day for Camp. May the same kind providence who has hither to watched over him, continue to preserve him from all harm. It is believed that another battle is impending at Fredericksburg. O! when shall we again here the joyful sound of Peace? God alone can give us the victory from such over whelming numbers

27ᵗʰ Continued bad weather for seven or eight days which has prevented a second attack on our army at Fredericksburg which was contemplated by Gen Hooker

Feb 13 A negro girl twelve years of age was hung at this place to day for attempting to kill a little white boy. She showed perfect indifference, said she wanted to die and after the rope was put around her neck, she jumped from the cart, and broke her own neck. Truly a strange case

14th A letter came from John enclosing $15 which was handed him by a gentleman saying it was money put in his hands for me, that John must ask no questions about it, he could only tell him it was for me. I have not the least idea from quarter it comes. It is certainly acceptable for we have not enough to pay our board much less supply ourselves with necessary clothing.

23rd A heavy snow storm covering the ground for five or six inches.

27th   Continued bad weather although the winter has been generally mild we have had three opportunities for putting up ice, so our poor sick Soldiers will be well supplied this summer.

March 2nd Perfectly delightful spring weather. Now we may look out for stirring news from South & West.

8th Bad weather. Every thing at a stand

16th Nothing but rain. No advance by the enemy either at Fredericksburg– Vicksburg or Charleston

17th Emily left us to day to make John a visit in Richmond.

20th A violent snow storm lasting a day and night–snow a foot deep. Our soldiers have a hard time–on less than half rations–indeed starvation stares us all in the face. The flour in the country has been impressed by the Government as well as many other articles for the army. Bacon selling at $1.50 a pound. Butter $3.00 & c &c

24th Came from Hanover on my way to Charles City to be awhile with Annie, but from the freshet in the River and the state of the roads find I cannot get there for a week. It causes me great uneasiness. The gloomiest state of weather I ever saw.

26th Richmond to Hanover as I could not get down the country. I know that my poor child feels greatly troubled & disappointed.

27th This day has been appointed for Fasting & Prayer by the President & has been generally kept. I trust the admirable sermons on Exhortion may have the desired effect for as long as it prevails we can expect the blessing of the Almighty upon our unhappy country

30th Again in Richmond hoping to get to Annie but a night's hard rain has again stopped me. The earth is completely saturated. But few have been able to sow Oats or attend to their gardens. The Apricot trees are just blooming. The Spring is unusually backward. Felt depressed to leave my poor husband for so long a time but as he has employment he will not feel so lonely

1st April Cold enough for snow.

2nd This has been a memorable day for the Capital of our Southern Confederacy and one that will injure us more in the eyes of the Yankees than any thing that has occurred. A Mob of women assembled on the Square and from there march to the different stores on Main St on the pretense of [*MS. illegible strikethrough*] seizing the necessaries of life for which they were starving but it proved to be a wholesale robbery–taking every thing they could lay their hands on even from the Jeweller. They were accompanied by men of the worst character who no doubt were at the bottom of this infamous proceeding. The worthy women among our poorer class had no concern in it. This is but one of the disgraceful attendants upon this unholy & in my opinion unnecessary war.

6th Left Richmond to day for Charles City on the York River Railroad. The river at the 'Forge' was so high and dangerous, some pickets who were there carried us over in a boat and then drove the wagon through. We reached Mr Waddill's about nine o'clock at night. I was so thankful to find Annie pretty well and the mother of a little Boy born the night before (the 5th). As I have the privilege of naming him I have called him Willie Marshall after our poor lost Soldier boy.

15th Annie & the baby have both been very unwell.

17th Received five letters to day. One from John telling me of the arrival in town of my Uncle Robert Copland from New Orleans. Hope to see him before he returns.
John expects to be sent to the army among the other Government Clerks who have been conscriped. For the sake of his family I trust he will not be taken

30th Expected to have left for Hanover to day but a hard rain has stopped me. Such continued bad weather the farmers have not planted corn yet

May 2nd Arrived in Richmond to day in a Buggy. Mr Wight feeling uneasy about me came down in the Cars. We are staying at John's and as it is believe Gen Hooker has commenced his attack it is best we should be here until we know the result.

3rd The whole town in a state of the greatest excitement–a large number of Yankee Cavalry have gotten in the rear–of our army have cut our Telegraph wires and torn up portions of our Railroads so as to cut off all communication with our army. So many flying rumours we don't know what to believe.

4th Couriers have arrived saying the Yankees are within four miles of the place. Bells now tolling to call out our citizens as nearly all our soldiers have been sent off to reinforce Gen Lee. I can not and will not believe yet that our beautiful Capitol is to fall into the hands of those Vandals. If we could only be certain of the safety of our dear Charles, we could bear better a mortifying defeat dreadful as that would. O! may GOD in his infinite mercy spare him to us Afternoon–A Dispatch from Gen Lee says we have gained a great victory and driven Hooker & his army across the Rappahenah [*Rappahannock*]. That means were not taken to prevent this Cavalry raid is disgraceful affair on our part and we must give our enemies credit for carrying out a bold and well executed plan for they came this morning within four miles of Richmond without meeting any to oppose them. Gen Stoneman commanded. They have now gone back and the panic is somewhat over. We cannot get home as portions of the Railroad have been destroyed.

6th Road easily repaired over [*MS. illegible*] Meadow Bridges so we returned in the Cars to day to Hanover Ct House–found the Depot entirely destroyed–no injury done to private property, except to take away all the horses and many of the servants. The raiders still going through this part of the country at their pleasure. It is too bad.

9th Great anxiety to hear from Charl[*es*]

10th News of his safety through a letter from a friend. How much cause we have for gratitude.

12th A letter from Charles telling us about the battle–out of one hundred & sixty the number in his Regiments they lost sixty–in killed [,] wounded & missing but every thing is now swallowed in grief at the loss of the Greatest as best General the world has ever seen. Gen Thomas J Jackson–the idol of the army the nation. But GOD permits no people to look to any man as the giver of Victory. He alone is the GOD of battle and he saw best to remove this Christian Warrior from the field of strife to a haven of rest. When told he must die his reply was "It is all right"   This is but the beginning of sorrow I fear to our Southern Confederacy who now as a nation worship <u>Money</u> and instead of aiding and supporting the Government as they did at the commencement of this war hold provisions and every article necessary for the comfort of the nation at the highest possible price. Patriotism laid aside for love of gain. We are to be punished for it yet.

13th The Northern papers have to acknowledge that Hooker has been defeated. We wish it had been a rout but they got over the river again.

22nd Have just recovered from a sharp attack of sickness. For the first time all my children were away but my husband nursed me tenderly as well as my kind friends in the house. Have written for Emily to come up from Charles City for fear she may be caught in Yankee lines.

25th Great anxiety felt with regard to Vicksburg our stronghold on the Mississippi river. It is now surrounded by the Yankee fleet and Grant's army.

26th No news of importance. Cold enough for fires after ten days of hot, dry weather. Many farmers still planting Corn. John & Emily arrived unexpectedly this morning from Charles City.

28 Weather continues very dry. News from Vicksburg encouraging–enemy has been repulsed several times with great slaughter but the seize still continues. All quiet on the Potomac.

29th Made my first purchase at Confederate prices–Shoes at $15. I have never given more than 1.50. Stocking[s] sell now at $5 per pair–nine penny Handkerchiefs at, 2.50 & 3.00.

31st The hot & dry weather still continues–it has lasted more than three weeks with the exception of two light showers. Gardens burning up.

4th June Letter from Charles saying they were under marching orders since heard Gen Lee had gone with a portion of his army towards Culpeper.

6th Exciting news of the Yankees being in King William burning & destroying but I have no fear that they will be here as Gen Pickett & Gen Wise have been sent after them with their commands. No Mail or papers from Richmond to day as the Cars were filled with Soldiers going up towards Fredericksburg.

8th Vicksburg still holds out bravely. We have defeated the Yankees at Port Hudson and killed all but thirteen of a negro regiment. They were cruel enough to put in front. Dry weather continues.

10th John came up this morning and brought us a letter just received from Julia who is still in Connecticut the hot bed of Abolitionists–poor child! she says she longs to get home but I fear she will not be able. We are so concerned that she and her dear children should be shut up with them miserable Yankees.

11th News of a great Cavalry fight in in which we were surprised by the enemy but after six hours hard fighting we drove them over the Rappahanock [*Rappahannock*]. There must have been some negligence on the part of Gen Stuart or we should not have been taken unawares.

12 A few lines from Charles written with a pencil near Culpeper Ct. House. Then had marching orders for Tuesday morning but this Cavalry raid & fight perhaps interfered with Gen Lee's plans. We are very anxious to hear from him again Ann left us this evening.

13 News to day that the Yankees are advancing up the peninsula but can get no reliable information.

15th Emily left us to day on a visit to her uncles family in Goochland. I miss my dear child dreadfully.

16th Mr Wight and I commenced an experiment to make Envelopes for sale by quantity[*?*]. If successful we shall be enabled I trust to make a support, at best during the war. Give $35 for the Ream of paper.
Received news of the capture of Winchester by our forces under Gen Ewell.

18th Been a great deal with one of our neighbors Mr P Winston who is very ill.

22 Who should walk in this morning but Charlie. A most delightful surprise. He was sent down in charge of the Officers (~~prisoners~~) taken at Winchester but obtained leave to make us this little visit. He looks well & is very cheerful seems to have perfect confidence in the success of Gen Lee's army wherever he may go. Charles returns to his regiment to morrow. My sorrow at [*MS. Illegible*] is much mitigated[*?*] for I have reason to believe he has placed his truth in the Rock of Ages and what greater comfort can a mother have in parting with her soldier boy to encounter the horrors and dangers of the battle field.

26th We were all sitting quietly at our work when about two thousand Yankee Cavalry came upon us like a perfect hurricane. The whole household were in commotion hiding all the silver and valuables. They had orders not to disturb private property so we began to breathe rather more freely but they spread themselves all around us and in every direction taking all the Government Stores at the Depot & destroying them—every mule and horse they could find—tearing up a portion of the Railroad. They then went up to the Junction but were stopt at the Bridge by about eighty of our soldiers who defended it bravely and did not surrender until they lost eight or nine men. Hearing we had troops above they were afraid to proceed further. They soon returned bringing their prisoners, killed & wounded and some of ours, as well as Negroes Waggons & c in abundance. In addition to all this they went to Mr Wickham's and took Gen Fitzugh [*Fitzhugh*] Lee (who was badly wounded at the fight at Kelly's Ford) out of his bed and brought him by in a Carriage as prisoner and carried him on to the White House (his old home) where there camp now is. After remaining here four or five hours they retired with horses mules Negros and all their plunder.

27 A quiet day but I have felt quite sick for a week past.

28th My good friends the Nelsons left us to day for poor old Fredericksburg their former home. To see such utter ruin and desolation will be a sad sight for the refugees.

29th This is my darling Willie's Birthday, his 20th year. GOD grant I may not be called to mourn the loss of another son before this dreadful war ends

30th My fifty fourth Birthday. A long and useless life ashamed and self condemned am I when I reflect upon the past. May GOD in mercy forgive me and help me to act a better part the few remaining years of my life.

1st We hear that Gen Lee with our army has gone into Pensylvania [*Pennsylvania*]. ~~and~~

4th Another visit from the Yankees. They have come this time with Infantry as well as Cavalry–the road is blue with them. Two of the young men who belong to the Quarter Master's Department had not time to get off so they have hid themselves in a closet upstairs, but I see they have set a guard around the house to protect it so we are safe from a search. They are behaving very well for enemies–kept in bounds no doubt by some of the Staff Officers who are here. The Cavalry has gone to destroy the road at the Junction but I hope we have sufficient force there to prevent it

5th They have just returned–had a skirmish lost some eight or ten men and were [*MS. illegible*] to retreat without accomplishing their purpose except to cut across to Ashland and destroy a small amount of Government property there. After breakfast they recrossed the River burning the Bridge behind them–carrying off nearly all the servants from one of the neighbors (Mrs. Winston) besides destroying her wheat and taking her provender. They are persuing a fine course to bring about <u>reunion</u>. News has reached us the we have gained a victory at Gettysburg but not Official

7th Two Yankee deserters have come in to give themselves up to our pickets–they seem anxious to stop fighting
Report of an intended attack on Richmond from the peninsular but they will find us prepared for us there in addition to a large force under D H Hill all the militia in Richmond have responded to the call and now man the Batteries.

7th Bad news–that Vicksburg has surrendered & Lee been compelled to fall back. Can't believe either yet awhile

10th John came up unexpectedly to day bringing with him Johnny to stay with us awhile. He confirms the sad tidings about Vicksburg–they were literally starved out. We have not much to encourage us from the South West–for we rarely have good news from that quarter. As to Gen Lee's army, no one believes that they have been whipped but that he fell back to Maryland for some good reason which we shall see here after. Yet we are very anxious to receive a report from him.

*11th A rumour that he has gained a Victory but it needs confirmation.

12 No battle, but he has made a stand at Hagerstown and has not been followed by the enemy which proves the victory they claim was not a very glorious one.

13ᵗʰ News from Charleston. We have again whipped the Yankees there. * John came up and brought Johnny to stay with us awhile. he is a good child and much company for us. I only wish we could keep him altogether.

14ᵗʰ A long spell of cloudy, rainy weather

15 Another attack on Charleston but have been repulsed up to this time

16ᵗʰ A letter from Charlie written on the 3ʳᵈ at Winchester–expected to leave for our Army in Maryland the next day–a Victory at Gettysburg but it is not official. We are on the life too of anxiety & expectation

7ᵗʰ Two

18ᵗʰ Charles did not reach Winchester in time to go on and engage in the battle of Gettysburg which was the most terrific one of the War–and in which our loss in Officers & soldiers was appauling.

20ᵗʰ We have had no Cars since the Yankee raid–had to send to Ashland for our mail. Mr W and I have been hard at work upon our Envelopes hoping to have them ready for market by the time the railroad is completed

22 A letter from Charles dated at in the Valley of Va he only got as far as Hagerstown in Maryland

24ᵗʰ Emily returned to us from [Ingleside] . I am delighted to have her back again. It has made me feel better already. We finished 8,000 Envelopes to day. News reaches us that Gen Lee is falling back & Gen Meade in Culpeper. The future is dark to us now we know not what to anticipate

26ᵗʰ The cars have commenced running again & brought down a number of prisoners. The sound of the whistle is really cheering. I hope the Government will station[?] of sufficient military force here to save the road from a fifth attack.

28th A rumour has reached us that Gen Lee has resigned. Of all misfortunes that could have happened to us this is the greatest. We hope most sincerely it m[a]y not be true. The attack on Charleston continues.

29th Gen Lee has not resigned and as long as so good and great a Man has charge of our army in Virginia we will not despair. This is Court day quite a lively scene around us but no drunken riots

31st Heavy rain continue to fall every day. The roads are as bad as in Winter. Indeed there is a gloom over our country just all the news we receive is depressing except from Charleston and that still holds out against overpowering numbers. The love of gain which has gotten entire population[?] of our people has brought this dreadful punishment upon us.

1st News has just reached us that Morgan (our great guerrilla Chief of Cavalry) has been captured during an extensive and destructive raid he was making in Ohio & Indiana. Poor fellow! his will be a hard fate

2nd We cannot hear the exact position of either Army. It is said that the Yankees in Va are to be reinforced by a portion of Grants army from Vicksburg. We have just received the proceeds of our Envelope scheme, $57 Net at $10 a thousand. I am very willing to try it again even at this price as I consider it clear gain - having no other employment on which I could make one cent. Times are gloomy enough in every way. Articles of every kind continue to rise–a lady cannot get a calico or any kind of dress for less than thirty dollars–Shoes even for children twenty–Gents seventy five & more. Watermelons from $5 to 10 Pears $1 a dozen Peaches $2 Tomatoes eight cents a piece and so on. What are we coming to?
John has come up to spend the day hopes to be able to get a situation for his father in one of the Departments in Richmond. He leaves Johnny with us awhile longer.

4th The hottest weather of the season for several days. Thermometer in the shade 96 degrees and upwards hard upon those poor soldiers who have any marching to do. We are exceedingly anxious to hear again from Charles - Who up to this time has preferred walking to giving the enormous price that has now asked for horses six[,] seven & nine to fifteen hundred dollars–and very scarce. The weather has been fine for the crops they are spoken of as being remarkably good. A great mercy when so much depend upon it.

7th No news of interest–every thing seems to be at a stand. The enemys gun Boats have been up the James River within sixteen miles of Richmond but were driven back by our Cannon (planted on the shore to receive them) in a disabled condition–One [*MS. illegible*] Lincoln has issued a most infamous proclamation–That for every negro taken in battle by us and executed he will kill two of our Southern soldiers so that will compel us to shoot them all instead of taking them prisoners. That is Northern humanity!! We have not seen the worst of this unnatural war yet.

8th I have received a letter from my Uncle William C[*opland*] telling me of the death of his niece and my cousin–Mrs Margaret Munford, of Consumption. Her first husband was my brother-in-law–Edwin Wight. In consequence of a difficulty in the family which occurred after his marriage, he left his property (having no children) after the death of his wife, to the family of Barton Haxall of Richmond.

9th Attended service at the Episcopal Church this morning–the first time for six weeks–kept at home by indisposition

11th A long and gratifying letter from our dear Charles written from Orange County. Notwithstanding the reverses we have met with in the last few months, he and the most of the army are still hopeful. The weather for the last ten or twelve days have been so excessively hot (the Thermometer varying from 92 to 98 in the shade) that both armies seem to rest in quiet for the present–neither having energy enough. I suppose for the grand & decisive battle.

12th The oppressive weather still continues.

13 We had a fine rain to day which refreshed every thing in the way of gardens & crops, but has not cooled the air.

14th Letters from John[,] Annie & Charles. The president has appointed the 21st of Aug as a day of fasting and prayer. Surely we are now being punished for our great wickedness. O may the cries that spread that day from those who put their trust in GOD alone be answered in mercy and deliverance given us from our enemies

15th A case of Diptheria has occured in the home. A little child was taken with it yesterday and died last night. It is truly an awful disease.

19th A delightful change has taken place it is almost as cool as October. Johnny has left us for his home after being with us six weeks. He is a smart boy has warm affectionate feelings and if properly managed will make a fine boy.

21st Another case of Diptheria–A young lady (Ms Campbell) who has been staying with us sometime was taken yesterday and is now very ill.

23rd Been engaged in nursing most of the time. I do not fear this dreadful disease myself but am very uneasy about Emily altho' she has no symptoms of it now.

24th Bad news from Charleston. Fort Sumpter [*Sumter*] has about fallen into the enemies hands. The south and east side are a map of ruins. The city is now being shelled

26th Miss Campbell continues very ill. Three more new cases. The neighbors are afraid to come near us. Much of my time is spent in nursing.

27th Some of our Infantry have taken several Gun Boats in the Rappahanock [*Rappahannock*] which I hope will enable us to take some of these Blockade runners who are coining money and keeping up every article we need to these fabulous prices–Gloves $10 Stockings $5 Calico dress $40 Shoes & Garter $35 & c & c
28th Charleston not taken yet. The bombardment progressing slowly.

29th Poor Susan died last night after great suffering - her last words were "I am choking to death" Yet she had expressed no fear and seemed unconscious of her danger. She had been a professor of Religion some years. We have had eight cases altogether the neighbors are afraid to come near the house. I don't wonder at it for it is truly alarming. The physicians say they consider it worse than small pox.

31st It continues as cool as October–fires are comfortable. A long gratifying letter from Charlie. he writes me that they have preaching every day in Camp. Surely the Almighty will not permit an army of Christian soldiers (as a large proportion of our are) to be subjugated by a parcel of hirelings and negroes. I have strong faith yet - we may have to pass through a fiery ordeal but I pray we may come out refined & purified. My husband returns from Richmond to day and tells me, our poor little Johnny is very sick. I feel so concerned with it–be strong enough to go and nurse him but I trust it is nothing serious.

Sept 1ˢᵗ Delightful weather. No news from any quarter. All our armies seem to be resting, or gathering new strength for another great onset.

2ⁿᵈ Two new cases of Diptheria but my dear Emily still escapes

3ʳᵈ Greatly relieved to hear Johnny is better. The papers contain no news. Charleston holds out yet.
   We can't obtain paper to make Envelopes–it is taken to make Cartridges for the army.

4ᵗʰ My husband last year bought a farm in this neighborhood. The purchase money was to be paid down by the aid of a friend. After the contract was duly signed & acknowledged the owner thought he had sold too low. after trying in various ways to get off he said he would take nothing but gold & silver!! which the law gave him a right to demand as cash in as the (customary) term used in the contract but which various things proved he had no expectation of receiving when he sold it. Mr W has been advised by many to sue and has determined to do it since selling one half the Contract to for $2500 to a young man Capt Smith they will bring suit next month.

5 Am very anxious to find a school for Emily. Have written to day to my old friend Mr Frank Watkins of Farmville to look out for one for us.

7ᵗʰ We hear that two Divisions of Gen Lee's army are to go either to Charleston or to the help of Bragg in Tennessee but we feel confident he will not leave Richmond unprotected or leave Virginia to be overrun by the enemy. We shall see

9ᵗʰ Fort Wagner & Morris's Island have been evacuated by our men but our Flag still waves over the ruins of Sumpter [*Sumter*]–and Charleston has not been reached.

11ᵗʰ The Cars are passing[,] every few loaded with our Troops going South (we suppose). Our papers keep silent on the subject that the Yankees may remain ignorant of our movements as long as possible. Charles writes to know whether he shall try to get a furlough now or wait until the winter. His Pa then wrote him to wait until October and then come & go down to Charles City with us. I trust the Yankees will not cut us off from poor Annie before that time.

12th We have been trying in vain up to this time to find a school for Emily within our means. The charges are from $600 to $1000 the full term. I don't know what we are coming to–Calico dress fifty to sixty dollars and a worsted one cannot be obtained under one hundred and every thing is rising. This Confederacy must go to ruin if this extortion is not stopped.

13th The Division of our army which passed have not gone to Tennessee but are stationed not far from Richmond. The news this morning is depressing. The enemy have gotten possession of Knoxville eastern Tennessee and in a heavy skirmish with our Cavalry in Culpepper [*Culpeper*] they have whipped us and taken possession of the Ct House. It is hard to think that the wickedness of our people will cause us to be subjugated. The South is divided into two classes. The patriots & Extortioners and I begin to fear the last are greatly in the majority.

17th The long desired rain has at last come–every sign of an Equinoxtial storm. This may stop the Charleston fight for a time. It has been about forty days since the attack was commenced.

18th Capt Smith has paid my husband $2500 for half of that Contract. It is more than we have had in our possession for many a long year. They have now gone to town to see about the suit. Capt S[*mith*] pays the lawyer so this is clear gain to us. And what we should have done without it I know not.
This is my dear Emily's seventeenth birthday–many years may she yet be spared to us. We are yet on the look out for a school for her & I trust the way may be made plain and that we shall be guided for her good.

20th Mr Wight went to Richmond to day & brings me word that all three of John's children are sick with chills & fevers. I shall go down in a day or two.

22nd This is Charles's twenty second birthday. How merciful GOD has been in sparing him to us through all the dangers of twenty battles and giving him a heart to love and trust Him. Continue O Lord to protect & save our beloved children. I have written to our poor Julia who is still at the North with her children and urged her to come South this Fall if she can get a permit for she can safely promise never to return at least until the war is over.

24th Great news from Tennessee. Bragg with the aid of Gen Longstreet has defeated Gen Rosancrans[*Rosecrans*]. The first good tidings we have had from the West.

26th Western news confirmed but as it did not amount to a rout we rejoice with fear & trembling. We have decided to send Emily to Farmville to school.

27th Wrote my last letter to Charles before we leave for Charles City which will probably [be] next Monday but every thing is so uncertain now we can not make any calculations as to the future.

28th Very busy preparing Em for school. I am to be her escort.

29th Left Hanover to day.

30th Remained in Richmond until this morning when we went to the Danville railroad expecting to reach Farmville by night but found after getting in the Cars, there was no connection and that we should have to stop at Burkeville five or six hours but we concluded to go on & reached our journeys end between eleven & twelve at night. We went to the Hotel and in the morning I met with several old friends I had not seen for many years. I then walked over to the school–was much pleased with the teachers and appearances generally. I paid Mr Preot $450 for the first session four & a half months. Leaving my dear child I prepared to return home but found the Cars had just been taken to transport our troops back from Western Virginia so that to return home at the appointed time I had to go to Lynchburg from there to Charlottesville to reach the Central Road but had a pleasant trip meeting & making agreeable acquaintances. I reached Hanover on Saturday evening

5th Oct We left for Richmond on our way to Mr Waddill's. Took the York River Cars and at Tunstalls station we continued with considerable difficulty to get across the country (twenty miles) and reached Annie's about sunset. There we spent nearly four delightful weeks altho' leading a very quiet life. Our little grandson Willie afforded us much pleasure.   We spent one day in Richmond on our return about the last of the month.

1st Dec My diary has been interrupted for some weeks–in that time important events have transpired in our army. The battle of Chickamauga in Georgia has been fought & won by Bragg. This revived us greatly but soon a reverse came in the Battle of Lookout Mountain Ten[nessee] where we were defeated and driven back losing many men artillery & baggage. Longstreet who had [MS. illegible] from Gen Lee's army, had been sent by Bragg to attack Grant at Knoxville and it is believed to be in consequence of that we lost the Victory. Bad management and bad Generalship have ruined us in the West. ~~About~~

15th Two weeks ago Meade crossed the Rapid Ann [*Rapidan*] with a large army. Gen Lee confronted him in life of battle expecting an attack after viewing each other for two days the Yankees under cover of a dark night escaped the River to the surprise of our army. In consequence of this cowardly withdrawal (I suffice they think it) the Government at Washington have removed Gen M & put temporarily Gen Pleasington [*Pleasonton*] in command. Whether we shall have any more fighting this winter is it impossible to conjecture but starvation we must have if the present prices continue - $125 a Barr for Flour $16 a Bus for Meal $35 a load for Wood $30 for Coal & every thing in proportion–Ladies Shoes $50 & 60 children's not to be had Cotton $6 a yard Gloves $20 - Bonnets from $50 to 250! and no prospect of peace so what are we coming to

19th We commenced making more Envelopes about the 24th of last month. To day we have completed 10,000 ready for sale. My husband has obtained a place in the Quarter Master's department $75 a month and rations so we hope now to be able to meet our board and have a little over.
No truth in Gen Meade's removal.

22nd Emily has come to spend the Christmas holidays.

24 This evening John, Ann, and Annie with her dear little baby arrived. It is a joyful meeting with us all but saddened somewhat by a letter from Charles saying he could not get a furlough at this time as they were only granted to those who urged important business.

27th John spent but one day with us. On his return to Richmond sold our Envelopes for $200. We had sent 10,000–a month's work $162 profit. My husband gave me half for my work.

31st The weather bitter cold. How our poor soldiers must suffer. Many of those who have been pursuing Gen. Averell through the mountains have been frost bitten. There is great suffering for Socks and Blankets.

Jan 3rd Still intensely cold–it has extended over the whole country and is the worst severe spell we have had for many years. Annie left us to day. Emily was to have returned to school but seems very unwel with fever and cold.

4th To day her sickness proves to be Measles. It has come out thickly. I hope and pray my dear child will get through it safely. I have always dreaded her taking it.

9th Em seems to be getting over this disease much better than I feared she would. No movement in the Army. Nothing can be done such weather as this unless it is a raid from some of Butler's forces below.

16th So busy making more Envelopes I have but little time for any thing else.

21st Mr W has been ordered to Beaverdam Depot to send off Hay. He met with some <u>cheap</u> Shoes at a country Store which I got him to buy on Speculation that we might make enough to purchase a pair for Emily.

25th The weather is now charming as mild as Spring.

28th I have just finished the last of this set of Envelopes–3,300. John has been fortunate in getting us a hundred lbs more of paper so that if we keep our health we shall be able to make a support and help Ann Eliza too who has also to work for her living. I shall give a list now and then of the price of articles for there is an advance every day.

29th A letter from Charles saying he hopes to be with us next month. As Em has taken cold in some way I can't let her return to school yet awhile. Mr W still absent. Charleston still hold and bravely. Congress has tendered Gen Beauregard & all his command a vote of thanks–for their noble conduct. It is the greatest siege of modern or ancient times. Such continued disappointment must be provoking to our Yankee foes.

1st of Feb The weather has been and still is clear and delightful–no bad roads this winter–some portion of our Western army seems to be moving all the time but no great move just now.

March
10 Feb Went down to Richmond on a little visit. Saw a good many of my old friends[,] stayed with Ann in her little attic room. Sold $125 worth of Envelopes. The cost of every thing increasing daily. Returned home on the 15th.

16th We were cheered by the sight of Charles this afternoon. He looks so well and happy it did my heart good. He has a furlough of twenty days so cheerful as to our prospects and thinks this spring will bring us decided victories.

19th C[harles] went to town with Emily & then up to his Uncles in Goochland for a day. He had to give $100 for a Hat & Em $90 for a pair of Gaiters. How can any people get along at this rate.
Congress has just made public the change in the Currency–we are to have a new one on the 1st April until then the old notes may be used except the $100 which must be invested in Bonds or lost. There is of course great confusion in the money market and want of confidence. Most persons think it the most judicious scheme that could have been planned.   Prices–Bacon=8 lb Butter 8 Bale Cotton from 80 to 100 Flour $250 Bar Meal $4 pt Corn 150 Bar[?] & c. How the poor live is a perfect mystery

28th A rumor that the Yankees are on a Raid.

29th Wakened up about 2'o'clock in the night by a courier telling us the Yankees were between this place and at Ashland[,] we made Charles go into some place of safety until we could find out the truth of it. We heard firing up the road but they passed two miles below us which we were glad enough of. They however took care to tear up a portion of the railroad at the Meadow Bridges of course stopping the cars. Gen Hampton's Brigade passed here in persuit came upon them about night–defeated and took many prisoners. Gen Dahlgreen [Dahlgren] was in Command–he escaped there with a portion of his men and got over into King William. There he encountered some of our Cavalry and the Home Guards who surprised them killing Dalgreen [Dahlgren] and taking many more prisoners. On his person was found a program of the East. One part under Kilpatrick went to the James River about Goochland destroying Mills and provisions as they went. They were to meet in Richmond with the prisoners who were to kill Davis and the Cabinet and then sack the town!!

1st They having destroyed a small portion of the Railroad between this place & Richmond. Charles is still with us.

4th All being right again our dear son was obliged to leave for Camp when if ever to meet again. GOD only knows.

7th Emily has left us too to spend some time in town with her aunt and sharring expenses the board here being so heavy.
A letter from John telling us that he was one of the City Batallion who drove the Yankees back on the plank road six miles west of Richmond only one killed & twelve wounded on our side. I am so thankful he was not among them. My Uncle Robert Copland aged sixty four was also in the fight–a volunteer.

10th A sad death has occurred in the house. A young & beautiful widow leaving two little children. She was a great sufferer–and I felt that her death was almost a mercy.

15th The enemy have all retired from these parts for awhile and will probably not molest us again before the spring. Every thing seems to be swallowed up just now in the worthlessness of the money and difficulty of getting provisions which gets worse & worse. We hope that in April when the Currency is revolutionized that the state of things will improve a little.

20th My husband, the Doctor and Ann have just come into possession of $7000 each. It was left to Mrs B Haxall & children by then brother Edwin Wight at the death of his wife. In consequence of some wishes expressed at his death bed we all thought that had he been able at that time to make another Will he would have left it to his family. Mrs H (her husband consenting) has given up all right & title to it believing they had the best right to it. It certainly comes at a good time for I do not see how we should have next our board.

27th Hearing that Emily cough continued very bad I determined to go to town. I find her looking thin but better than I expected. It has been rainy for several days. I fear we shall have a disagreeable spring. Spent three days in town very pleasantly in Ann's snug little room.

29th Returned to Hanover but we have determined to leave and seek a cheaper home. The weather continues bad.

1st April Snow and rain–great freshet–Can't imagine what the poor soldiers do.

6th A letter from Charles–says they have one pound of Beef or Bacon for four Officers & two servants with some Beans to help out!! starvation fare that–But all seem bright & hopeful and bare up with these privations nobly. Grant has been put in command of the Army of the Potomac but they do not fear him.

From the Northern papers an immense army is to be concentrated for this next ground effort to take Richmond. But I hear no one express any fears as to the result.

7th The sun has cheered us to day after continued clouds.
I am packing up to go to Richmond while Mr W goes up the road to look out a home for us. This roving life does not suit old people but if we can manage to live without debt while this war lasts we must be thankful.

8th My husband returns unsuccessful so I am going to town for awhile & he to the Junction until we know what to do.

9th We leave old Hanover Ct House to day where I have spent some pleasant times in the last two years. I wish the board had been within our means for in many respects its suited us better than any other boarding place.

11th Emily and I are now with Ann in her little room. I wish we could live in this way. I should then feel that we had a home but as nearly all our necessary articles of furniture are in Norfolk which is now in possession of the Yankees we cannot well go to room keeping.

14th Still in Richmond dividing my time between John & Ann.
Em has gone off very suddenly to Annie. The Wagon was sent for her as the roads are too bad for the carriage. I feel anxious about her as its commenced raining some after she left and she is so delicate.

19th Have been working hard on my Envelopes ever since I came to get them prepared for some ladies to make. We hear regularly from Charles–every thing quiet, as yet. News from the West and S.West, good we whip in every skirmish.

25th Was much startled this morning by a messenger from Charles City for Vaccine saying that Emily[,] it was found had varioloid. I cannot believe it but shall leave in the morning.

27th Found Em with Chicken Pox–greatly relieved. She has it lightly. Annie looks so thin, it really distresses me and she is certainly not as strong as [s]he used to be. I sometimes fear that all of our children are to be taken from us–but GOD knows which is best. I can only pray that if consistent with his holy will he will in mercy spare them.

29th News has reached us that the Yankees have quite a large force in New Kent and that there are a number of transports down the James so I must hurry up for fear of being cut off–As they are pressing all the horses and mules in Richmond except those belonging to Market Carts. I am going up in a little wagon with a <u>Surgeon</u>.

May 2nd Have gotten back to town find John has been quite sick with cough & fever but is out again. Anxiety is kept up about the health of my beloved children <u>all</u> the time.

3rd A letter from my husband telling me he has obtained board with Dr. Thompson's in the upper part of Hanover for the present.
Rumors of an advance by Grant on Gen Lee–no anxiety is felt as to the result but if GOD is not with us in this unequal contest as to numbers, vain is the help of Man. I cannot but believe that the fervent, heartfelt prayers sent up by devoted Christians–daily–will be heard and <u>answered</u>–and that we will not be visited according to our sins. If we were we might despair indeed.

4th Arrived at Dr T's to day–my husband joined me at the Junction. It is an old fashioned country place[,] fine Elm trees and large green yard but I doubt whether we shall remain long for the mistress of the house (a sister of Dr T's showed evidently by her manner that it was not agreeable to her to have boarders. But we shall have to remain until we can make some other arrangements as Mr W is obliged to return to the Junction. it seems lonely altho' the other ladies in the house are very kind.

5th <u>Firing</u> is heard to wards the army. The cars bring news that the fight has commenced and up to this time we have been successful and that Ewell was the first to encounter the enemy who were driven back - my poor Charles ! what a time of anxiety for us and we can't hear from him for days.

7th News in the paper cheering driving them back at every point but with great loss of life to us as well as them. O what dear bought victory.
We hear this afternoon that a large force is advancing up the peninsular and James river and that there is great commotion in Richmond but I believe we are prepared for them there.

8th We are looking anxiously for news to day. The ladies have gone to the Depot–wounded are being brought in every time.

8th My husband came up this morning bringing good news but the fighting still going on. On James river we have repulsed and driven them back to their gun boats after taking one and destroying another. Beauregard and Pickett have command of our forces. I fear Annie & Emily are in their lines as they have landed on the north as well as southside of the river. My hope is they will be so hurried to get off, they will not have time to plunder and destroy.

9th After we retired last night Mr Thompson and another soldier arrived with the body of one of their comrades who was killed in the fight in the morning poor fellow! he was married since the war commenced. Mr W was telegraphed just about dark to go to Beaverdam Depot as stores were to be sent there to be Wagoned to the Army now in ~~Spotysallwakened~~ Spotsylvania.

10th He went over this morning and returned about sunset–said that immence stores of Bacon, Meal[,] Sugar[,] Molasses & sc had been brought up by the Cars, which were still being unloaded. We had scarcely been here more than half an hour when someone came up in great haste to tell us the Yankees were there. then came some of our soldiers in great alarm enquiring where they could go for safety that they had come on (fifty in number in charge of about three hundred prisoners when the Yanks in very large force had come upon them suddenly and recaptured them which of course they had to make them escape as best they could. we dared not take them in here, and spent (all of us) a sleepless night thinking it not improbable they might make us a visit.

11th A morning of anxiety & restlessness hoping every moment to see some of our own troops coming. I forgot to mention that they set fire to all our army stores, a tremendous fire blazed all night. We see them now burning a hundred cords of rail road wood about a quarter of a mile off. We keep a close watch upon their movements. Some of them are coming this way there is no escape for us. Doctor T. went last evening fearing they might take him so my husband is our only protector. They rode up to the door and demanded whiskey, when told there was none, said would search the home, went into the rooms, closets, drawers, trunks, and took some of the Doctor's clothes. I stood by mine and told them they were mine if they chose to take them but they did not. I believe it is the best plan always to go with them. But that did not save the Bacon to which they helped themselves to largely. Unfortunately one of them found a Revolver and said immediately that the house must be burned down such were their orders. We thought it all over then but after much entreaty they gave it up and rode off to our great relief.

They had hardly left when the sound of firing was heard again in the direction of the Depot. We were of course all anxiety again and soon saw some horsemen flying in this direction but could not tell whether they were friend or foe soon the blue coats were visable and we saw they were giving way before our men. This took place the most exciting scene I ever witnessed–a race over hedges, ditches, & fields for at least a mile, our men following hard after –firing all the time. But at the top of the hill the Yankees rallied and he goes to fire upon our Cavalry whose horses were so completely worn down by a forced march they were compelled to fall back–but immediately formed a line of battle just around the yard and garden. After waiting awhile the Yankees concluded to retire which we did not regret. As it was they left some twenty wounded and dead not far from us. Most of the former were taken into houses but one or two were allowed to lie on the ground exposed to the inclement weather for days before any one had humanity enough to give them a shelter. We need not talk so much of Yankee cruelty when we allow wounded and dying men to suffer altho' they are our enemies. Gen Stuart followed them in and this evening we hear firing.

12 We are all anxiety to hear about the raiders. We are told tonight that Gen Stuart has been mortally wounded and our men repulsed with the loss of a Battery. They have about fifteen thousand and we about eight. On the Yankees go toward Richmond.

13th Soldiers now and then coming in. Picketts men meet the raiders about the fortifications and drive them back - our Cavalry hurrying them all the way but obliged frequently to fall back as the odds are great and they are no doubt greatly dispirited as the favorite leader Gen Stuart is dead.

14th Instead of the Yankees going into Richmond as it appears to us they might have done from what we hear they have gone down towards the peninsular to join Butler who is making an attack on the Southside. With Gens Beaureguard [Beauregard] & Pickett to meet them on land and Drewry Bluff to protect the River. Good news from Gen Lee–fighting every day, always with success. our poor men must be completely worn out.   Bad weather. It has been raining almost constantly for four days.

15th The railroad has been repaired But no news from any of our dear children. this state of suspence is dreadful. Gen Lee has had another terrific fight again repulsed Grant yet we lost heavily. What has become of our poor Charles. I cannot believe that he has been taken from us. GOD only knows.

My husband (who has returned to the Junction) writes me to come to him there and I am thankful to do it for I shall never have a home feeling here. It is not the old Hanover Ct House. Gen Johnson's [*Johnston's*] command from Tennessee is on its way to join Gen Lee and Gen Thomas to reinforce Grant so there is no hope of the fight being over shortly.

17th Thank GOD! my husband has heard from a wounded soldier that our dear Charles was safe on the 13th after that fearful fight on Thursday and a long letter from John too saying that in consequence of being sick he was not in the fight so that our anxiety in that quarter is greatly relieved.
It is not true that Gens Johnson [*Johnston*] and Price have come to Virginia. O! that Gen Lee could be reinforced   this is the seventeenth day of the fight. Our poor men must be completely broken down. Large numbers have been twice added to the Yankee force.

18th Came down this afternoon to Hanover Junction and from there to Mrs Dejarnettes about their [*three*] quarters of a mile off. She does not wish to take more boarders but consents to let me remain here with my husband until this dreadful struggle is over. He has just returned from Richmond where he heard most shocking news from Charles City which has increased my anxiety about my poor girls tenfold. The negroes have killed three gentlemen there, that we know and whipped another dreadfully!!! Many of the others had to make their escape leaving their families to their fate. GOD is their protector and to Him alone can we look. Truly there is nothing but sorrow and trouble over our whole land and those who brought this bloody, cruel war about have a mountain of guilt resting on their hands.

20th A letter from Charles–well but so tired having been in line of battle fifteen days. Gen Breckinridge's command has arrived at the Junction having whipped Gen Seigle's [*Sigel's*] Division in the Valley on their way to reinforce Grant. News that the Yankee Cavalry are again advancing up the peninsular

21st All excitement   Our troops ~~cavalry~~ Artillery and Infantry being sent down to guard the Bridges–the Yankees having reached ~~the~~ Hanover Ct House
        Been listening all day for the sound of cannons but hear they returned after a slight skirmish finding we were ready for them. We are very sorry to hear that Mr. Chisholm was ruined by them–all his furniture broken up and every thing destroyed also Mrs W. O. Winston & Dr Price–cannot learn the particulars as they have torn up a portion of this Railroad. Fortunately the Fredericksburg is still open.

22nd After breakfast this morning who should come in but Charles. I cant express how surprised & happy I felt. Gen Hancock's Yankee Corps having moved in this direction. Gen Ewell's Corps has been sent after him and has just gotten as far as the Junction. Mr W in Richmond and was not a little astonished to find Charles here. He heard in town from a Charles City gentleman that those blacks had been to Mr. W[addill]'s but had not disturbed them so this is some relief to our anxiety. If I could only have them with me how thankful I should be.

23 Our whole army is on the move finding the Yankees were pushing in this direction -- thousands are coming in. Gen Lee has arrived and has been riding around all day so we may have a fight about here after all. Charles is so unwell his surgeon has given him a certificate to remain until fit for duty. It is such a mercy that he got to us. A Division of our troops (Rhodes [*Rodes*]) are on the march. I have been in the woods with Mrs Dejarnette to see them pass. They are all so cheerful and confident of whipping Grant yet. The firing this evening is constant. We hear it is near the railroad bridge over North Anna river. Gen Gorden [*Gordon*] rode here for an hour this evening to see his wife who came this morning.

24th My poor child is still very unwell and as the cannonading comes nearer & is almost incessant. I fear they may reach the Junction yet and cut us off. What a time of anxiety & suspense about children & country.
9 o'clock Mrs Gorden [*Gordon*] who arrived yesterday is advised by the General to move to Ashland nearly all the ladies in the neighborhood are fleeing from their homes. Soldiers are coming in constantly. They tell us that Gen Lee is in line of battle & threw up breastworks from one railroad to the other but they do not seem to think that Grant will attack him. We will wait awhile to see what is to be done. The roar of the cannon is constant–skirmishing they say.

25th The whole of our army is extended along our Central road–it front of our windows it is a busy and novel scene. Cutting down trees, making breastworks planting her cannon around the top of the hill on which this house stands. They seem to think it as good a position as Gen Lee could have chosen. Mrs. Dejarnette shows herself a true patriot altho' her crops are being destroyed and her stock killed, besides the danger of her home being riddled by the balls she never utters a complaint–says she is willing to bear it all if Grant can only be whipped.   Charles still feels very badly and has left to find his surgeon at Taylorsville–perhaps to go to Richmond. We have no way of leave and don't know what to do.

26th We have no Gen Ewell's Corps in front of us–the right wing of our army. The Yankees are opposite to us about a mile & a half off. Every thing is quiet to day we hear that Gen Grant sent in a flag of truce to bury their dead killed in the skirmish on Tuesday but it may be a ruse on their part as we hear from a scout that they are also fortifying. So it is doubtful when the fight will come off. It is wonderful to see how cheerful our men are no one would believe that they were just on the eve of another deadly combat and so orderly too[,] no noise no confusion. I have not heard the first oath, but have heard them this morning singing hymns of praise unto GOD. With such an army may we not look for his blessing? Every here and there one can be seen with his Bible in his hand–on the other hand Grant is ~~given his men~~ receiving large amounts of whiskey to give his men when the fight comes on to make them fight. Many of the Officers think Grant will not attack so strong a position but will move on towards Richmond. This evening or tonight will decide it. Mr. W has gone to see how Charles is, then we shall decide what to do.

27 Mr W walked over towards Camp to find Charles–hear he has gone to Richmond to the Hospital, so we must follow him. We hear that Grant is moving lower down the Pamunkey our breastworks are rather too strong for him perhaps. It is a pity he will not make the attack here as Gen Lee says it is one of the strongest positions he has ever had–Artilley and musketry still sounding in our ears.

28th As no conveyance is to be had Mr W and I took our satchels (leaving all the rest of our Baggage with Mrs Dejarnette) and set out on a walk to Taylorsville to take the Cars a distance of two miles. Just we reached the main road we found ourselves in the midst of Gen Ewell's Corps who were on their way to meet some of the enemy below so we walked side & side nearly to the railroad. It does me good to be with and talk to our brave and veteran troops. Got to Richmond in the afternoon–found Charles was at John's and had been very sick but is now on the mend altho' very weak. I shall remain with him.

30th Sounds of war from the armies. The Yankees reach from Hanover Ct House below Old Church–ours between them and Richmond. We are staying at Johns.

31st Every thing as quiet here. No one would would [repeated] suppose that an army of one hundred thousand Yankees were within a few miles aiming to burn and destroy this devoted City.

June 1ˢᵗ Charles continues to mend—we are thinking of getting a room for
we hear the Cavalry raiders have cut & destroyed much of the railroad so we
cannot return for some time to our house where I have left all of my clothes.

June 2 The fighting has fairly commenced. Grant has again tried his
Spotsylvania plan bringing up his men to our breastworks to be slaughtered.

3ʳᵈ Good news continually from our front—we have repulsed every assault losing
comparatively few but amongst them many valuable Officers. We can not feel
thankful enough that our dear Charles escaped <u>this</u> fright as his brigade has
suffered greatly.

4ᵗʰ John came in just now and told us his Battalion was ordered off. My poor
son is not strong enough I fear—to stand the exposure—but there is no help for
it we can only hope and pray for the best. He has gone to Bottom's Bridge for
which point the enemy seem to be aiming.
I have been so much relieved and comforted by a letter from Emily who is with
Annie in Charles City—she writes that the Yankees (black) have never been on
the place at all although every one around them has suffered[,] some have been
killed, homes burned and nearly all the gentlemen taken prisoners. The only
way in which I can account for there except is Mr Waddill's great kindness and
likeability to all classes. Emily says that Annie and herself have all the cooking
and work to do so I fear the servants have either run off or been stolen. I can't
get a letter to them. My great fear is that if Grant gets possession of that country
with his great army of perfect savages.

5ᵗʰ The Union prayer meetings (which take place every afternoon) are largely
attended by all denominations—and are deeply interesting. Surely the fervent
prayers thus offered up to Him who is mighty to save will be heard and
answered, even unworthy as we are. Charles is well enough to go with me and
seems to enjoy them.

6ᵗʰ We have rented a room for the time we are compelled to remain in town.
A basement room in the same house that Ann lives in—give $25 a month and
intend to purchase our own provisions. It is comfortable to be in a place to
call our own. My husband dislikes so much being in town but we can't leave
now. I will give the prices we have to give for articles purchased -- $18/ ½
lb Bacon 16/ lb Butter 8 ½ pint of Molasses <u>Black</u> Tea $28 a lb $2 a qt[?]
Potatoes $1 large Roll of bread 5.50 for ½ lb Lard $11 lb Sugar. There are no
doubt many, many now on the verge of starvation in this City.

7th Charles reported for duty to day and leaves us for the army this evening. I had hoped to keep him a little longer but I could not urge him when he thought it his duty to go. John writes that he is well and all quiet at Bottoms Bridge. Indeed both armies seem to be taking a resting spell. I suppose this calm proceeds the storm.

8th I wanted to visit some of the poor wounded soldiers to day but Ann is quite sick, and my husband too is complaining greatly of his head.

10th All better, but the news to day is rather depressing. The enemy have gotten possession of Staunton and another party has made an attack on Petersburg–got inside the fortifications and but for the reinforcements sent to our militia (who fought bravely) would have taken the Cockade City. Sheridan has also started on a raid with eight or ten thousand so we may look for stirring times soon altho' the two great armies are still confronting each other in a state of glorious inactivity.
The prayer meeting this evening was largely attended.

11th All quiet. Mr W has gone up the Railroad this afternoon to spend two days with a friend. There is so much bustle and confusion in town I cannot have a settled feeling. It does not compare to the sweet quiet of the country. Had an opportunity of sending a letter to the girls to day–the first time for six weeks.

13th News that Staunton has been taken by Hunter has occasioned considerable. It is too bad that all that rich region of country should fall into the hands of the Yankee for we hear they have no stores but are feeding upon our people   Gen Breckenridge [*Breckinridge*] has gone up and our Cavalry too to meet them. Grant has quit his fortifications and gone lower down.

14th We hear that Gen Early's Corps has gone on some secret expedition so Charles with it. We shall no doubt hear of it in the right place. Gen Hampton has badly whipped the Yankee Cavalry commanded by Sheridan at Louisa Ct House but Hunter got to Lexington with his forces and destroyed the Military Institute–the pride of our state. They aimed for Lynchburg but that was saved by strong fortifications and Gen Breckenridge's [*Breckinridge*] Division. They dared not venture.

15th Gen Grant has reached Westover on James River–having persued the same unfortunate rout that McClelland [*McClellan*] did. Gen Lee keeping parallel with him protecting Richmond but unwilling to sacrifice his men by acting on the offensive.

16th An attack has been made on Petersburg again and the outer fortification gained by driving back our militia but reinforcements have been sent over we shall expect soon to hear better news. The news from all the counties visited by the raiders is sad in the extreme having destroyed and taken off provisions of every kind and laid waste the growing crops so there is real suffering for food among those who were once rich as well as the poor. We have purchased one pound of meat to day and a few Potatoes for a rarity which cost us five dollars and that is not enough for three of us with out a little rice & bread making our dinner about $7.

18th Gen Early is in Lynchburg it is said if so we shall soon hear of a victory by Gen. Breckinridge and himself over Hunter who has eighteen thousand men. The railroads all being cut the information from the various portions of our army come in slowly except from Gen Lee - he as well as Grant has a portion of his army on the south side–where there is now a fight going on but we can't here any thing yet. The Union prayer meeting for the success of our cause every evening are largely attended and very interesting. John came up this afternoon from Chafin's [*Chaffin's*] Bluff–but returns again in the morning. The clerks from the Government Department being absent has caused almost a suspension of business–even the Post Office–no letters have been delivered for a week which has caused great dissatisfaction.

20th My husband left me this morning for the Junction again where I shall rejoin him in a few days.

21st Busy all day preparing to leave. Heavy skirmishing between our lines on the other side–we, gaining the advantage every time Petersburg safe yet. Early has had a fight with Hunter near Liberty who is retreating towards the mountains rapidly I hope we may be able to cut him off yet.

22 Left Richmond about 3 o'clock and soon reached South anna river–the bridge being destroyed my husband met me with an Ambulance and I reached Mrs Dejarnette's about dark every thing so quiet and peaceful–a different scene from what it was when I left. I sometimes fear I am going to have a spell of sickness. I have felt badly for some days.

23rd No rain for a fortnight and the weather very warm.

25th Every body and every thing wilted under the extreme heat–poor soldiers! what a time they must have standing in the trenches and no doubt suffering for water. We shall no doubt hear of the death of many. I can't hear a word from either of our boys or the girls–it keeps me so uneasy–no mails any where.

26th We hear that Gen Early is in the neighborhood of Charlottesville but we are at a loss to know who or what he is waiting for there. Weather still awfully hot no one has energy to do any thing. I still feel very badly

27th A severe hail storm which has cooled the air delightfully and given us renewed strength, but we had not rain enough for the crops or gardens. No war news but of raiders trying to cut off our southern communication by which we draw most of our supplies and they have succeeded for the time but they will be baffled yet. We have provisions in Richmond to last months–for the army and Grant has a good deal more to do before his famous siege commences.

29th This is my poor Willie's twenty first Birth day.
I have at last received letters from the girls, but sad indeed are the contents every thing stolen in the way of provisions, horses, mules, hogs, fowls, crops, every thing but furniture. What a war! What a war! I had hoped to the last that they would be spared, but no one escapes. I enclose their letters here. All is confusion and darkness when I think of the future prospects of our family–but we suffer less than we deserve.

30th This is my 55th birth day–a long and most unprofitable life. I have reason to humble myself in dust and ashes when I think of it.

1st July A letter from Charles dated near Staunton. He says none of them know where Gen Early is going but we suppose into Maryland & Pennsylvania time will show

2nd Good news from the Southside the Yankee cavalry have been repulsed & routed in two or three different places and Sherman has been repulsed by Gen Joe Johnson [*Johnston*]. John with the other Department Clerks has been ordered back to Richmond after being on service a month. His health much improved by camp life. Sold our months rations for $100. Mr W pays now $95 a month board for each of us.

3rd No news from any quarter yet awhile.

4th Weather continues excessively hot and dry–two showers in five week We occupy a little attic room with one window and find it very oppressive. O' for a great snug home of our own–how delightful it would be but it is no easy matter for any one to keep home now. Flour $400 a Bar Bacon $10 a lb - Cabbages $5 a head–Tomatoes $10   Many of the poor must starve and no prospect of peace. The shelling of Petersburg still continues. Most of the women & children have left - many in tents around the town

5th No rain yet

6th Gen Early & Corps has reached Martinsburg–taken the stores and the garrison prisoners.

8th The Northern afford us our only information of Gen E's advance. They are greatly mystified at the appearance of a 'large rebel force' on the borders of Maryland. I hope we shall accomplish something great now.

9th Still hot & dry–gardens burnt up

10th John came up to see us this morning bringing a letter from Charles near Winchester. He does not know their destination but we hear that since his was written we have taken Harpers Ferry.
We have been distressed to hear of the destruction of our great privateer the 'Alabama'. Capt Semmes who for the last two years has been such a source of annoyance to the Yankee vessels–destroying nearly one hundred. She had been repaired in Cherbourg Harber [*Harbor*] France and came out to have a fair fight with a Yankee craft of the same size that had been waiting for her. After a hard fight she was struck below water mark and sand in a few minutes–fortunately Capt Semmes and forty of his men were picked up by the boats of a British Yacht which had been a spectator of the fight and carried to England a neutral port.

13th We hear that Gen Early has entered Maryland for the third time. Every thing in confusion & alarm there. Militia ordered out to defend their homes–for us to fight for ours is an act deserving death

14th We have had a fine shower.
Early's army advancing steadily towards Baltimore & Washington. Grant is lost sight of entirely since our advance into the enemy's country. It is wonderful that he does not make an attack upon Gen Lee now. He is afraid for he knows he will be whipped again

16th We have captured seven thousand horses–four thousand Beeves
and quantities of stores of every sort which are being brought off by Gen Breckenridge [*Breckinridge*]. Had a fight and took many prisoners at Monacary [*Monocacy*] bridge in Maryland. No news yet from Charles.

17th Went to 'Fork Church' to day one of the oldest in the State–met with some old friends

18 Received a letter from Emily which makes me more anxious than ever to get Annie and herself away from that sad & desolated country. As long as the enemy hovers around them there is no possibility of their leaving–and poor little Willie has been so ill too and I not able to get to him.
Wrote to Charles by an Officer who was going from this neighborhood

19th Gen Early has returned to Virginia–encountered Gen Hunter at Snicker's Gap on the Shandoah [*Shenandoah*] and routed him. Grant keeps quiet
Have heard with great surprise of the removed of Gen Joe Johnson [*Johnston*] in command of our Army now defending Atlanta, Georgia.
Gen Hood has been put in his place and as he was put there because Gen Joe did not think it best to fight we shall expect to hear of a great battle in that quarter in a very few days. We think that Sherman will be the sufferer on that occasion.

20 Went three miles up the railroad to pick Blackberries to day–A fruit scarcely noticed before the war but now in great demand selling at $3 a quart.

21st Spent the day with Mrs Chisholm at the Ct House. It looks dreary and lonely enough there[,] not a boarder in the house.

22 A letter from John telling me his little Bob is sick I shall go down if he does not get better. Finished six thousand Envelopes to day.

23rd Received a telegraph this evening from John telling me to come down

24th Reached Richmond this morning about nine found poor little Bob extremely ill with dysentery but had the comfort and relief to find Emily there– she looks well–the account she gives of the Yankee savages at Mr W's [*Waddill*] and throughout the whole country is truly distressing they killed every thing except the cows[,] took every thing they had to eat so that as long as they remained near them they suffered from hunger[,] helped themselves to clothes bed clothes and every thing else they wanted–and yet they make a great outcry at our going to Maryland and taking a few horses & cattle.

25th Sat up with Bobby last night–he is in great danger. I have felt greater anxiety than usual about Charles hearing that Gen Ramseur has had a fight in which he lost three hundred men killed[,] wounded and missing. We have not heard the particulars.

27th Some slight improvement in B[*obby*] Grant has crossed over a large number of his forces to the Northside & reaches across the White Oak swamp so my dear Annie is again cut off from us. John's Batallion is ordered off but he is allowed to remain on account of sickness in his family. He has lately moved into a comfortable home on Clay St–rent $2200.

28th Gen Early has routed Crock [*Crook*], Averil [*Averell*] & Muligan [*Mulligan*] near Winchester and drove them across the Potomac is now persuing them into Maryland. Bob's disease has been arrested but is now running into <u>Typhoid</u> so that he may be in this feeble state for weeks so I shall return home to-morrow.

29th Arrived at the Junction this evening just as a letter was received giving us the distressing intelligence that our dear Charles is a prisoner   It was a great shock but we had so much cause for gratitude that his life had been spared. We here he has probably been sent off to Camp Chase in Ohio. We can form no idea when our poor child will be restored to us again but will be spared the dangers of the battle field for awhile.

30th They are fighting at Atlanta. We feel great anxiety with regard to the result. Grant is evidently preparing for some great & speedy move. Every thing depends upon the issue of these two great battles.

31st A house full of company not much like the Sabbath. Weather still very warm & dry

August 1st Grant has blown up one of his mines making a gap in our breastworks of a hundred and fifty feet and killing some of our men besides gaining possession of the works and a few guns. But this success was only temporary. Our forces soon recovered from the confusion occasioned by the explosion–retook the fortifications–one of the Generals and many hundred prisoners. After that complete failure what will he do next! I think he had as well give up.

2nd Aug We had a delightful rain this evening of two hours which greatly revived man & beast as well as crops and gardens.

3rd Mr W went to Richmond to day and put in a notice in the Enquirer to Charles. I hope my poor boy may see it and send up word where and how he is.

4th Spent a pleasant day at one of the neighbors. Came home late in the evening on the Hand Car–had a delightful ride.
End of my first Book

M	F	Winston[?]	$ 1.00
Rachel		(ditto)	1.00
Mary		Dogier[?]	1.00
S	V	Tinley	1.00
A		Dalby	1.00

FIRST PAGE OF 2ND VOLUME
   Continued from the [*MS. illegible*]

   Clear & pleasant
20 Cloudy
21 Clear
22 Changeable[?] warm
23 Cold & cloudy

1864
Augt 5th News has reached us that Grant has sprung a mine under some of our works near Petersburg which they immediately took possession of killing many of our men and taking prisoners. But as soon as we recovered from the surprise,

we regained our fortification killing thousands of them so the Yankees gained nothing by that last effort

6th Emily arrived from town to day

7 The oppressive weather still holds on. It has been early two months since we have had rain sufficient to wet the ground more than three or four inches. I fear our corn crop will be greatly shortened

9th Too warm to work, write or do any thing–no rain.

11th Heat greater than ever

14 Went to church at Taylorsville to day. Thermometer–100 in shade–A delightful shower after dinner.

15 Grant has again moved some of his forces to the North side

16th A sharp skirmish in which we lost one of our General's Chambliss. Therm r 101–in shade I can't see how our poor men stand it
News of a naval fight at Mobile in which we have been defeated. They had a force of twenty vessels Iron clad & gunboats–we only [*blank section*]– Commodore Buchannon [*Buchanan*] mortally wounded.

17 Frequent fighting between Hood and Sherman but Atlanta safe yet

18th Rejoiced by the sight of a letter from our poor Charles written from Camp Chase in Ohio. He says he is well treated which is a great comfort to us. John is again ordered below with his Brigade. There has been constant skirmishing they have gained nothing. A fight yesterday near the Railroad beyond Petersburg in which Gen Heth whipped and drove the enemy several miles.

19th We are blessed by a heavy rain so much needed.

20th It continued all night and to day Have just finished plaiting thirty six yards of straw to make Emily a Hat.   The prices have fallen a little–Flour from $350 per Barrel to 250–Bacon from $10 to 7–Butter 8 But dry goods as high as ever. Ladies Gaiters $100–six dollar dresses for $150–Country made straw hats $50 Common Umbrella's not to be had at any price.

22nd Continued showers.

Another fight near Petersburg

Fighting occasionally on same line which the Yankees have extended to and beyond the Weldon road.

24 No news from any quarter

26th Another letter from Charles–says he is comfortable (except that he wants clothes) and has a plenty to eat. We have written to him and his father enclosed $5 in Green backs equal to $40 in Confederate–afraid to send more in an open letter. One came from poor Ann[ie] she says she knows nothing of what is going on. The Yankee Pickets between us.

27th Spent the day with Mrs Catherine Winston an old friend. I hope through her Emily will get a situation as teacher which on many accounts is more desirable than writing in one of the Government Departments for the winter at least as board in Richmond will be so high. We have had a Cavalry fight twelve miles beyond Petersburg in which we drove them back taking twelve hundred prisoners and eight pieces of Artillery

29th Gen Early is driving the Yankees before him after giving them a whipping. We may soon hear of his being across the Potomac. Have written to day to Annie & John.

31st Great anxiety is felt to hear who is the nominee of the Chicago Convention (Democratic) We think peace or continued war depends on it. It met on the 29th

Sept 1st Really cold this morning

Mr W goes to Richmond to see something about his suit against Mr Coleman. He has given me $112–half of what he received for 15,000 Envelopes. No news of importance from the army. Shelling still going on at Petersburg & Atlanta

3rd Have decided at last to take a little trip to the mountains–very busy packing

5th Mr W & I took the Train for Staunton. Emily went down to Richmond as we could not afford to take her with us. We had a pleasant days journey. My husband enjoyed it not having been as free for thirty years. But the sight of the miserable corn crop was depressing these war times. We found our good friend Mr. Catlett at the Cars who carried us to his house after concluding not to go above Staunton for fear we might be cut off by some raiding party we agreed to remain a few days with Maria & Bettie

7th Walked over to the Hospital to see an old acquaintance (Mrs. Fannie Johnson) who is matron of it. Every thing about the place looked so clean & comfortable and the grounds are so beautiful but all saddened by the sight of so many of our young & noble soldiers maimed for life

8th Left this morning to look for a boarding place somewhere on the central road. We stopped at Mechum's River but after getting off the cars 'bag & baggage' the old bachelor proprietor told us he could only accommodate us one night He had other lady boarders but evidently wanted to get rid of the whole of them. Finding we could not get in else where we turned our faces homewards and arrived here this evening after a weeks absence. Have not heard a word from any of the children since I left

11th Attended church at Taylorsville to day–heard a good sermon from a Baptist Minister. There was communion and never before have I been with [*MS. illegible*] who did not extend a cordial invitation to all professing Christians to unite with them. I have never been with the Baptist on such an accasion and we, with the balance of the congregation, were literally [*MS. illegible*] because not having been under the weather we could not partake of the Supper of our Lord which the common[?] did all who love Him to keep in rememberance of Him. Is this in accordance with Scripture? My darling Emily has been persuaded by others that it is her duty to unite herself with this Church. If she feels it consciously her duty I cannot [*torn page*] any thing more but I should be [*MS. illegible*] were she willing to unite with any of the others but to know then she is a true child of GOD will make up for mere forms.

12th There has been such a change in the weather that it is almost cool enough for frost. Not being able to have a fire we shall have to look out for another home.

14th There seems to be a gloom cast over everyone just now, even the most hopeful. It certainly seems to be the darkest period of the War. Altho' a perfect calm it certainly preceeds a dreadful storm–nothing but the mercy of GOD can save us. Grant is collecting an overwhelming force for the last grand onslaught. He has cut our communications is making railroads & cutting a canal thro' Dutch Gap to facilitate his operations October or November will probably decide our fate God grant we may not be delivered into the hands of our cruel enemies.

15 John sends me another letter from poor Charles he says in his prison the time drags slowly along, but I am thankful now that he is there, he has certainly borne his part in this dreadful contest & I am glad to have him out of the coming conflict. I am perfectly yearning to see my dear Annie but my husband is afraid that I may be cut off if I go now. What are the poor to do this winter Flour is now from $250 to 300 a Barr Meal 30 to 40. Wood 60 & 70 a cord Coal $100 for 25 Bus–Shoes $100 to 125 - Stockings 10 & 12–Pocket hand 12 (common). Almost every lady in the country is braiding straw to make Hats & Bonnets. I have finished one for Emily. And am now wondering what I shall do to help my husband make a support.

17th Letters from all four of our dear children Emily has obtained some writing to do and will remain in town for the present with her brother.
[*sent letters to all: written in margin*]

18th This is Em's eighteenth birthday

19th Rumors of a raid upon the Central road. Cars stopped to see the truth of it. Gen. Hampton captured 2500 Beeves from the Yankees in Prince George Cty. A great help to our poor soldiers, but Grant will now take from the Citizens in that region of country every thing they have. The suffering this winter will be intense

20th The Yankees burned a Bridge over the Rapidan & retreated. All quiet on the road again.

21st Bad news from the Valley. Early has been defeated by Sheridan. Rodes, one of our best Generals has been killed. Have not heard the particulars but it is a most unexpected blow to us.

22 Our poor Charlie spends this, His 23rd Birthday in a Northern prison.

23 We have now something of an Equinoxial storm–dark & raining.
Our men under Early fought (near Winchester) with the greatest bravery from morning until night [*MS. illegible*] & killing a large number. There were ten thousand Yankee Cavalry the flower of their army before which our men were compelled at length to retire. Many are already talking of "Reconstruction" if

McClelland [*McClellan*] is reelected. I was for the Union until the Yankees wanted to force us back) heart & soul, but when I saw that so many of our best men, ~~who~~ thought the Southern cause was a just one and that the Almighty blessed our efforts with success all my feeling became enlisted on our own side. Now I begin to doubt whether there was just cause for the heart rending sacrifice of so many near & dear to us, so that our whole land is one of mourning.

25th Every prospect of our Railroad (the Central) being destroyed. A heavy Yankee force is advancing upon Gordonsville and we have no one to oppose them.

26th News of another attack upon Early by Sheridan at Fisher's Hill -- we were compelled to retire leaving twelve cannon in the enemy's hands. It is said we lost both battles by the cowardice of our Cavalry but we must not judge them too harshly before we know all the circumstances. They certainly outnumbered us three or four to one

27th There is a rumor that the prisoners at Camp Chase overpowered the guard and escaped I cannot believe they would be so rash for it would be impossible for them to get safely through Ohio & Kentucky without detection. We look anxiously for another letter from Charlie–now to prove it is not true

28 A report now comes that we have gained in a little fight with Sheridan but we get nothing definite except that three Brigades of Yankee Cavalry are in Staunton. Commenced reading my Bible through again. Wrote to John & Emily

29th Another letter from Charles of the 10th He had at last heard from us. They won't allow the poor fellow to receive clothing I don't know what he is to do when the cold weather comes on if he is not exchanged.
There is news that we have whipped a portion of the Yankee Cavalry near Waynesborough [*Waynesboro*].   Cannonading was heard last night & this morning towards Richmond
Afternoon–The enemy have come over the North side of the river twenty thousand strong and have advanced upon our first line of fortifications[,] every man between sixteen & fifty have been sent to the front from Richmond. All excitement there. We are all anxiety to hear more

1st   The roar of cannon has been heard all the morning and very heavy firing for an hour. My dear John, may our Heavenly Father in his great mercy spare him to us & his little family–and stretch forth now His omnipotent Hand to save us from this mighty host

2ⁿᵈ   We drove them back with heavy loss yesterday but it was not a general engagement. A heavy rain is fallen to day and through it all, comes the distant booming of artillery. After severe fighting they got possession of Ft. Harrison which gave us command of the Canal. Butler is digging through 'Dutch Gap'. On the South of Petersburg they have also gotten hold of the 'Vaughan Road' by which Gen Lee draws his supplies from this South. This is their great aim. John is on the 'Osborn' [*Osborne*] Turnpike below Richmond. He has been made Lieut of his company.

3ʳᵈ No church today. Have been much interested in reading a work of Dr Robert Breckinridge's on 'Romanism'. It contains a great deal of information, But his bitter feeling against the South (of which he is a native) takes a great deal from the respect once felt for him.

5ᵗʰ Every thing quiet no fighting both parties busy preparing for the last great contest for Richmond before the Northern presidential election in November

6ᵗʰ Went over to a neighbor's this evening to see the operation of making Sorgham from Chinese Sugar Cane. It is very simple and quite as good as the N Orleans or West Indies. There are quantities made throughout the country. It will be such a good substitute for which is not very abundant. It sells at this time for $30 a Gallon.

7 I have come down to Richmond to see what I can do about getting Emily a place in one of the Departments. Have seen several of my old friends who advise me to make personal application to the heads of the Bureaus. Will try first to get it through Col Catlet[*Catlett*] one of Charlie best friends.
Attended one of the daily prayer meetings–very interesting & solemn a large congregation.

8 John is still in camp. I regret so much not being able to see him. Col Catlett says he will do all he can to get Em a place and thinks he will succeed. She is so delighted at the thought of doing something for herself these hard times.

9 Attended Dr Hoge's Church this evening heard an excellent sermon. Went to the United Prayer Meeting at Dr Moore's Church in the Afternoon.
Have spent a good deal of my time with Ann who is room keeping again & on the lookout for some employment

10th Came up in the Fredg [*Fredericksburg*] Cars. Mr W met me at the Bridge we have to walk across the river on a foot bridge as the other has not been rebuilt since the Yankees burnt it.

12 Very busy. Weather fine.

14th Commenced my Envelopes again hoping to get 10,000 ready this month to help with our board

15th A fight last night & this morning below Richmond repulsed the enemy four times, they lost heavily, we but few. John not in it.

16th The weather cool for the season but delightful

17th A letter from Charles. He says my mothers brother Charles who lives in Zanesville Ohio went to Camp Chase to see him but was not allowed to. That was too hard but just like them. He left a note and some money for him. He is a feeble old man, it was so kind in him

19th We heard that Gen Early whipped Sheridan in the valley on the 15th

20th A letter from Annie–poor child she says Butler says that all who do not take the Oath in that part of the country must be sent thru' the lines, so there is no telling when they may be driven from their home   Sorrow and trouble on every hand and yet we are blessed our children so far spared to us and in perfect health

22nd Still busy on Envelopes–at night plat Straw. Weather fine. Situation of affairs in Georgia still envolved in mystery. Gen Beaureguard [*Beauregard*] has command of that Department.

24 A letter from Emily Has not received her appointment yet but certainly expects to get it.

26 Bad news from Gen Early–has been defeated by Sheridan after whipping him, and taking eighteen hundred prisoners by our men struggling off to plunder the Yankees returned suddenly and took thirty pieces of Artillery from us including eighteen we had just taken from them. Our poor fellows I suppose were hungry but I trust we may punish them for it yet. Great rejoicing in Yankeeland of course

26th Quiet reighns every where[,] no news

26th Went to Taylorsville Church.

27th A great deal of interest expressed on the Northern election for president– between Lincoln & McClelland [*McClellan*]–many think that if the latter is elected there will be a greater prospect of peace   Walked out with one of the ladies to gather Walnuts, which are now selling for $1 a dozen!
Weather charming.

28 Still very busy with my Envelopes no news of importance

29th Received a letter from my dear Emily to day telling me that she had been Immersed and had united herself with Dr Jeter's Church in Richmond. Altho' it would have been a great pleasure to me to have had my beloved child go with me yet after many conversations on the subject and ~~having~~ feeling satisfied that she is governed by what she considers her duty with regard to the mode of Baptism I could not object as she has waited so patiently for months. To feel that she is a [*MS. illegible*] Christian is all I ought to ask or wish. May our Heavenly Father guide & direct her steps for her everlasting good.
She also writes me that she has obtained a situation in Gen Kemper's Department at a salary of $4000 a year. This will be a great help to her as her father's income does not support us all three

~~30~~ Wrote to E and Annie–feel dreadfully at being cut off from A[nnie] perhaps for the Winter.
Went to Fork Church and heard a very fine Sermon from Mr Stringfellow.
Weather still delightful

Nov 1st Every thing goes not greatly with us now. Once in awhile the sounds of a few shells are heard. This perhaps is but the precussor of a fearful storm. No satisfactory news from Georgia. Price is driving every thing before him in Missouri. Sent a letter to Charles to day. His father is trying to have him exchanged before the winter sets in.

2nd We hear that our nephew Willie W Wight is to be married to day to Miss Nannie Cunningham

3rd At least we have a change in the weather–rainy & cold

4th Still cold & a drizzling rain. Made six hundred & eighty five Envelopes to day.

5th Bright and windy. Received a sweet happy letter from Em to day. I wrote to John.

6th Sunday No preaching. Rode to a neighbors to see a sick child

7th Rainy & disagreeable, poor soldiers what a time they have in the trenches.

8th A great day at the North. Lincoln & McClelland [*McClellan*] the candidates for the presidency. We can't hear for some days. Cloudy & warm. Wrote to Emily

9th Warm & sultry. Just packed 10,000 Envelopes -- ~~ready~~

10th Weather still warm but clear at last. My husband has just brought me a letter from poor Annie. The Yankees have just carried off her husband and taken mules, cows & nearly every thing left before. What is to become of my poor child I don't know & I am perfectly miserable about her and don't know how I can possible get down there. To think of her being all alone no protector and no comforts or even necessaries is too dreadful. She says she has bread still that is probably all she has left. O! if I could only get to her. Weather pleasant

11th Received a Telegraphic Dispatch from John telling me that he was in Richmond for a day or two and wanted me to go down

12th Came down by the Central called by the Department to see Emily. She looks very bright & happy. I never saw John in finer health–camp life certainly agrees with him. He is detailed every now and then by those who employ him to attend to their business. I shall remain two days, and so much enjoy the society of my dear children. If my poor Annie could only be with us or I even knew that she was not alone or suffering in any way I should be so comforted. Weather cold & clear

13th This is a memorable & interesting day. Our Church which has been for twenty seven years divided into Old and New School has been reunited and this morning the five Presbyterian Churches in town assembled at Dr Moore's to celebrate the supper of our Lord. The body of the Church was filled to overflowing with Communicants. The Clergy and Elders occupying the pulpit & platform around it. It was truly a delightful scene. There was no regular sermon preached but five or six most appropriate addresses were made by the different ministers.   At night I went with John to hear a sermon to the Unconverted from Dr Hoge. It was a very solemn one. Cold & cloudy–some snow

14th Mr W came down to day and brought our 10,000 Envelopes.

15th Returned to the Junction to day and my dear John to the army Em will remain at his home until Jan. Cold & clear   paid Mrs D[ejarnette] up to the 10th

17th Very busy making a calico for Em which cost $160!! worth 12 cts[?] a yard[?]

19th Cold & rainy.

20th No Church raining all day
Can't hear from Annie except that she has made two attempts to get into the enemies lines to see about her husband with out success–my poor child I think of her night & day & can't help her.

21st Kershaw's Division passing down from the mountains to reinforce Gen Lee. Cloudy & rain.

22 Bought a pound of Tea for $50 hope in the course of a month or two to make enough on it to help pay for a dress which I am going to have woven. I have only spent $50 in the last two years on my clothes.
Dreadful weather–raining steadily for twenty four hours and snow too–very cold.

23 Cloudy & damp

24th Anniversary of our Marriage
Thirty three years we have been spared to each other when so many of my old friends have either been taken or are widows

25th Still cloudy & disagreeable

26th Have not heard from any of the children. This separation is dreadful. Since Lincoln's reelection no hope of peace–no bright prospect for the future.

27 Weather still threatening–no church the armies below Richmond are as quiet as if there had been an Armistice.

28th Commenced upon my Envelopes again. It is clearing off warm.

29th Mild & bright

30th Weather delightful–like Spring. Made 1000 Envelopes to day

1 Dec Mild & clear. Emily writes me that wood is $100 a Cord and almost impossible to get Coal–she is now room keeping–had to give $200 for <u>half</u> Barrel of Flour. Ladies shoes $150 Calico $16 Flannel $25 and every thing else in proportion. A horse sell from $2000 to $3000. A Cow $1500 to 2000– Chickens 5 to 8–Tallow Candles $2 a piece. Nothing under a dollar unless it is an Apple. Eggs $<u>1 a piece</u>!

2nd Still pleasant. No war news.

3rd Clear

4th Letters from all the children, the greatest comfort I have when separated from them. Annie writes me that by <u>hiding</u> she has saved enough provisions to last her some time. That she feels it her duty to stay at home and take care of what little the Yankees have left unwilling that when her husband does return he should find a desolate home. She is right. Charles poor fellow is anxiously looking for an exchange. John still on the fortifications at work on the Bomb proofs. Weather delightful

5th News from Sherman in Georgia still vague & indefinite. He seems to be slowly making his way to the Sea coast. If he does reach there without being whipped the North will have reason to boast. Still clear

6th We hear that Sheridan has reached the Potomac and coming down the river to reinforce Grant. Weather clear

7 The Cars are going up to bring Early's forces down to Gen Lee. Weather good

9th Trains are constantly passing filled with our soldiers. Clouding up

10th Still they come but it is now so cold my heart aches to see many of them sitting on the open Flats exposed to the piercing wind - are no shelter or fire when they get to Richmond.

11th Bitter, bitter cold but how can we complain when we see how our brave soldiers have to suffer to night a heavy sleet is falling and through it all the loaded trains are passing–every thing frozen. Mr W & I sleep in a small room without any fire but it is best for our health as we are perfectly free from cold. The only thing we have to cheer us is the news from Georgia that we have Sherman surrounded. I pray it may be true and that the whole of his army may have to surrender

13th Persons are putting up ice. Cold ground covered with snow

14 Cloudy & disagreeable

15 Finished to day our Government Contract for envelopes.

16 Another letter from my poor Annie. Has heard of her husband and the rest who were taken. They went through the greatest hardships–walking through mud knee deep for miles some times half the night. Butler had sent for Mr W[addill] and said he might return if he would take the oath. I hope he did while in their lines for what is to become of my child and his children if he does not get home?

17th Cloudy & warm. Another Corps of Early's men have passed down to Gen Lee. No one can tell whether there is to be a battle between Grant & Gen Lee this winter or not. The weather and roads render it almost impassable. Bad news from the South Sherman has managed to reach the sea coast a little south of Savannah. What a shame–Gen Hood has gained a victory over Thomas at Franklin a town in Tennessee but with of <u>thirteen</u> <u>Generals</u>!! six killed & six wounded one a prisoner–besides a number of privates. A dear bought victory. Weather still cloudy and threatening

18 Cloudy & warm

19th Bad news. Hood has been badly whipped by Thomas near Nashville–a number of prisoners and cannon taken. Yankees still persuing. These are truly dark days for us. Damp

20 Turning cold. Mr W has just bought 400 lbs of White paper to make Envelopes on our own account

21st Rained very hard all night. Heard that Emily went down to Charles City in a <u>Cart</u> on Saturday evening–hearing that Annie was sick travelled all night. I am exceedingly anxious about both

21st It is intensely cold–a North easter blowing. A very large Yankee fleet had just sailed for Wilmington it is supposed. They seem to be gaining foothold at the South. Savannah is safe yet, but how long can she hold out?

22 The Yankees are coming toward the Central road near Gordonsville. Our troops are being sent back to check them. What the poor fellows must suffer this bitter weather. Savannah surrendered

23 Cold & clear. Our men drove the enemy back are persuing them towards Madison.

24th Clear–Moderating a little. Our soldiers are now going back again

25th Christmas day. A sad one to me   It is the first time since we were blessed with children that all, or some of them were not with us, but not one now. Nor can I hear a word from my girls. I fear they are <u>both</u> sick and I [*MS. illegible*] from them. All I can do is to leave them in the hands of One who knows what is best for me and them. The streams are so high that all communication seems to be cut off for the present. If I could only get to them I should not feel this great anxiety. I had a long, affectionate letter from John which was a comfort to me. Weather clear & warm.

26th Dismal rainy weather again. The ground perfectly saturated. No great news from any quarter

27 Cloudy cold

28th Cold & clear. No news yet from the children. It is decided to give a New Years dinner to Gen Lee's veteran troops. Many provisions are pouring in.

29 We have purchased White paper at $3 a pound to make Envelopes–have sold seven packs already at $2 a pack. At that price we can make a very comfortable support. Snowing fast.

30th Very cold. It is the worst winter we have had for many years. The great Yankee fleet and land forces that started with the certainty of taking Wilmington NC did not accomplish this object and made an inglorious retreat to the great mortification of the Yankee Nation. We hear of the death of Gen Streling [*Sterling*] Price the best General we had west of the Mississippi river. Clear & cold

31st The last day of another year. What sad reminiscences it brings up. Who would tear aside the veil to look into the future? I would not if I could. GOD is merciful in hiding from us the sorrows that may be in store for us. clear–ground covered with snow

1865
Jan 1st A bright, cold New Years day. O that we may lead a better & more useful life than we have yet done. May our Heavenly Father in his infinite mercy bring peace once more to our troubled country and bring us all to look to Him for of ourselves alone we can do nothing.

2nd It is so bitter cold I cannot work at my Envelopes. What suffering there must be. Wood is $100 a cord in Richmond & Coal not to be had

3rd No news. It is impossible for fighting to go on such weather as this.

4th Can't hear a word from Annie, Em or Charles. I feel heart sick but try to leave them in His hands–knowing that he can and will care for them.

5th Worked upon my Envelopes.

6th This cold, rainy gloomy day we cannot feel thankful enough for the comfort of a home and good fires when we think of the thousands exposed to the weather

6th Em arrived after another dreadful night journey. It is such a comfort to feel that she is safe & well & that Annie is getting along pretty comfortably not withstanding all her hardships & losses.

10 She returned to Richmond.   No army news

11th John has been detailed to take charge of a Government Wagon Train

15 Made a little visit to Hanover Ct House. Engaged two ladies to help us make Envelopes.

16th Found John at home on our return waiting orders

17th Another letter from our poor Charlie written quite cheerfully. He seems to have resigned himself to his fate

18 Ft Fisher has fallen so our only port is closed–every thing has gone up higher than ever. Wilmington must ultimately be evacuated I fear

20 We have been fortunate to engage 2 Barrs of Flour from our friend Mr Catlett of Staunton at $350 now selling in Richmond at $700 - part of it is for Annie if we can ever get it to her.

22nd Mr Sedden [Seddon] Secretary of War has resigned

24th Our little Fleet went down the river hoping to reach City Point & destroy the stores there but had to return
25   without accomplishing any thing in consequence of obstructions placed by the Yankees in the River.

27th Came to Richmond to see Em who is not well–suffering from the effects of that terrible trip. I feel so anxious about her whenever she has a cold. Found a letter from Annie. Her husband has been allowed to return she seems perfectly happy now.

30th We have sent our Commissioners to meet Lincoln & Seward to see whether we can come to any terms that will bring about peace. The whole country is waiting with greatest interest the result

Feb 1st As Em seemed quite well again I returned home after five days absence. It was so bitter cold I could go out but little. I never have seen such a winter in my life. Every thing frozen for upwards of two (2) months. But the weather does not prevent Sherman's steady advance thro' N Carolina. I feel confidant he will be whipped before he gets much further altho' at this time a gloom has spread over us all as

2nd Our Commissioners after having an interview with Messiers Lincoln & Seward and at old point have returned with out accomplishing any thing. We only asked an Armistice to give time to see what could be done they would agree to nothing but an immediate surrender which of course we cannot agree to. All we can do now is for every man to shoulder his Musket, look to GOD for help and fight for his liberty or be a slave. We must be a unit now there is hope of nothing but a conquered peace

5 We have had a pretty severe fight south of Petersburg. Three Corps on the side of the enemy against two Divisions of ours. They gained back little considerable loss on both sides. Among our losses was that of Gen Pegrum [Pegram] of [MS. illegible] Brigade. He had been married only three weeks to Miss Cary of Baltimore. This has been the sad fate of many during this war

6th Congress is going to take all into the field now so my husband will probably lose his situation as the Quarter Master at the Junction will come in under that Law. Our Envelopes will hardly make us a support.

8th Every thing frozen up–snowing & sleeting. What suffering every where.

10th Emily came up most unexpectedly this evening. She has a dreadful cough and feeling badly she came up to stay a day with us. O! that we only had a home for our poor children to come to. But I will not complain we might be so much worse off than we are. She has taken a room at our cousin's William Johnsons and is very pleasantly fixed. She felt badly to leave John's house on his account for she devoted to him but there were reasons which made it best. Her cousins are very affectionate to her and then she will have such pleasant society

13th Em left us to day feeling rather better than when she came. O Lord in mercy restore her health and spare her to us.

14th We hear it to day that a general exchange of prisoners is to be made so our dear Charlie will soon be with us again. We have so much cause for gratitude that his health has been spared.

16th Mr W took down seven thousand Envelopes to sell. We shall see then what we have to depend on.
Gen Breckinridge has been made Secretary of War. His sister married Charles Parkhill a cousin of mine as noble a fellow as ever lived. Both died the second year of their marriage

17 Sold Envelopes for $350.
Weather too bad for any war movement. My husband is quite sick to day.

18 Still in bed. I pray he may not be ill

20th He was brought down stairs to day on a bed into a room with a fire still very sick–a sad time in every way. Charleston & Columbia are in the hands of the enemy. Gen Lee has gone South. Gen Johnson [*Johnston*] reinstated.

22nd The Doctor has come. My husband rather better but very sick. I am so anxious too about Emily. She has had a cough for six weeks

24th Mr W continues very sick

26th John has come up on his way to the Rappahannock. Em better. All is gloom & sadness. Sherman has taken Charleston & Columbia & is marching steadily on cutting our Railroads as he advances. But scanty supplies for our army from any quarter of course they are on very short rations. And where are we to get any? Richmond may have to be evacuated unless we can whip them shortly. A battle beyond Petersburg is expected. The exchange of prisoners is going looking for Charlie every day. My husband is a little better but kept so anxious about the times. I cannot yet believe that Richmond will fall. GOD only can save us. Let us all look to Him.
Gen Johnson [*Johnston*] has been restored to the Command of the Army of the Carolinas[,] Georgia & Florida at the urgent wish of the Army and people.

28th Mr W is sitting up again. I have so much cause for gratitude

March
1st Weather dreadful. John leaves us for the 'Northern Neck' on Government business.

2nd All news of Lee's Johnson's [*Johnston's*] & Sherman's movements are suppressed so we are all in the dark from those quarters but a Telegram has informed us that Sheridan is coming with a force twenty thousand strong towards Staunton and we have a mere handful there to oppose him. Large contributions had been made up there of provisions for our suffering army in answer to a call from Gen Lee which I fear will be lost.

3rd They have reached Staunton and destroyed all the stores and are now in Charlottesville. Bridges all blown up. Later news tells us that Gen Early undertook to check them with only eight <u>hundred</u> men–of course we lost nearly all against such tremendous odds. If Gen Johnson [*Johnston*] does whip Sherman there may be a ray of hope yet but War & famine are evils stare us now in the face.

4th A day set apart at the North for a general rejoicing over our losses & ruins. One of Charlies' fellow prisoners has written us from Richmond so we look for him every day.

5 This has not appeared much like Sunday. It has been a day of great excitement. The Yankees are reported to be advancing in this direction. We are greatly at a loss what to do or where to go

6th Greatly relieved by hearing they have not come farther down than Charlottesville. We suppose they have crossed over to Lynchburg. The papers are still perfectly silent upon the war movements

7th We had all just begun to feel secure when the news reached us this morning that the Yankees were in large force at Fredericksburg so again we are on the 'qui vive'. They remind me of the locusts of Egypt and are certainly destroying all the sustenance we have. Some arrangement had been made (a very singular one) with a Mr Singleton[?] from Washington & supposed to be with the sanction of Mr Lincoln to send them Tobacco for Bacon so a large quantity of the former is being carried to Fred^g [*Fredericksburg*] to the purpose of exchange. Perhaps they have come to take that a way.

8th The Tobacco burnt that could not be carried off. Our Wagons & teams gone. Why do we trust the word of such a people

9th They have all gone back so our fears are relieved from that quarter for the present. We are in utter ignorance of what the other raiders are doing as our papers are still silent. There is a rumor that a portion of Sherman's army has been whipped by Hardee. I have gotten to that state now that nothing good or bad seems to move me.

10th This is a day set apart by the President as a day of Fasting & Prayer never did a people need more the help of an Almighty hand although we deserve not the least of all his mercies. We can only pray for pardon & deliverance from our oppressions & that he make us His own people. We have no preaching near us. It is unfortunately a real March day–Cloud Rain & hail.

11th More excitement. Sheridan has returned from the river to the Railroad and is advancing in this direction

12th Still they come on & we don't know what to do–the Bridges will be destroyed and we shall be cut off from Richmond if we remain here.

13th Packed up and came down to the Court House on the Cars were all leaving the Junction. Felt sorry to part with my kind friends there but we are running about from pillow to post now–no home and no rest for the soles of our feet

14 Find all frightened & hiding every thing to keep them out of Yankee hands as they are destroying every thing on their march. Constant & wild rumors.

15 Here they come! I never dreaded them more. Have secreted all that I could. Stay about here all day. Finding they had commenced searching the rooms I asked Mr C[hisholm] to let me call for an officer, ask for a guard which was granted & the home soon cleared of their presence. They have a fight with some of our men at Ashland fell back towards the Junction and burn it

16 Fitz Lee comes with our Cavalry. Longstreet with a portion of his Corps also Rosser and McCusland [McCausland]. The Yankees go forty miles round & cross the Pamunky [Pamunkey]. Our troops came on this side of the river, they on the other. The Camp fires of both visible. Our Generals waited for pontoons all day.

17th We did not or make bridges to cross the river in time and Sheridan with all his men wagon train & prisoners goes on his way rejoicing. Shameful! Leaving nothing but misery & destruction in his wake.

18 Our dear prisoner boy has come. A happy meeting. He looks thin and no wonder not having had enough to eat at any one time for eight months. And were not allowed to buy any thing. Slept on a plank with a Blanket for a covering all the winter–but had a plenty of fire

19th Em got a furlough and made her appearance but my pleasure was dampened by finding her still with a cough & quite unwell

20th John is here too so once more we are blessed by having all of our children with us but my poor Annie. John has just returned from Westmoreland on Government business. Soldiers all gone towards Richmond All quiet again

22nd Em has been detained by sickness

23 Charles & herself leave to day for town

27 C[harles] came back.

28 News of a fight beyond Petersburg. Gen Gordan [Gordon] made a successful attack upon the Yankee fortification–took many prisoners but was at last had to retreat. Charles in town again

30th Fighting on the lines. Sheridan has gotten round towards the South side rail Road which has brought on a general engagement. All the forces have been with drawn from this side of the river.

31st We are in constant suspense hearing the most conflicting rumors.

April
2 A day never to be forgotten poor old Richmond given up to the Yankees!!! I never could believe that this was to be its sad fate but it is so   I was aroused a little after day by several loud explosions & soon a servant told me Charlie had come again. I knew at once that something dreadful had happened. He told us that Pres Davis had been called out of Church to receive a Dispatch from Gen Lee telling him the City must be evacuated immediately. Instantly

all was bustling turmoil. But few could leave as there was but the Danville road in operation and that was taken for the Government. Emily decided to remain with her cousins the Johnsons as they got some provision that evening from the Commissary. Charles had to come off without being able to get his clothes as the Yankees were expected every moment, and could not tell us where John was going or what he would do with his family. I never was so completely cast down except by some family affliction before. It was so sudden–so unexpected to me. Now all is chaos & confusion was there ever a country in such a condition for just now we have no Government & no currency. No one will touch Confederate Notes about here now. The fighting is still going on but have had the worst of it so far. Petersburg is also the possession of the enemy. Gen Lee pulling back–towards Amelia Ct H. What is to become of us? I have never despaired before but I fear our course is almost hopeless now. Charles, poor fellow got his horse and went off he knew not where for he is on parole still of course could not join his regiment. We had no spare to give him & he went without overcoat or any thing to protect him from the weather. His sad face at parting haunts me still. O Lord watch over & preserve my darling children & enable them to look to Thee.

3rd News has come that Richmond has been on fire for forty eight hours nearly all the business part of the town destroyed on Main & Cary Streets. Ann's houses among them. This will be very hard upon her as their rent was her support. I wish we had a home to share with her. The loss of property in town can only be estimated in millions and has ruined hundreds. It was caused I believe by our own people setting fires to the Public Warehouse containing Tobacco. It ought not to have been. So many persons have been ruined by it

4th Wrote to Emily by a gentleman going to town but can't hear from her or for any thing from our army except depressing news told by deserters to justify their leaving. I'm sorry to say numbers are continually passing.

5th Kept in a constant state of anxiety by not being able to hear any thing reliable. Some tell us that Gen Lee is whipped which we won't believe. Have just received a most unexpected & cordial invitation from Mrs Gen Rosser to go over to her Mother's (Mrs Winston's) and stay while we remain in the neighborhood. We have no reason for declining and shall accept. As our Confederate money is utterly worthless now & we have nothing else. Our situation is very unpleasant. Nor can we get either to Richmond or to Annie's. Mrs Chisholm was very kind & altho' she knew we had nothing to pay board said as long as she had any thing she would share it with us. My husband is so unwell. I constantly fear he will be laid up. How blest those are who have a home.

6th We are most comfortably fixed for the present at Mrs Winston's. It is a sweet place and every thing on her table is as good as it can be and has less the appearance of <u>war</u> times than any place I have been to. Mrs Rosser seems to feel that we will be a protection to them in case they should have another visit from Yankee raiders.

8th Firing was heard the whole night and continues to day. We are at a great loss to account for it and have a little hope that Gen Lee is driving them back–but we must wait.

9th Cloudy & gloomy. Mr W very unwell

10th Wrote to Emily by Willie Dabney[,] trust I shall hear something from her.

11th Went with the ladies to the Depot.

12th This evening I heard there the startling rumor confirmed Gen Lee has surrendered!!! The die is cast. After four years of bloodshed, horror and misery we are compelled (mortifying and humiliating as it is) to succumb to our bitter enemies. Whether this war ought not to have been commenced by the South or whether for the sins of our people (which are grievous) we have suffered this great afflictions we cannot tell perhaps both. We have certainly been thro' a furnace of fire. I shall ever think we had not sufficient pervocation for breaking up our once glorious Union. What is our condition now? Virginia particularly. Lands laid waste and dissolute, mills, barns burnt & dwelling homes, servants gone nearly all the horses taken. Confederate money nothing but waste paper and but one in a hundred with specie. no prospect at making any thing or going any where, and all this for nothing–<u>nothing</u>. The firing was in consequence of Gen Lee's surrender.

13 Leut Winston returned to day. He tells us that after the evacuation of Richmond the men deserted by hundreds & thousands–leaving Gen Lee with only eight thousand and being surrounded by the Yankees–his soldiers too having nothing but parched corn to eat he was compelled to give up. They are now parolling our men but what the conditions will be we cannot imagine they can require any thing they please we are utterly powerless. If we had only

remained as we once were. We should have been saved all this humiliation & distress. Charlie is on his way back again. We are all without money and know not what to do.

15 Charles returned mortified & depressed at the result. He had reached Campbell Co^{ty} with the train when he heard of the surrender. He is unwilling to take the 'Oath' if he can possibly avoid it. He has his parole as a prisoner and on that has gone to Charles City to see his sister. It is all over I fear with our poor old State but the Country is not subjugated yet.

16 Have just heard from Emily though some ladies who have come. She asked for a parole to go down to Charles City & being refused by the Authorities went to Head quarters. Gen Wetzel [*Weitzel*] who not only gave her one but allowed her to go down the River on one of their Yankee Boats and be put off wherever she wished. We hear they are treating the inhabitants of Richmond with great civility & kindness - a very politic measure. The negros are flocking to them & they are setting the men to work & sending many of the women back to their homes to remain for the present which proceedings are very unexpected to the blacks some of them are now trying to get away from their new friends. Mrs Winston is very anxious that some of hers should go but they seem to know their own interest too well. Virginia will no doubt be a free state & if the negros are allowed to remain what a terrible condition we shall be in.

17th We hear cheering news from Yankee authority. Gen Johnson [*Johnston*] (who did not surrender) has whipped Sherman badly & taken much ammunition & many wagons. The fight is said to have been in N Carolina. We hear heavy guns all the time & can't account for it

18th Gen Rosser came to day on a visit to his wife. Gen Johnson [*Johnston*] has not had a fight. He has quite a large army but as that is the only one on this side of the Mississippi of any size there is but little hope of our gaining our independence now. So I wish we could come to terms & settled with the North as best we may.
Horrible news! Hearing minute guns a few days ago, there came a report that Lincoln was dead. It has proved to be true. He was assassinated in the Theatre on the 15th by some person unknown who made their escape. Shot through the head. At the same time Seward (who was ill from having his arm & jaw bone broken by being thrown out of a carriage) was stabbed in his breast while in bed. We shall hear something more. This seems the beginning of a "reign of

terror" our <u>Domestics</u> being told by the Yankees that they are free are in a state of perfect insubordination. Work or not as they please. This murder of Lincoln will cause us much sorrow I fear. They seemed from policy inclined to be lenient to us but now we have nothing to expect but the hardest terms.

20th Great excitement at the North about Lincoln's being killed. Seward it is thought will recover his two sons (who were stabled at the same time) are getting better.

22 The papers filled with Lincoln's assassination. And the Southern government is getting the credit of it but it was no doubt the work of a few desperate characters

24th We are anxiously looking for a letter from Richmond to seeing whether we can go through to Charles City with out my husband's taking the oath.

26th Every thing in town is under Yankee rule, but they are behaving well towards the inhabitants

27th Mr W could wait no longer and ventured to go on the cars. We had but $1.25 in specie every cent we had in the world just enough to buy his fare from the Ct H[ouse] so I am to remain until he sees what can be done

28th A letter telling me he had no difficulty in getting transportation down the river & without taking the oath for us both so I leave my kind friends this evening to join him in Richmond

29 Got to town late so that I could not see any of my old friends except William Johnson's family where we staid all night & left this morning a little after day to walk down to Rocketts. To walk through those once familiar streets and see nothing but charred & blackened ruins was indeed a sad sight. I could not tell where I was. When we reached the Steamboat we found crowds of other 'rebel' passengers but all subjected to a rigid examination of papers before we were allowed to go on board. It is very hard to keep quiet under such rule but we must bear it as best we can. The river is filled with vessels of every size & description. We were detained hours at Bermuda Hundred & City Point and then again at Fort Powhatan from which place we crossed over in a row boat manned by Yankees to Weyanoke (Maj Douthat). It was then so late we remained there all night. He sent us over here the next morning

30 Annie saw us coming all hands were gathered to meet us. It was indeed a joyful season. Annie, poor child looks badly enough and no wonder after all she has gone through since we were together last. Willie is a noble, smart fellow & Annie keeps but one servant of course has a vast deal to do, too much for her strength. As soon as Mr W[*addill*] has means I'm sure he will get more help. <u>No one</u> has money now. How people live I can't imagine. And what they are able to acquire is liable to be taken from them by the negros who consider themselves free to do nothing or take what they please. A most horrible condition of things. If they are allowed to remain in the country and no one to control them, what is to be come of us. We heard salutes the day we came down the river and were told that Gen Joe Johnson [*Johnston*] had surrendered with his Army to Sherman so that ends the war and all who now act as guerillas will be delt with as high way robbers. This is but the beginning of the end I fear.

May 2 Charles thinks he must teach for a living for the present at least and can at the same time study Law

3rd We do not see the papers regularly. A reward of $100,000 is offered by the Yankee Government for our poor fugitive President under the pretense of being accessory to the death of Lincoln as well as traitor which I am sure scarcely one of them believe. I trust he will escape.

5 We shall be in a terrible state with the negros who have all been told they were free but were to remain here and work for their former masters but exact their own wages. I can't see how we are to live in any comfort or peace. I wish we could all go out of the country. All the regulations & rules adopted by the Yankees show <u>we</u> are to be kept in perfect subjection to their whims.

6th Emily has left us to make Mrs Graves a visit for a week.

8th John has come again. He loves the country, poor fellow so much I wish he had a little farm. Now he is entirely out of employment. He had a situation offered him as clerk by a Yankee if he would take the <u>Oath</u>, but he could not make up his mind to it yet.

11th All our days are just alike. Talking of sorrow of the past and anxiety of the future.   The price of every thing is higher than before the war and money <u>very</u> scarce. We have not been able to get a <u>cent</u> of interest

June 16th My diary has been at a stand for a month past. In that time our poor President Jeff Davis was taken prisoner in Georgia.

EPILOGUE 1878

Jan^y

Another year has passed and I am left alone
After forty six years of married life our Heavenly Father saw best to take my
beloved Husband from me. I cannot murmur however desolate I feel when
I know he was translated from a life of sorrow and sadness here to one of
inexpressible happiness. His affliction (almost perfect deafness) which shut
him out from social intercourse he so much enjoyed) proved to be a blessing
in disguise. He was always fond of reading, tho' never books of a serious
character but in the past year he was mysteriously led to take up The Bible and
read it thoughtfully and with increasing interest. Altho' he read other works
particularly Hodge[s] 'Way of Life' which he read over twice and pronounced it
strong reasoning he told he preferred to take the Bible as his guide. And a short
time before his death when Charles held it up before him he held out his hand
caught hold of it and held it so firmly as if he realized it as the best of Books

During his last & short illness his mind seemed contantly occupied with
regard to his preparation for the quiet & solemn event he fully realized. He said
he was afraid he was too great a sinner to expect mercy. He prayed constantly,
even after he ceased to speak I could see his eyes raised to heaven evidently
in prayer. Once when he saw me on my knees he called out 'pray for me'. My
precious precious husband I feel so assured that his earnest supplications were
heard and answered through the merits of a blessed Savior I can only pray that
my end may be like his

I have thought since his death, if there had not been so many constantly
around and a strange nurse he might have expressed himself more freely
to me but he had not been willing from the first that others should know
he felt on the subject. Not for a moment that he was ashamed of it but he
said he might be deceived in himself and not feel as deeply interested as his
children might think. I am perfectly satisfied that all was peace at the last.
He made all earthly arrangements even who was to officiate at his funeral
& where he should be buried until I died and then both to be carried to the
family burial ground in Richmond which my dear Annie can carry out or
not as she chooses. We can remain close to her, or not while she lives here as
she thinks best but I should love the remains of my darling Jennie to be laid
near us wherever we are

I would not recall him to the sorrows of this world even if I could but O I
should be so thankful to have him know how many many acts in our long life

to-gether I mourn over from my very heart and would feel it such a mercy to recall but it is all passed now. I think of him night & day yet I dare say those around think he is almost forgotten as I appear cheerful and take an interest in all that concerns the dear ones left to me. It is a relief to me to spend my time alone thinking of the past & the future.   Yet it would not be right so I try to be of some use to those around me. Yet when night comes again I feel that [*MS. illegible*] is still wrapped up in a napkin for which I shall be called to on account O that my latter days may be guided & directed for my ever lasting good.

I have written this with regard to my dear husband as it has been a relief to me as I cannot now speak about him to any one but no one knows how constantly I think of the past. I appear cheerful and show an interest in all around me tho' I often feel inclined to shut myself up and dwell upon my past life which has been so unprofitably spent but I have duties to perform as long as life lasts. I pray this may be made clear to me for I walk in the dark and often feel I can do nothing but pray.   I never saw a clearer case of answers to prayer than in the conversion of my beloved Husband for tho' <u>constant</u> & <u>earnest</u> yet there prayers were wanting in perfect faith for (sinful human nature) could not see how a change was to be brought about as he had never had shown the least interest in any thing of a serious nature tho' I believed all things were possible with GOD and that all hearts were in his hands. But I saw & believed that the fervent & trusting prayers of our dear children & of his brother & sister were mercifully answered to his eternal salvation. O' if I could have that faith which is never clouded by a doubt.
His death occurred on the 1 Sept 1877

Other sad afflictions we were called to mourn a few months before in the loss of our dear daughter Julia & <u>her</u> daughter Gertrude Henlet[*?*] a month after <u>her</u> mother ~~after her mother~~. Oh it was so <u>very</u> <u>very</u> sad and so unexpected in Julia's case she had an attack of Jaundice but we had heard she was better then came the shock the dreadful news. But we almost feel it was a merciful dispensation for had she lived to see her only daughter & her little grandson taken from her she could scarcely have stood the terrible blow. She had been for years a devoted member of the Episcopal Church as was my dear Gertrude who I was told died a calm & peaceful death expressing her resignation to GOD's will and begged her devoted husband to try and bear the sad separation with submission. They had not been married quite twelve months after an engagement of four years. Had just gone to house keeping in Orange NJ with every comfort indeed luxury around them with every prospect of a long & happy life. We must all try to remember that.

Man proposes but GOD disposes and he knows what is best for his creatures tho' mysterious providences to us.

Guy, Julia's only son started not long after her death on an extensive business tour to the East Indies [,] Australia [,] Japan & ec to be absent eighteen months. The last accounts we had of him he was well & succeeding, yet I cannot help feeling great anxiety about him among strangers so far from all who love him should he be sick

23 Jan My book seems likely to be filled with sad events. Emily writes me of the death of her mother in law Mrs. Graves dear old lady–when we parted in the Fall her last remark to me was 'we may never meet again'. I felt as she did but wondered <u>which</u>? I am spared a little longer to prepare for the great event for which she had been for so many years ready and waiting.

   O that I could be ever free from temptations and doubts which are often fearful–nothing but darkness all around me no silver lining to the clouds yet <u>sometimes</u> I feel that my prayers have been heard and a merciful Father delivers me from them for a season. It is no doubt intended for my good that I may feel more & more my need for a blessed Savior.

Feb 14 Yet another death of an old friend and connexion the Rev George Woodbridge who died very suddenly from heart desease. How startling there sudden calls are. They ought to come home to each one of us and make us feel how all important it is to be ever ready. He married my cousin Rebecca Nicolson.   Was pastor of the Monumental (Episcopal) Church in Richmond for many years–was truly a good man and greatly beloved by his people.

22nd Received a letter from Charles telling me of the most unexpected marriage of my grandson Robert Wight a most imprudent step as he is not yet twenty & his income not $500. If his wife proves to be a plain & sensible girl it may prove for the best. But I don't know any thing about her or even her name. It distresses me but it can't be helped now.

March 13th A letter from Charles tells me he, as his Wife's Trustee has bought "Ohenham" [*Oakenham*] her old family residence in Middlesex. She did not wish it to pass into the hands of strangers as it had always been her home and her parents were buried there. He will rent it out and still keep his Professorship.

17th I went to Manoah Church yesterday. Mr. Lamb preached on the uncertainty of life. There have been so many proofs of it lately–it is passing stranger we do not realize it more.

My state of mind now is dark indeed. GOD alone knows what a miserably wicked being I am. I pray that HE may enable again to have a clean & bright faith in His blessed Son. I dread the thought of going more into the world again. Retirement is best for me if I thus can employ my time for GOD's glory.

My dear husband same month before his illness said <u>his</u> prayers would be of no avail he was too great a sinner -- that only the Christians ~~that~~ could be heard. I urged upon him the importance of praying <u>himself</u> for pardon so I copied the enclosed verses from the Old & New Testament that he might see we are commanded to ask if we hope to receive a blessing & thanks to GOD he did feel the necessity of it, and prayed I believe with his whole heart

27th A letter from E has announced the birth of Charlie's little daughter on the 23rd. I am rejoiced to hear it.

1st April Julie & Nannie (Annie's step daughters) have gone on a visit to Baltimore

A sweet letter from Charles telling me about his little Mary. I am so glad he gave her his oldest sister's name for she would, indeed I almost believe, she did sacrifice her life for her brother's. She said her great desire to enter the Culpepper [*Culpeper*] Hospital was that if her brothers should be wounded she would be there to nurse them and there she contracted Typhoid fever from one poor soldiers to whom she devoted herself night & day and in a few weeks was removed from all suffering and anxiety. My darling child she [*knew*] not what it was to spare herself if she could in any way help others even the poorest.

I have been reading (to me a very interesting Book by an old friend Mr Samuel Mordicai called 'Richmond in By Gone days').   I recalled to memory so many events, persons & places I had entirely lost sight of. It is a sad pleasure to recall the days that are past

June 27 After a visit of four weeks from Emily and her little ones they left us today for her home. Mr Graves spent only a few days. The house seems almost deserted since they took their departure altho' we have still a family of <u>eleven</u> left.

30th Have reached my ~~sixtieth~~ sixty ninth Birth day nearly three score years and ten. Mercy has followed me all the days of my life notwithstanding my constant sinfulness and ingratitude. Trials have been sent me but I have been enable to see the Lord's hand in most of them. My great trouble arises from the doubts, darkness & wickedness of my own heart. O that ~~the point~~ my iniquities ~~of my past life~~ may be blotted out and that the short balance of my unprofitable life may spent more and more in accordance with Thy Holy Will. I ask this for the sake of They blessed Son who died to save the worst of sinners. O Lord enlighten my mind with Thy Holy Spirit that I may <u>see more clearly</u> my own vileness and thy infinite goodness and prepare me for that solemn hour which cannot be far distant when I shall be called to enter in presence of one mighty & willing to save

July   An affectionate letter from my dear Charles just before leaving for the Orkney Springs asking me to join them there and he would pay my expenses if that was my difficulty about going. I really cannot afford it and am not willing that he should pay as the board for his family will cost him no small sum. If my health should make it necessary to leave home I will have to accept his kind offer

Aug 1st   Our little Julia has been very ill for several weeks with Malarial fever which does not yield to nay of the remedies so to day the 29th Annie took her to Baltimore to try change of air. Maggie went also to live at her Aunt Emily's for the winter and attend one of the Public Schools

1 Sept   This is the first sad, <u>sad</u> anniversary of my beloved husband's death. I have gone over all the sufferings of his last days with his wonderful patience. O! that my end my be like his fully prepared and shall ever believe he was and in the enjoyment of such perfect happiness now–<u>such </u>a contrast to his life here. I cannot wish him back altho' I do so miss him all the time and have him ever before me
    I have just finished reading the life of Dr. Guthrie a celebrated Presbyterian Minister of Scotland. It is deeply interesting. He was certainly a model of a preacher and Philanthropist. His compassion was so [*MS. illegible*] for the poor miserable uncared for children of his country that by untiring exertions he established 'Ragged Schools' in Edinburg which spread to London and other large cities and was the cause of saving many, very many young outcasts from a life of imprisoning and the gallows. That was only one of his great works for the benefit of others. This book was loaned me by a Baptist preacher who enjoyed it as much as I did

6th Annie has returned[,] little Julia looks better but is not clear of chills yet. I trust the cool weather will stop them

The Yellow fever is raging in New Orleans and other Southern cities. The mortality is fearful a large proportion of those who die are children. We can't be thankful enough that we are spared this dreadful scourge. The accounts are heartrending. May our Merciful Father speedily remove this terrible disease from those poor suffering people

Oct 20 I have at length taken for Goochland on a visit to William and Hattie Wight and from there to Staunton to see my very dear and old friend Maria who is the last living person who was present at our marriage. Never was friendship more lasting and sincere than ours has been. She is a noble woman. No one is perfect but she comes nearer to being so than any one I know. I can truly say that from an intimacy of more than fifty years. I feel a great desire to be with my other precious children but a sadness comes over me when I think of leaving those behind also so very dear to me. And then the grave of my beloved husband is here. When I stand and look at it I feel that the casket is still with me tho' his soul is in the presence of his merciful Savior. The more I think of the patience and fortitude he [*MS. illegible*] during his illness, the more I am satisfied that he prayed for and received help from above. His sufferings must have been excruciating from the nature of his disease and not able to move or be moved for days and nights together. A wonderful strength was given him to bear this agony without a murmur.

Sept 26th   I have at length decided to leave home & spend at last a part of the winter with my other dear children but will go to Goochland & Staunton first

27 William Wight's carriage met us (I took Emily) at the Wharf and took us that evening to Dover. They were very kind and affectionate. We spent ten days there & then made Hattie a visit of a week. She was also as sweet to me as if I were indeed her own aunt. I am very glad I went it was the wish of my dear husband that I should and I may never be able to go again.

Oct 12th I came down to Richmond and from there took the Cars to Staunton to see my old friend Mrs Breckinridge & her sweet family there again I was received with the greatest affection–how gratifying this is to 'old age'. There I spent ten days meeting old friends & making new. Yet this roaming life does not suit me it confuses my mind and a quiet life seems almost necessary for my best interests now therefore the country suits me best

19th Arrived in Baltimore. C[*harles*] met me at the Depot but I came to Emily first. O how I wish all mothers were blessed with as affectionate children as I am.

27ᵗʰ After spending two days at Mr Graves' came over to C[*harles*]'s. Their dear little Mary is one of the finest children I ever saw and a perfect idol with her father as I knew she would be he is so fond of children generally

29ᵗʰ Guy Gardner & his bride spent one evening and night with us on their return from their wedding trip. We like our new niece and grand-daughter very much

Mr Moody the great English Evangelist is now preaching in Baltimore to over flowing houses[?] and with great effect. His manner is plain, earnest & solemn, no attempt at oratory but what he says the young may perfectly understand and is well calculated to fix the attention of all. Every one is an interested listener. He is a pure Gospel preacher with touching illustrations of his subject nothing more

Dec 9   I've again returned to Emily's after a visit of five weeks to C[*harles*] & J[*uliet*] where every thing was done to make me happy

Decʳ   Christmas draws near and it's a pleasure to see my dear little Grandchildren looking forward to it with so much delight but to me it is not unaccompanied with sad thoughts both of the past and the future. I feel that every year as it rolls round brings me nearer to my end. Sometimes I feel that it would be a happy change   then again clouds and darkness surround me. O that I could feel secure in a Savior's love and ready to go at any moment. I know that only He can save me but I don't <u>feel</u> it as I ought and wish. There is something wrong in my wicked heart for GODS's promises are sure. I often think that I'm the 'barren fig tree'

25ᵗʰ   Christmas Day   A Happy time with the young ones and the old cannot help participating in their enjoyment. They have a beautiful xmas tree and all of us many presents as mementos of love. I do not feel well having taken a heavy cold.

Jan 1ˢᵗ 1879   Another year has passed attended with blessings innumerable and undeserved and found me with the same cold ungrateful heart. I pray that the Holy Spirit may never leave me again but give me faith <u>at all times</u> to trust in Him alone for pardon

8ᵗʰ   We have had a weeks spell of intensely bitter weather every thing frozen up and on the water, among the vessels caught in the Ice the suffering and loss of life has been fearful and heartrending to read. I had not felt it much being in a warm home to which I am still closely confined by my cold

10th   News from Annie to day. The first for a fortnight she says James River is closed by ice and will probably not be open for a long time but they hope to get letters by land

Charlie's baby has been very sick but I have not been able to get over but I'm thankful she is so much better now. I feel more and more every day how entirely unable I've become to help my children. They have just to look upon me as a child to take care of the short remainder of my days

This is a month set apart for prayer by Christians all over the World for the promotion of the Redeemers cause. I have not yet been able to attend a single meeting but hope to yet before the month closes

Mr Graves' nephew about fourteen years old (whose father is Missionary to China) joined the Baptist church a few nights. He became deeply interested under Mr Moody preaching. He attended regularly all the meetings. There was nothing exciting.   The addresses plain & solemn so that all could understand.

20th I have had a wretched cold for nearly a month but am getting over it now. I hardly feel that I could stand much severe sickness a little weakens me so.

A letter containing joyful news from Annie. She is doing well after the birth of another little girl on the 11th. I can't be half thankful enough that she has been spared to her husband & children and all those to whom she is so dear

22   My weak feelings still continue although my cold is well. My children think a physician can benefit me. I do not as my case is one of chronic Dyspression which often varies, as is generally the case. It affects my spirits so that I often wish to be alone and it requires an effort to enter into conversation. It is not right to give way to these feelings unless carried by the disease. I wish my dear affectionate children would not be so troubled about but let me follow my own inclination. The constant effort to keep up is painful to me. They forget that old people cannot rally as the young do. Nature must gradually give way and as I am now bordering on seventy years of age the allotted time of man on earth I cannot & do not expect much if any increasing strength the rest of my days. I do wish to die where my dear husband did and to be laid by his side

Feb 20th   I am thankful to have recovered my usual health and am now looking forward to returning home but I will not leave until all are well. Emily's children have both been ill but are out of danger. This has been a most trying winter bitter cold and changeable, scarcely any two days alike. There has been great mortality among old people mostly accasioned by pneumonia. I think in one week there were twenty deaths, the average age 75 years

3rd March   Hearing that Annie and one or two of the children were very unwell I decided to shorten my stay after a happy sojourn of five months with my two child[ren] and leave for home. On arriving in Richmond I went to our cousin's Mrs Woodbridge where I remained until the next morning ~~where~~ I had a delightful visit. The next day I returned to my old quarters and found a hearty welcome from all. My health is quite good again which I had no reason to expect and hope I'm thankful as it is one of the greatest of all blessings. I do so enjoy the country

April 15th The last month has passed quickly but one sad event has occurred the death of Robert's wife & child–poor fellow he is deeply afflicted I hear. I pray that his heart may be softened by this unexpected blow and he enabled to look to Him for comfort who only heal the wound. I have never heard whether Ida was a Christian or not she being almost a stranger to me

May 10   We have just heard that Annie's dear daughter has made a profession of Religion and united with the Baptist Church in Baltimore Dr Bitting's Maggie is a child of much character. I pray she may by example have a happy influence on her sisters & brothers by setting them a bright example of faith & firmness in the many temptations she will meet in her Christian course

June 30   My seventieth birthday! I have reached the period allotted to man "And if by reason of strength they be fourscore years yet is their strength, labor & sorrow." I have no expectations of reaching that period but ever feel that I am hastening to my end. And what has my life been or busied to but nothing, nothing have I done for the glory of GOD. I can hope for nothing but through a crucified Redeemer. O that I could feel the love of Him shed [*MS. illegible*] abroad in my heart which I have sometimes had in a slight degree, but O so tempted

The first of this month Charlie's wife presented him with another daughter, a little Juliet. I pray they may both be spared to be blessings to their parents

NOTES

Chapter One

1. K.M. Kostyal, *1776: A New Look at Revolutionary Williamsburg* (Washington, D.C.: National Geographic Society, 2009), 11–12.
2. Koystal, 14.
3. Catherine B. Hollan, *Virginia Silversmiths, Jewelers, and Watch and Clockmakers 1607–1860* (McLean, Virginia: Hollan Press, 2010), 311.
4. The Colonial Williamsburg Foundation issued a detailed archaeological report on the Geddy house originally entitled "The James Geddy House and Silversmith Shop Block 19, Building 11, Colonial Lot 161 (61)" by Catherine Schlesinger in 1986. A revised *Colonial Williamsburg Foundation Library Research Report Series—1450* in 1990 is available online at http://research.history.org/DigitalLibrary/View/index.cfm?doc=ResearchReports%5CRR1450.xml.
5. Hollan, 312.
6. Ivor Noel Hume, *James Geddy and Sons: Colonial Craftsmen* (Williamsburg, Virginia: Colonial Williamsburg Foundation, 1970), 36.
7. Hollan, 312.
8. Kostyal, 20.
9. Hollan, 314.
10. Hollan, 314–15.
11. W. Hamilton Bryson, ed., *The Virginia Law Reporters Before 1880* (Charlottesville, Virginia: University Press of Virginia, 1977), 87.
12. W. Hamilton Bryson, ed., *Miscellaneous Virginia Law Reports 1784–1809* (Dobbs Ferry: Oceana Publications, Inc., 1990), 25.
13. W. Hamilton Bryson, *The Virginia Law*, 87.
14. Albertina (Brown) Parker, *The History of John Francis Deane and members of his family in Virginia, Montana, and California* (Missoula, Montana: A.B. Parker, 1963), 12–13.
15. W. Hamilton Bryson, *The Virginia Law*, 25.
16. Ibid., 88.

17. Jean Edward Smith, *John Marshall: Definer of a Nation* (New York: Henry, Holt & Company, 1996), 130.

18. W. Hamilton Bryson, *The Virginia Law*, 26.

19. The Colonial Williamsburg Foundation issued a detailed archaeological report on the Nicolson house that includes significant detail about the personal life of Robert Nicolson and some of his contemporaries. The report, entitled "Robert Nicolson House Archaeological Report, Block 7 Building 12," (originally entitled: "The Nicolson House—Report on the 1982 Archaeological Investigations") by Patricia Samford was written in 1986. The revised report of 1990 by the Colonial Williamsburg Foundation Library Research Report Series—1083 can be reviewed online at http://research.history.org/DigitalLibrary/View/index.cfm?doc=ResearchReports%5CRR1083.xml.

20. Janice Nicolson Holmes, "The Nicolson Family of Virginia, 1655–1975," *Virginia Tidewater Genealogy Bulletin* 8 (1977), 53.

21. Patricia Samford, "The Nicolson House—Report on the 1982 Archaeological Investigations Block 7 Building 12" accessed May 3, 2013), http://research.history.org/DigitalLibrary/View/index.cfm?doc=ResearchReports%5CRR1083.xml.

22. Samford, 3.

23. Colonial Williamsburg Foundation, *Colonial Williamsburg Official Guidebook & Map* (Williamsburg, Virginia: Colonial Williamsburg Foundation, 1972), 99–100.

24. Holmes, 132.

25. Ibid., 134.

26. James Winnefeld and Fredda Coupland Winnefeld, *A Copeland/Coupland Genealogy* (Baltimore: Gateway Press, Inc., 1997), 6.

27. Winnefeld, 39.

28. Holmes, 165.

29. E. Lee Shepard, "Sketches of the Old Richmond Bar: Charles Copland," *Richmond Quarterly* 3 (Spring 1981), 30.

30. Shepard, 30.

31. Michael L. Nicolls, *Whispers of Rebellion: Narrating Gabriel's Conspiracy* (Charlottesville: University of Virginia Press, 2012), 26.

32. Shepard, 31–32.

33. Margaret Wight's mother was referred to as both Mary and Maria Brown. When she signed her will, Mrs. Brown made a notation stating "Maria Brown or properly Mary Brown."

34. Original manuscripts of Charles Copland are located in the Archives of the Library of Virginia. Some are also available on microfilm.

35. *Pianoforte* here simply refers to a piano.

36. William Ward Wight, *The Wights: A Record of Thomas Wight of Dedham and Medfield and of His Descendants, 1635–1890* (Milwaukee: Swain & Tate Printers, 1890), 27.

37. William Ward Wight, 46.

38. Ibid., 78.

39. Ibid.

40. Various original manuscripts of Hezekiah Lord Wight are located at both the Library of Virginia and Virginia Historical Society in Richmond.

41. National Park Service, U.S. Department of the Interior. "Shockoe Valley and Tobacco Row Historic District," accessed May 15, 2013, http://www.nps.gov/nr/travel/richmond/ShockoeValleyTobaccoHD.htm.

42. Jessie Ball Krusen, *Tuckahoe Plantation* (Richmond, Virginia: Krusen, 1990), 17.

43. Goochland Historical Society, *The Story of Goochland* (Goochland, Virginia: Goochland Historical Society, 1973), introduction.

44. Litchfield Historical Society, "The Ledger: A Database of Students of Litchfield Law School and the Litchfield Female Academy," accessed April 9, 2012, http://www.litchfieldhistoricalsociety.org/ledger/students/2793.
45. Several original handwritten letters of Ann Eliza Wight to Mary Venable Carrington are located at the Virginia Historical Society in Richmond.
46. William Ward Wight, 237.
47. Ibid., 142.
48. Some inconsistencies were found regarding the name of Mary Wight. Some sources show her as Mary E. and Mary Elizabeth, where others use a middle name of Mary Hamden or Mary Hamilton Wight. Her handwritten letters signed "Mary H. Wight" confound the issue.
49. Questions existed regarding the gold embossing on the cover of the first volume of Margaret Wight's diary. Discovering that her daughter, Mary, worked in the Norfolk Public School's Fourth District provides an interesting link to Mrs. Wight's first volume; the cover reads "DISTRICT NO. 4. SECOND FEMALE DEPARTMENT."
50. Henry Smith Roer, *History of Norfolk Public Schools 1681–1968* (Norfolk, Virginia: H.S. Roer, 1968), 49.

Chapter Two

51. Edward Porter Alexander, *Military Memoirs of a Confederate: A Critical Narrative* (New York: Charles Scribner's Sons, 1907), 6.
52. Mrs. Wight does not seem to tackle the complex subject of slavery in any direct fashion. Her references to the subject are primarily focused on those she called "servants" and "negroes" who either "ran off" or were taken as "plunder" by the "Yankees." She did express direct concern about slavery at war's end. "Virginia will no doubt be a free state & if the negros [*sic*] are allowed to remain what a terrible condition we shall be in." Again, after the war, Mrs. Wight expresses a question about slavery: "No one has money now. How people live I can't imagine. And what they are able to acquire is liable to be taken from them by the negros who consider themselves free to do nothing or take what they please. A most horrible condition of things. If they are allowed to remain in the country and no one to control them, what is to be come of us."
53. Drew Gilpin Faust, "The Civil War Homefront" in *Rally on the High Ground*, (National Park Service, 2010), accessed May 12, 2013, http://www.cr.nps.gov/history/online_books/rthg/chap6.htm.
54. Joan E. Cashin, "Into the Trackless Wilderness," in *A Woman's War: Southern Women, Civil War and the Confederate Legacy*, Edward D.C. Campbell Jr. and Kym S. Rice, eds. (Charlottesville: Museum of the Confederacy and University Press of Virginia, 1996), 29.
55. Ibid.
56. Ibid., 36.
57. Drew Gilpin Faust, *Mothers of Invention: Women of the Slaveholding South in the American Civil War* (Chapel Hill: University of North Carolina Press, 1996), 45.
58. James M. McPherson, afterword in *Religion in the American Civil War*, Randall M. Miller, Harry S. Stout and Charles Reagan Wilson, eds. (New York: Oxford University Press, 1998), 409.
59. Ibid.
60. Faust, *Mothers of Invention*, 180.
61. McPherson, 409.
62. Faust, *Mothers of Invention*, 180.

63. Robert Lewis Dabney quoted in *Moses Drury Hoge, Life and Letters*, Peyton Harrison Hoge, (Richmond, Virginia: Whittet & Shepperson, 1899), 139.

64. Harry A. Stout and Christopher Grasso. "Civil War, Religion, and Communications: The Case of Richmond," in *Religion and the American Civil War*, Randall M. Miller, Harry S. Stout and Charles Reagan Wilson, eds. (New York: Oxford University Press, 1998), 316.

65. Letter to Reverend T.V. Moore, D.D., November 15, 1861, Rare Book Collection, University of North Carolina at Chapel Hill, Call Number, 4173. Also included is this collection is the complete text of Moore's sermon published by Hargrave White in 1861. Electronic edition accessible at http://docsouth.unc.edu/imls/mooretv/moore.html.

66. Stout and Grasso, 319.

67. Drew Gilpin Faust, "Without Pilot or Compass," in *Religion and the American Civil War*, eds. Randall M. Miller, Harry S. Stout and Charles Reagan Wilson (New York: Oxford University Press, 1998), 252.

68. Ted Tunnell, "A 'Patriotic Press': Virginia's Confederate Newspapers 1861–1865" in *Virginia at War: 1864*, William C. Davis and James I. Robertson Jr., eds. (Lexington: University Press of Kentucky, 2009), 36.

69. Ibid., 37.

70. Ibid., 35.

71. Ibid., 39.

72. Ibid., 42.

73. Bradford A. Wiseman, "Trains, Canals and Turnpikes: Transportation in Civil War Virginia, 1861–1865," in *Virginia at War: 1864*, William C. Davis and James I. Robertson Jr., eds. (Lexington: University Press of Kentucky 2009), 67.

74. Ibid., 69.

75. Ibid., 68.

76. An excellent description of railroad construction in the Civil War Era can be read in Edwin A. Pratt's *The Rise and Fall of Rail Power in War and Conquest*. The summary of railway construction was derived from this source. For an exciting primary source that describes the challenges of keeping the Virginia Central Railroad on track during the war, Charles S. Anderson's, post-war memoir, *Train Running for the Confederacy, 1861–1865: An Eyewitness Memoir, Union Cavalry Raids—Incidents—Troop Actions and Train Wrecks.*

77. J.C. Swayze, "Hill & Swayze's Confederate States Rail-Road & Steam-Boat Guide, Containing the Time-Tables, Fares, Connections and Distances on all the Rail-Roads of the Confederate States; also, the Connecting Lines of Rail-Roads, Steam-Boats and Stages. And Will Be Accompanied by a Complete Guide to the Principal Hotels, with a Large Variety of Valuable Information," in *Documenting the American South* (1863) http://docsouth.unc.edu. imls/swayze/swayze.html (accessed April 8, 2013).

78. Ibid.

79. Wiseman, 74.

80. John Steele Gordon, "The High Cost of the U.S. Civil War," in *Barrons*, accessed Feb. 12, 2013, http://online.barrons.com/article/SB50001424052970203990104576191061 207786514.html.

81. *Daily Richmond Examiner*, March 31, 1863.

82 Faust, *Mothers of Invention*, 81

83. Ibid., 80.

84. Ibid., 91.

85. Ibid., 89.

86. Margaret Loughborough and James H. Johnson, *The Recollections of Margaret Cabell Brown Loughborough: A Southern Woman's Memories of Richmond, Va. and Washington, D.C. in the Civil War* (Lanham, Maryland: Hamilton Books, 2010), 74.

87. "Confederate Papers Relating to Citizens or Business Firms, compiled 1874–1899, documenting the period 1861–1865," in *fold3*, accessed Feb. 8, 2013, http://www.fold3.com/image/58538721/.

88. James I. Robertson Jr., *Civil War in Virginia: Battleground for a Nation* (Charlottesville: University Press of Virginia, 1991), 110.

89. Caroline E. Janney, "Mourning during the Civil War," in *Encyclopedia Virginia* (Virginia Foundation for the Humanities), accessed Dec. 4, 2012, http://www.encyclopediavirginia.org/Mourning_During_the_Civil_War.

90. Judith White Brockenbrough McGuire, *Diary of a Southern Refugee During the War: By a Lady of Virginia* (Richmond, Virginia: J.W. Randolph & English, 1889), 251–52.

91. Bill Bryson, *At Home: A Short History of Private Life* (New York: Random House, 2011), 469.

92. Dorothy Denneen Volo and James M. Volo, *Daily Life in Civil War America* (Greenwood, Connecticut: Greenwood Press, 1998), 245–46.

93. McGuire, 251–52.

94. Ibid., 244.

95. Loughborough and Johnson, 88–89.

Chapter Three

96. Robertson, *Civil War in Virginia: Battleground for a Nation*, 28.

97. Thomas Cooper DeLeon, *Four Years in Rebel Capitals: An Inside View of Life in the Southern Confederacy, from Birth to Death; from Original Notes, collated in the Years 1861 to 1865* (Mobile, Alabama: Gossip Printing Company, 1890), 88.

98. Shenandoah Valley Battlefields, "Preserving the Valley's Historic Civil War Landscapes," accessed June 2, 2013, http://www.shenandoahatwar.org/The-History/The-Battles.

99. "Historical Overview," in *A Survey of Civil War Sites in Hanover County, Virginia* (County of Hanover and National Park Service, 2002), introduction.

100. DeLeon, 86.

101. Anonymous, quoted in Faust, *Mothers of Invention*, 146.

102. Heros Von Borcke, *Memoirs of the Confederate War for Independence*, Volumes 1–3 (New York: J.B. Lippincott & Company, 1867), 59.

103. "The Stranger's Guide and Official Directory for the City of Richmond Showing the Location of the Public Buildings and Offices of the Confederate, State and City Governments, Residences of the Principal Officers, etc.," Richmond: n.p., 1863.

104. Loughborough and Johnson, 84.

105. DeLeon, 87.

106. Hanover Tavern Foundation, "History" (2013), accessed May 10, 2013 http://hanovertavern.org/tavern/history.

107. Martha McCartney, "A Documentary History of the Hanover Tavern Tract" unpublished monograph, December 2002. (Hanover Tavern Foundation Archives), 98–102.

108. *A Survey of Civil War Sites in Hanover County, Virginia*, (County of Hanover and National Park Service, 2002), 66.

109. McCartney, 98.

Chapter Four

110. Faust, *Mothers of Invention*, 92.

111. Phoebe Yates Pember, *A Southern Woman's Story* (New York: G.W. Carleton & Company, 1879), 5.

112. Faust, *Mothers of Invention*, 92

113. The assumption that Maggie Haley penned the eulogy is based on the fact that it was signed "Her Friend Maggie" and that both women served at the Culpeper Hospital at that time.

114. "Compiled Service Records of Confederate Soldiers Who Served in Organizations from the State of Virginia," in *fold3*, accessed April 6, 2013, http://www.fold3.com/image/10909687/.

115. Richard M. McMurry, *Virginia Military Institute Alumni in the Civil War: In Bello Praesidium* (Lynchburg, Virginia: H.E. Howard, Inc., 1999), 227.

116. "Compiled Service Records of Confederate Soldiers Who Served in Organizations from the State of Virginia," in *fold3*, accessed Feb. 19, 2013, http://www.fold3.com/image/9892784/.

117. McMurry, 39.

118. Superintendent's Order Book April 1-20, 1861, Order No. 64 (Virginia Military Institute Archives, Originals in volume 1861–1863), 38-43, accessed Feb. 24, 2013, http://www.vmi.edu/uploadedFiles/Archives/Records/Order_Books/Orders_1861_May_June.pdf.

119. McMurry, 37.

120. *Superintendent's Order Book*, 38–43.

121. Charles Copland Wight, *Recollections of a Confederate Soldier, 1843–1897*, Wight Family Papers (Richmond: Virginia Historical Society).

122. Ibid.

123. Ibid.

124. Colonel J.C. Wise, "In Memoriam," in *The Cadet*, 1913 (Lexington: Virginia Military Institute Archives), 2, 5.

125. National Park Service, "The First Battle of Manassas" (June 19, 2013), accessed May 15, 2013, http://www.nps.gov/history/history/online_books/civil_war_series/17/sec5.htm.

126. The coatee that bears the name "Wight" on the inside of the collar is on display today at the Manassas Battlefield National Park. It has been placed there by the family of Charles R. Norris, who wore it on the day he was killed in the First Battle of Manassas.

127. "Compiled Service Records of Confederate Soldiers Who Served in Organizations from the State of Virginia" in *fold3*, accessed May 15, 2013, http://www.fold3.com/image/10909687/.

128. Lee A. Wallace, *First Virginia Infantry* (Lynchburg, Virginia: H.E. Howard, Inc., 1984), 14.

129. Charles T. Loehr, *War History of the Old First Virginia Infantry Regiment, Army of Northern Virginia* (Richmond, Virginia: Wm. Ellis Jones, Book and Job Printer, 1881), 9.

Chapter Five

130. Robertson, *Civil War in Virginia: Battleground for a Nation,* 51–52.

131. Von Borcke, 11–12.

132. Michael C. Hardy, *The Battle of Hanover Courthouse: Turning Point of the Peninsula Campaign, May 27, 1862* (Jefferson, North Carolina: McFarland & Co., Inc., 2006), 2.

133. Von Borcke, 59.

134. Wallace, 34.

135. William Marshall Wight was born on July 29, 1843. He was seventeen, a few weeks shy of his eighteenth birthday, when he volunteered for military service in May of 1861.

136. Henry Wyatt Wingfield, "Diary of Capt. H.W. Wingfield: 58th Va. Reg. 4th Brigade, Early's Division, Ewell's Corps," in *Two Confederate Items*, ed. W.W. Scott (Richmond: Bulletin of the Virginia State Library, Vol. XVI, Nos. 2 and 3, 1927), 17.

137. Robertson, *Civil War in Virginia: Battleground for a Nation*, 77.

Chapter Six

138. Letter from William Leeds Wight to Secretary of War James A. Seddon, April 18, 1863, *Compiled Service Records of Confederate Soldiers Who Served in Organizations from the State of Virginia* National Archives Records Administration, in *fold3*, accessed May 14, 2013, http://www.fold3.com/image/13114546/.

139. Charles A. Anderson, *Train Running for the Confederacy, 1861–1865: An Eyewitness Memoir, Union Cavalry Raids—Incidents—Troop Actions and Train Wrecks*, ed. Waldbrook D. Swank (Charlottesville, Virginia: Papercraft Printing and Design Company, 1990), 56–58.

140. Robert Edward Lee, *Recollections and Letters of General Robert E. Lee* (New York: Doubleday, Page & Company 1904), 96–100.

141. Although Mrs. Wight says in her diary that "Rooney" Lee was wounded at Kelly's Ford, it was during the fighting at Brandy Station.

142. Letter from General Robert E. Lee to Jefferson Davis, August 8, 1863, United States War Department, *The War of the Rebellion: a compilation of the official records of the Union and Confederate armies* (Washington, D.C.: Government Printing Office, 1890–1901).

143. Letter from President Jefferson Davis to General Robert E. Lee, August 11, 1863, United States War Department, *The War of the Rebellion: a compilation of the official records of the Union and Confederate armies* (Washington, D.C.: Government Printing Office, 1890–1901).

144. The origins of St. Paul's Church in Hanover County date to the Colonial era; the building that Margaret Wight would have visited was built around 1840. During the Battle of Hanover Courthouse, in 1862, the church's Bible was stolen. It was found in a California bookstore in 1967 and returned to the church. Today, St. Paul's Church in Hanover is a Virginia Historic Landmark and on the National Register of Historic Places.

145. Mrs. Wight described Susan Campbell as a "professor of religion." She likely meant that Campbell had been one who had placed her faith in the "Rock of Ages" as Margaret would say.

146. All of the details about Farmville Female College and its term of 1863–1864 are taken from the bulletin published August 10, 1863 by E.A. Preot, President of the College. The material is the property of the Academic Affairs Library, University of North Carolina at Chapel Hill. (Available at http://docsouth.unc.edu/imls/farmville/farmville.html.)

Chapter Seven

147. "Southern Claims Commission Approved Claims, 1871–1880: Virginia," in *fold3*, accessed April 19, 2013, http://www.fold3.com/image/222352295/.

148. James Branch Cabell, *The Majors and Their Marriages* (Richmond, Virginia: The W.C. Hill Printing Company, 1915), 142–53.

149. Haxall's role in the milling operations of the company is described in Northern Miller, Minneapolis, Minn., January 20, 1882.

150. Robertson, *Civil War Virginia: Battleground for a Nation*, 149–52.

151. National Park Service, "Battle of Wilson's Wharf," Heritage Preservation Services, "The American Battlefield Protection Program," accessed June 5, 2013, http://www.nps.gov/hps/abpp/battles/va056.htm.

152. Ulysses S. Grant, *Memoirs of U.S. Grant* (New York: Charles L. Webster & Company, 1886), 262–63.

153. *A Survey of Civil War Sites in Hanover County, Virginia* (County of Hanover and National Park Service, 2002), 66–67.

154. Wingfield, 40.

155. Wingfield, 41.

156. Robertson, *Civil War Virginia: Battleground for a Nation*, 149–52.

157. Driver, 66.

158. Robertson, *Civil War Virginia: Battleground for a Nation*, 158.

159. National Park Service, "Battle of Rutherford's Farm," Heritage Preservation Services, "The American Battlefield Protection Program," accessed June 3, 2013, http://www.nps. gov/hps/abpp/battles/va115.htm.

160. Wingfield, 44.

161. "Camp Chase," in Ohio History Central, accessed May 12, 3013, http://www. ohiohistorycentral.org/w/Camp_Chase.

162. Grant, 308–12.

163. "Southern Claims Commission Approved Claims."

164. Letter from James H. Christian to General Benjamin Butler, November 18, 1864 (Richmond: Virginia Historical Society).

Chapter Eight

165. Letter from General Robert E. Lee to General Ulysses S. Grant, April 9, 1864, United States War Department, in *The War of the Rebellion: a compilation of the official records of the Union and Confederate armies*.

166. National Park Service, "Appomattox Courthouse—The Surrender" (May 23, 2013), accessed June 19, 2013, http://www.nps.gov/apco/the-surrender.htm.

Chapter Nine

167. John M. Coski, "The New Old Order in Charles City County: Reconstruction and Race Relations, 1865–1900" in *Charles City County, Virginia: An Official History*, eds. James P. Whittenburg and John M. Coski (Salem, West Virginia: D. Mills, 1989), 77.

168. Charles Copland Wight, 143.

169. Virginia Military Institute Archives has a variety of documents related to Charles Copland Wight. These sources offer insight about his years as a VMI cadet as well as personal details regarding his postwar activities.

170. Charles Copland Wight, 238.

171. Michael B. Chesson. *Richmond After the War 1865–1890* (Richmond, Virginia: Virginia State Library, 1981), 18.

172. John O. Peters, *Richmond's Hollywood Cemetery* (Richmond: The Valentine Richmond History Center, 2010), 182.

Selected Bibliography

Alexander, Edward Porter. *Memoir of a Confederate: A Critical Narrative.* New York: Charles Scribner's Sons, 1907.

Anderson, Charles S. *Train Running for the Confederacy, 1861–1865: An Eyewitness Memoir, Union Cavalry Raids—Incidents—Troop Actions and Train Wrecks.* Edited by Waldbrook D. Swank. Charlottesville, Virginia: Papercraft Printing and Design, 1990.

Blair, William. *Virginia's Private War: Feeding Body and South in the Confederacy, 1861–1865.* New York: Oxford University Press, 1998.

Bryson, Bill. *At Home: A Short History of Private Life.* New York: Random House, 2011.

Bryson, W. Hamilton. *The Virginia Law Reporters Before 1880.* Charlottesville: University Press of Virginia, 1977.

"Camp Chase." *Ohio History Central.* n.d. http://www.ohiohistorycentral.org/w/Camp_Chase (accessed February 20, 2012).

Cashin, Joan E. "Into the Trackless Wilderness." *A Woman's War: Southern Women, Civil War and the Confederate Legacy.* Edited by Edward D.C. Campbell and Kym Rice. Charlottesville: Museum of the Confederacy and University of Virginia Press, 1996.

Chesnut, Mary Boykin. *A Diary from Dixie.* New York: D. Appleton, 1905.

Chesson, Michael B. *Richmond After the War 1865–1890.* Richmond: Virginia State Library, 1981.

Colonial Williamsburg Foundation. *Colonial Williamsburg Official Guidebook & Map.* Williamsburg, Virginia: Colonial Williamsburg Foundation, 1972.

"Compiled Service Records of Confederate Soldiers Who Served in Organizations from the State of Virginia." *fold3.* 2013. http://www.fold3.com (accessed March 21, 2013).

"Confederate Papers Relating to Citizens or Business Firms, compiled 1874–1899, documenting the period 1861–1865." *fold3.* 2013. http://www.fold3.com/ (accessed May 16, 2–13).

Coski, John M. "The New Old Order in Charles City County: Reconstruction and Race Relations, 1965–1900." *Charles City County, Virginia: An Official History.* Edited by James P. Whittenburg and John M. Coski. Salem, West Virginia: D. Mill, 1989.

DeLeon, Thomas Cooper. *Four Years in Rebel Capitals: An Inside View of Life in the Southern Confederacy, from Birth to Death; from Original Notes, collated in the Years 1861 to 1865.* Mobile, Alabama: Gossip Printing Company, 1890.

Driver, Robert J., Jr. *58th Virginia Regiment.* Lynchburg, Virginia: H.E. Howard, Inc, 1990.

Faust, Drew Gilpin. *Mother of Invention: Women of the Slaveholding South in the American Civil War.* Chapel Hill: University of North Carolina Press, 1996.

———. "Without Pilot or Compass." *Religion and the American Civil War.* Edited by Randall M. Miller, Harry S. Stout and Charles Reagan Wilson. New York: Oxford University Press, 1998.

Goochland Historical Society. *The Story of Goochland.* Goochland Historical Society, 1973.

Gordon, John Steele. "The High Cost of War." *Barrons*, April 9, 2011.

Grant, Ulysses Simpson. *Memoirs of U.S. Grant.* New York: Charles L. Webster & Company, 1886.

Hanover County, National Park Service. *A Survey of Civil War Sites in Hanover County, Virginia.* Hanover: Hanover County, 2002.

Hanover Tavern Foundation. n.d. http://hanovertavern.org/tavernhistory (accessed June 12, 2013).

Hardy, Michael C. *Battle of Hanover Courthouse: Turning Point of the Peninsula Campaign.* Jefferson, North Carolina: McFarland & Company, 2006.

Hoge, Peyton Harrison. *Moses Drury Hoge: Life and Letters.* Richmond, Virginia: Whittet & Shepperson, 1899.

Hollan, Catherine B. *Virginia Silversmith, Jewelers, and Watch and Clockmakers 1607–1860.* McLean, Virginia: Hollan Press, 2010.

Holmes, Janice Nicolson. "The Nicolson Family of Virginia, 1655–1975." *Virginia Tidewater Genealogy Bulletin* 16 (1985), 12 (1981), 8 (1977).

Hume, Ivor Noel. *James Geddy and Sons: Colonial Craftsmen.* Williamsburg, Virginia: Colonial Williamsburg Foundation, 1970.

Janney, Caroline F. "Mourning during the Civil War." *Encyclopedia Virginia: Virginia Foundation for the Humanities.* n.d. (accessed June 23, 2013).

Johnson, Frederick, ed. *Memorials of Old Virginia Clerks.* Lynchburg, Virginia: J.P. Bell Company, 1888.

Jones, John Beauchamp. *A Rebel War Clerk's Diary at the Confederate State Capital, Volume 1.* Philadelphia: J.B. Lippincott and Company, 1866.

Kostyal, K.M. *1776: A New Look at Revolutionary Williamsburg.* Washington, D.C.: National Geographic Society, 2009.

Krick, Robert E.L. *Civil War Weather in Virginia.* Tuscaloosa: University of Alabama Press, 2007.

Krusen, Jessie Ball Thompson. *Tuckahoe Plantation.* Richmond, Virginia: Krusen, 1990.

Lee, Robert Edward. *Recollections and Letters of Robert E. Lee.* New York: Doubleday, 1905.

Litchfield Historical Society. "The Ledger: A Database of Students of Litchfield Law School and the Litchfield Female Acaledemy." 2012. http://www.litchfieldhistoricalsociety.org/ledger/students/2793 (accessed April 9, 2012).

Loehr, Charles T. *War History of the Old First Virginia Infantry Regiment, Army of Northern Virginia.* Richmond, Virginia: Wm. Ellis Jones, 1884.

Loughborough, Margaret, and James H. Johnson. *The Recollections of Margaret Cabell Brown Loughborough: A Southern Woman's Memories of Richmond, Va and Washington, D.C. in the Civil War.* Lanham, Maryland: Hamilton Books, 2010.

McCartney, Martha. *Nature's Bounty, Nation's Glory: The Heritage and History of Hanover County, Virginia.* Monroe, Virginia: Heritage and History of Hanover County, Inc., 2009.

McGuire, Judith White Brockenbrough. *Diary of a Southern Refugee During the War: By a Lady of Virginia.* Richmond, Virginia: J.W. Randolph & English, 1889.

McPherson, James M. "Afterword." *Religion and the American Civil War.* Edited by Randall M. Miller, Harry S. Stout and Charles Reagan Wilson. New York: Oxford University Press, 1998.

Moorhead, James Howell. "Religion in the Civil War: The Northern Perspective." *Princeton Theological Seminary, National Humanities Center.* n.d. http://nationalhumanitiescenter.org/tserve/nineteen/nkeyinfo/cwnorth.htm (accessed April 2013).

National Park Service, U.S. Department of the Interior. "Shockoe Valley and Tobacco Row Historic District." n.d. http://www.nps.gov/nr/travel/richmond/ShockoeValleyTobaccoHD.htm (accessed May 15, 2013).

Nicolls, Michael L. *Whispers of Rebellion: Narrating Gabriel's Conspiracy.* Charlottesville, Virginia: University of Virginia Press, 2012.

Parker, Albertina (Brown). *The History of John Francis Deane and members of his family in Virginia, Montana, and California.* Missoula, Montana: A.B. Parker, 1963.

Pember, Phoebe Yates. *A Southern Woman's Story.* New York: G.W. Carleton & Company, 1879.

Peters, John O. *Richmond's Hollywood Cemetery.* Richmond, Virginia: Valentine Richmond History Center, 2010.

Pratt, Edwin A. *The Rise and Fall of Rail Power in War and Conquest.* London: P.S. King & Son, Ltd., 1914.

Robertson, James I., Jr. *Civil War Virginia: Battleground for a Nation.* Charlottesville: University Press of Virginia, 1993.

Rorer, Henry Smith. *History of Norfolk Public Schools 1681–1968.* Norfolk, Virginia: H.S. Rorer, 1968.

Samford, Patricia. "Robert Nicolson House Archaelogical Report, Block 7 Building 12 originally titled 'The Nicolson House-Report on the 1982 Archaeological Investigations Block 7 Building 12,' 1986." *Colonial Williamsburg Foundation Research Report Series 1083.* 1990. http://research.history.org/DigitalLibrary/View/index.cfm?doc=ResearchReports%5CRR1083.xml (accessed May 3, 2013).

Schlesinger, Catherine. "James Geddy House Architectural Report Block 19 Building 11 Lot 161, 1968." *Colonial Williamsburg Digital Library, Colonial Williamsburg Foundation Research Report Series, 1450–1990.* 1990. http://research.history.org/DigitalLibrary/View/index.cfm?doc=ResearchReports%5CRR1450.xml (accessed June 10, 2013).

"Shenandoah Valley Battlefields, Preserving the Valley's Historic Civil War Landscapes." *Shenandoah at War.* n.d. http://www.shenandoahatwar.org/The-History/The-Battles (accessed June 2, 2013).

Shepard, E. Lee. "Sketches of the Old Richmond Bar: Charles Copland." *Richmond Quarterly 3*, Spring 1981.

Smith, Jean Edward. *John Marshall: Definer of a Nation.* New York: Henry, Holt & Company, 1996.

"Southern Claims Commission Approved Claims, 1871–1880: Virginia, National Archives Records Administration." *fold3.* 2013. http://www.fold3.com/ (accessed March 14, 2013).

Stout, Harry S. and Christopher Grasso. "Civil War, Religion and Communications: The Case of Richmond." *Religion and the American Civil War.* Edited by Randall M. Miller, Harry S. Stout and Charles Reagan Wilson. New York: Oxford University Press, 1998.

"The Stranger's Guide and Official Directory for the City of Richmond Showing the Location of the Public Buildings and Offices of the Confederate, State and City Governments, Residences of the Principal Officers, etc." *Documenting the American South.* 1863. http://docsouth.unc.edu/imls/stranger/stranger.html (accessed January 12, 2013).

Swayze, J.C. "Hill & Swayze's Confederate States Rail-Road & Steam-Boat Guide, Containing the Time-Tables, Fares, Connections and Distances on all the Rail-Roads of the Confederate States; also, the Connecting Lines of Rail-Roads, Steam-Boats and Stages. And Will Be Accompanied by a Complete Guide to the Principal Hotels, with a Large Variety of Valuable Information." *Documenting the American South.* 1863. http://docsouth.unc.edu.imls/swayze/swayze.html (accessed April 8, 2013).

Torrence, Clayton. *Winston of Virginia and Allied Families.* Richmond, Virginia: Whittet & Shepperson, 1927.

Tunnell, Ted. "A 'Patriotic Press': Virginia's Confederate Newspapers, 1861–1865." *Virginia at War: 1864.* Edited by William C. Davis and James I. Robertson Jr. Lexington: University Press of Kentucky, 2009.

Tyler, Gardiner D. *A History & Pictorial Review of Charles City County, Virginia.* D.G. Tyler, 1990.

United States Army. "Jackson's Valley Campaign." In *American Military History*, 220–21. Washington, D.C.: Office of the Chief of Military History, 1980.

United States War Department. *The War of the Rebellion: a compilation of the official records of the Union and Confederate armies.* Washington, D.C.: Government Printing Office, 1890–1901.

Virginia Military Institute Archives. *Superintendent's Order Book, April 1–20, 1861.*

Volo, Dorothy Denneen and James M. *Daily Life in Civil War America.* Greenwood, Connecticut: Greenwood Press, 1998.

Von Borcke, Heros. *Memoirs of the Confederate War for Independence, Volumes 1–3.* New York: J. B. Lippincott, 1867.

Wallace, Lee A. *First Virginia Infantry.* Lynchburg, Virginia: H.E. Howard, 1984.

White, Hargrave, complete text of Moore's sermon published by Hargrave White in 1861. "Rare Book Collection, University of North Carolina at Chapel Hill." *Documenting the American South.* n.d. http://docsouth.unc.edu/imls/mooretv/moore.html (accessed March 30, 2013).

Wight, Charles Copland. *Recollections of a Soldier, 1843–1897.*

Wight, William Ward. *The Wights: A Record of Thomas Wight of Dedham and Medfield and of His Descendants, 1635–1890.* Milwaukee, Wisconsin: Swain & Tate Printers, 1890.

Wingfield, Henry Wyatt. "Diary of Capt. H.W. Wingfield: 58th Va. Reg. 4th Brigade, Early's Division, Ewell's Corps." *Bulletin of the Virginia State Library*, 1927.

Winnefield, James and Fredda Coupland. *A Copeland/Coupland Genealogy.* Baltimore: Gateway Press, 1997.

Wise, Colonel J.C. "In Memoriam." *The Cadet*, November 29, 1913.

Wiseman, Bradford A. "Trains, Canals and Turnpikes: Transportation in Civil War Virginia, 1861–1865." *Virginia at War: 1864.* Edited by William C. Davis and James I. Robertson Jr. Lexington: University Press of Kentucky, 2009.

INDEX

X

Y

Z

CPSIA information can be obtained
at www.ICGtesting.com
Printed in the USA
BVHW041239010419
544231BV00017B/1256/P